# BIRTHRIGHTS

*Law and Ethics at the Beginnings of Life*

Birth has become a battleground. The impact of technological developments and sophistication, and the upheaval which they have wrought, present difficult and demanding questions to which there are no easy answers.

The timely publication of this original series of essays will contribute to and significantly influence the nature and direction of debate. The essays, aimed at the student and lay person alike, provide a stimulating and thought-provoking backdrop to the bill, recently published, which seeks to regulate the creation of life. Should we experiment on embryos? What guidelines are needed to control *in vitro* fertilization programmes? Should surrogacy be allowed? What should we tell the children born in the wake of the 'reproduction revolution' about their origins?

These are typical of the many issues addressed in a book which seeks to challenge the ethical basis for much of the legal regulation of matters surrounding birth. First published in hardback in spring 1989, *Birthrights* deals with a controversial area which continues to be at the centre of much public debate.

The editors' new preface, especially written for the paperback edition surveys important developments in legislation since the book's first publication.

Robert Lee is Director of Education at Wilde Sapte Solicitors and Derek Morgan is fellow in Health Care Law in the Centre for the Study of Philosophy and Health Care, University College, Swansea.

# BIRTHRIGHTS

*Law and Ethics at the Beginnings of Life*

Edited by
**ROBERT LEE**
and
**DEREK MORGAN**

London and New York

First published 1989 in hardback by Routledge

First published in paperback 1990
by Routledge
11 New Fetter Lane, London EC4P 4EE

Simultaneously published in the USA and Canada
by Routledge
a division of Routledge, Chapman and Hall, Inc.
29 West 35th Street, New York, NY 10001

© 1989 Robert Lee and Derek Morgan

Printed in Great Britain by
T.J. Press (Padstow) Ltd
Padstow, Cornwall

*British Library Cataloguing in Publication Data*
Birthrights: law and ethics at the beginnings of life.
1. Man. Reproduction. Scientific innovation. Ethical
aspects
I. Lee, Robert II. Morgan, Derek
174'.25

ISBN 0–415–01065–9
ISBN 0–415–00301–6 (cased)

*Library of Congress Cataloging in Publication Data*
Birthrights: law and ethics at the beginnings of life / edited
by Robert Lee and Derek Morgan.
p.    cm.
Includes bibliographical references.
1. Human reproduction—Law and legislation—Great
Britain.   2. Fertilization *in vitro*, Human—Law and
legislation—Great Britain.   3. Artifical insemination,
Human—Law and legislation—Great Britain.   4.
Parent and child (Law)—Great Britain.   5. Human
reproduction—Moral and ethical aspects. I. Lee,
Robert II. Morgan, Derek.
KD3340.B57 1990
344.41'0419—dc20
[344.104419]          89–70135

ISBN 0–415–01065–9
ISBN 0–415–00301–6 (cased)

# CONTENTS

# CONTENTS

# PREFACE

In the time which has passed since the initial idea to produce a book of essays relating to law and birth, reproduction has occupied an increasingly prominent role in the theatre of the personal. We hope that the audience will find in this volume an informative and critical review. However the essays which follow seek not merely to comment upon, but also to play a part in, the unfolding drama. Hence each writer raises as many questions as answers.

This is much as we hoped. It was never the intention to produce a definitive coverage of the area (although one essay on contraception which we should have liked to include, failed to materialize by the publisher's final deadline). We simply wished for our contributors to record their impressions on aspects of this contemporary morality play. As directors we are most grateful to them and our enthusiastic producer, Richard Stoneman of Routledge, for the time and trouble involved. To each of them we are enormously indebted.

Bob Lee
Derek Morgan

# PREFACE TO THE PAPERBACK EDITION
## Regulating reproduction: the human fertilisation and embryology bill

Since the appearance of the hardback edition of this book much has happened which bears directly upon the theme of *Birthrights*. In relation to abortion we have seen major developments in the USA, Canada and Ireland. In the USA the American Supreme Court upheld a Missouri State Law prohibiting any connection between State funds and non-therapeutic abortion. In the case, *Webster* v. *Reproductive Health Services*,[1] a mandatory viability test was also imposed where the doctor believes the woman to be more than 20 weeks pregnant. The preamble to the Missouri statute, which the Supreme Court allowed, asserted that life began at conception. Canada saw three attempts to restrain abortion via injunctions, following the Supreme Court of Canada's decision that the Canadian abortion legislation was unconstitutional and contrary to the Charter.[2] In Ireland in *Society for the Protection of Unborn Children (Ireland) Ltd* v. *Open Counselling Ltd and the Dublin Well Woman Centre*[3] the Irish Supreme Court upheld provisions of the Irish Constitution and refused rights of access to lawful abortion. Finally in France, the pill Mifepristone (RU 486) was placed briefly on the market. By blocking progesterone action it causes the uterine lining to reject the embryo if taken during the first 5 weeks of pregnancy.

In other areas, great controversy was caused when a High Court judge failed to express himself with the usual felicity and stated that 'I direct that leave be given to the hospital authorities to treat the ward to die ...' The wording was later revised to read 'treat the ward in such a way that she may end her life and die peacefully ...' Essentially this was upheld by the Court of Appeal[4] who authorized treatment, without specific instructions or directions as to its nature, that would relieve the suffering of the baby made a ward of court during the remainder of her life, even if the decision of the medical staff was that the relief of suffering was at the expense of a short prolongation of life.[5] In relation to the sterilization of mentally handicapped women, in *Re F*[6] the House of Lords ruled that there was no power emanating from the Royal prerogative to authorize *any* medical procedure on an incompetent adult.[7] This led to the conclusion, however, at common law, the courts could grant a declaration authorizing a sterilization in the best interests of the patient. The basis for such a rule, and the process by which it might be determined,[8] would need to form the subject of a separate essay.

The pace at which medico-legal development surrounding birth continue justifies the decision to publish *Birthrights*, but it renders it extraordinarily difficult to offer any preface for this paperback edition. Consideration of the issues raised above would fill far more space than is available. Consequently, we have taken the decision to devote the available pages to one topic which touches upon most of the other papers in this book: the introduction of a Bill to regulate human fertilization and embryology.

## INTRODUCTION

The relationship between law and scientific investigation, and between law and fundamental moral principles, is always open for debate and examination. Within the 41 clauses of the Human Fertilisation and Embryology Bill are some of the most difficult, most intractable and fundamental moral questions by which any society can become seized. What has characterized the twentieth century more clearly than any preceding is that we have assumed the power to cause death on a hitherto undreamt-of scale and, increasingly, to take scientific control of our own reproductive processes.

The moral skirmishes which followed the *Warnock Report* in 1984[9] suggest that the debates on, and eventual resolution of, the questions will involve bitter Parliamentary battles and even more intensive public lobbying. But there comes a time when fundamental moral disagreement collides with public and professional demands for certainty or consistency, however illusory these eventually prove to be. The nature and moment of scientific work in the past twenty-five years has ensured that new questions have been put upon the moral and legal agendas. Moreover, they have ensured that they will not go away. The continued pressure for abortion-law reform, which has surfaced again in the course of this Bill's passage,[10] exemplifies a simple point. Whatever Parliament here decides about, say, experimentation or research with human embryos, it would be mistaken to assume that pressure for reform would not immediately be gathered and the debate rejoined. We have, it seems, lifted some veils that can no longer be firmly drawn back. The Human Fertilisation Bill is a temporary marshalling of arguments, a transitory marker on continuing moral reflection.

## GENERAL PROHIBITIONS IN THE BILL

Clause 3(1) creates an offence of creating or keeping or using a human embryo outside a woman's body without a licence from the Human Fertilisation and Embryology Authority (HFEA). Clause 36 provides for the relevant penalties and for a 'due diligence and superior orders' defence. More gravely, it will be an offence, punishable with up to 10 years' imprisonment following conviction on indictment, to place any live embryo other than a live human embryo into a woman.[11] Clause 1(1) defines an embryo as a live human embryo where fertilization is complete. For the purposes of the Bill, that point is not reached until the appearance of a two-cell zygote (a duploid cell produced by the union of ovum and sperm).

The clause futher defines activities that are beyond the power of the HFEA to licence. For example, the Authority may *not* authorize the use or retention of a live human embryo after the appearance of the 'primitive streak'[12] (cl. 3(3) (a)). Unless the embryo is stored by way of freezing (see p. xiii), this is taken to be 'not later than the end of the period of fourteen days beginning with the day when the gametes are mixed'.[13] This much-criticized pragmatic solution was adopted by the Warnock Committee as the point when human life begins to matter morally.[14]

Similarly, the Authority may not authorize receipt of a human embryo, keeping or use of an embryo where regulations prohibit this, or nucleus substitution.[15] This is sometimes referred to as 'cloning' and occurs where the nucleus of the cell of an embryo (which contains the hereditary genetic material) is removed and replaced with the nucleus taken from a cell of another person, embryo, or later-developed embryo. The technique has been claimed to hold important prospects for work with genetically inherited disease and the production of immunologically identical organs for transplantation purposes; but it raises the spectre of the production of genetically identical humans, clones, or humans with specific characteristics. The Authority will not presently be able to licence such work.

Clause 4 provides more contentious reading. Clauses 4(1) (*a*) and (*c*) provide for offences of storing gametes (ova or sperm) and cross-species fertilization using live human gametes without an HFEA licence. But clause 4(1) (*b*) additionally provides for an offence, punishable with up to 2 years' imprisonment, of unlicensed use of sperm. Clause 4(1) (*b*) states that no person shall, except by licence 'in the course of providing treatment services for any woman, use the sperm of any man unless the services are being provided for the woman and the man together ...' This would seem to indicate that, unless specifically licensed, the insemination of a woman in a lesbian relationship would amount to an offence.[16] There are a host of queries on the wording used. One of the simplest, but politically most important, of the assisted-conception techniques is self-insemination. Is this to be outlawed? Or does the wording 'no person' as it relates to 'providing services for a woman' imply the presence of a third party? The definition of treatment services as 'medical, surgical or obstetric services provided for the purpose of assisting women to carry children'[17] might suggest that self-insemination would not be caught. However, the White Paper did suggest otherwise.[18]

Similarly obscure is the word 'together'. When are a man and a woman to be provided services together? It is less than clear whether this is intended to suggest some permanency of relationship between 'the woman and the man', although moves are apparently afoot to amend the bill in order to confine unlicensed treatment services to married couples only. As the wording stands, it seems that the donor of the sperm has to be provided services together[19] (whatever that means) with the woman, otherwise a licence will be required. The point is not an academic one as far as the donor is concerned, for otherwise he may aid and abet the statutory offence created by clause 36(2). In consequence, masturbation is criminalized where done in order to supply sperm for the purpose of an unlicensed insemination.

## THE LICENSING PROVISIONS OF THE BILL

The Bill proposes the establishment of a licensing authority, the HFEA (clause 5). The functions of the authority will depend in part on the legislative progress of the Bill, and the 'free vote' on the discontinuance or otherwise of research on live human embryos. Two possibilites are presented: restrictive provisions, which would in essence terminate all embryo research, and a permissive provision, permitting licensed work.[20] If the *restrictive* provisions of clause 11(2) are enacted, the authority will still have responsibility to grant, for a maximum of 5 years, 'treatment' and 'storage' licences. Licensed activities may be carried out only on licensed premises, under the supervision of the 'person responsible',[21] where proper records are maintained, and where the 'written consent' requirements of Schedule 3 have been complied with.[22]

### Storage licences

A storage licence will permit the freezing and storage of gametes (for 10 years, clause 14(2)) and embryos (for 5 years, clause 14(3)), after which they must be allowed to perish (clause 14(1)(c)). Gametes or embryos created *in utero* may be stored only if they are received from a consenting woman or other donor or from another licensed person. Embryos created *in vitro* by someone other than the licence holder may be stored only if acquired from another licence holder (clause 14(1)).

### Treatment licences

A treatment licence will provide for monitoring of the provision of 'treatment services'. A treatment service may only be provided to a woman following the opportunity for her to have proper counselling.[23] The types of treatment in question include the creation of embryos *in vitro*, the keeping of embryos and gametes (including storage by cryopreservation), and the keeping and storage of gametes.[24] Also included are the therapeutic screening of embryos for subsequent implantation purposes; the placing of an embryo in a woman; and the testing of sperm fertility by assessing its ability to penetrate the eggs of other species.[25]

Under the restrictive proposals, a treatment licence may *not* be granted for the purpose of alteration of the genetic structure of *any* cell (whether somatic or gene line).[26] The purpose of this provision is to prohibit even the therapeutic biopsy of embryonic cells developed to the 8-cell stage, during the first week after fertilization, and their replacement with other, healthy, genetic material. Under the permissive provisions, such a procedure would be allowed under licence.[27]

In respect of treatment licences, clause 13 provides that the authority may direct licence-holders to record information about the recipients of treatment, the services provided, and the identity of gamete-donors and of any child apparently born following treatment services.[28] A gamete-donor may be paid for his or her donation.[29]

Clause 29 requires the Authority to keep a register of information acquired from licensed centres, and clause 29(2) gives an applicant aged over 18 the power to obtain specified information.[30] If, from the information held by the HFEA, it appears that the applicant was or may have been born following treatment services, as defined, and he or she has been given a 'suitable' opportunity for counselling, the applicant may require the Authority to provide him or her with information. Precisely what information that will be is to be specified in regulations, but it is clear that while presently only non-identifying information is likely to be disclosed, the position will be kept under review.[31] Additionally, the regulations will provide that the applicant may require the Authority to disclose if she or he is genetically related to a person whom she or he proposes to marry. A minor who intends to marry may acquire similar information about the intended partner, but not the more wide-ranging information available from the age of 18.

## Licensing human embryo research

If the *permissive* alternative of clause 11(1) is adopted, the HFEA will have the additional responsibility of supervising and licensing *research* on human embryos. This is presently undertaken by the Interim Licensing Authority (ILA), established by the Royal College of Obstetricians and Gynaecologists and the Medical Research Council in 1986.[32] To April 1989 the ILA had approved 38 In Vitro Fertilization (IVF) centres in the UK, of which 17 are engaged in licensed research. This work involves the use of either 'surplus' fertilized eggs following a woman's superovulation as part of her fertility treatment or unfertilized eggs donated and subsequently fertilized *in vitro*.

To 1989, the ILA had licensed 53 research projects. The aims of these projects were either the improvement of existing IVF provision (on average only 1 in 10 IVF cycles successfully results in a live birth) or the treatment of infertility (an estimated 1 in 8 couples experience difficulties with conception), including the causes of miscarriage (of which there are some 75,000 annually in the UK). These activities are not themselves uncontroversial, but they are the first practical results of the research work that has been done in the last twenty-five years. Other applications to which research may be put include the diagnosis of genetic abnormalities in an embryo before implantation (there are 14,000 births annually of babies with genetic abnormalities), and the discovery of improved methods of contraception. The ILA has established voluntary guide-lines for such research work, which include provisions for donor consent and prior ethical-committee approval of the work. To 1989, only one projected protocol had been refused a licence, and that was because the procedure involved the transfer to the uterus of a woman of an embryo of unchecked chromosomal content following research.

The HFEA can grant a specific research licence for a maximum period of 3 years.[33] It must be shown to relate, broadly, to one of the existing categories of research which the Authority, using the guidelines in the Act,[34] is satisfied is 'necessary or desirable'. While a research protocol may seek to alter the genetic structure of a cell while it forms part of an embryo, a licence will only be granted in restricted circumstances.[35]

These provisions, even the restrictive ones, are far more

liberal than previous attempts to regulate embryo research work. For example, in the Unborn Children (Protection) Bill,[36] clause 1 would have prohibited the fertilization of a human ovum *in vitro* other than for the purposes of subsequent re-implantation, and then only for implantation in a specific woman authorized by the Secretary of State, and then only for a limited period of 4 months. Interestingly, however, the Bills would have allowed for the Secretary of State to permit the disposal of embryos not inserted, but whether this would have been by perishing was never determined. The person responsible under the licensing provisions of the present Bill has a responsibility to ensure that proper arrangements are made for the disposal of gametes or embryos that have been allowed to perish.[37]

## THE COMPLEXITIES OF CONSENT

The 'consent' requirements in Schedule 3 help determine otherwise unanswered points of principle and practice. Article 4(1) provides that the terms of any consent in the third schedule may be varied or withdrawn at any time, unless the embryo has already been used in providing treatment services or for research purposes.

Clause 12(c) requires that the provisions of the 'consent' schedule 'shall be complied with.' Failure to observe the provisions of Schedule 3 will breach the duty laid by clause 16(1)(e) upon the 'person responsible' for the licensed activities to ensure that the conditions of the licence are complied with. A breach of such duty – for example, by proceeding without an effective consent – is presumably meant to be one ground for revocation of the licence under clause 17(1)(c). However, that clause speaks of revocation where the person responsible 'is not discharging ... the duty under section 16 ...' This seems to refer to a *continuing* course of conduct, and suggests that revocation of licences may not be possible for single or past failures to meet clause 16.[38]

The 'consents' provisions of schedule 3 are not limited to the formal process of protection for the providers of treatment services. All consents must be in writing, and before consents to use or store gametes or embryos are given, a person must be given a 'suitable' opportunity to receive 'proper' counselling about the implications of such a step and 'such relevant information as is proper', including the right to vary or withdraw consent by notification unless the gametes or embryos have been used in treatment or research.[39] Good practice might dictate, at the least, that licence-holders reaffirm the consents before proceeding with any irrevocable treatments or research, and that 'relevant' 'proper' information include such matters as the procedures, success rates, degrees of risk, alternatives, and so on. More challenging is the proposal that, given a Centre's financial interests in these procedures, the counselling be provided by trained, professional counsellors, independent of the Centre concerned. Given the fiscal burdens that the proposed legislation places on licensees, this requirement seems to be fundamental.[40] In addition, the procedures of the Centre must ensure that 'inducements', such as a reduction or waiver of fees for the donation of 'surplus' eggs or embryos, cannot be countenanced.

Consents for the use of any embryo must specify to what use(s) it may be put and specify any conditions to that consent:[41] for example, whether gametes or embryo may be used only for the consent-giver, or for any other people requiring treatment services or for the purposes of research. In respect of gamete or embryo storage the maximum period of storage must be specified in the consent. In addition, and importantly, the consent must address the question of what is to happen to stored gametes or embryos if consent-givers die or become incapacitated and unable to revoke or vary their consents. The Bill does not provide for what should happen; it requires only that the consent-givers address the issue. This provision is inserted to obviate difficulties such as exemplified by the Rios embryos[42] in Melbourne, and also requests for use of the embryos or gametes after the death of one consent-giver.

It is to be hoped that the HFEA will use their powers of direction to cover certain specific questions. For example, in the event of death, does the surviving partner have the *right* of access to the gametes or embryos? While s. 27(4)(*b*) provides that a man whose sperm, or an embryo derived in part from his sperm, is used after his death is not to be treated as the father of any resulting child, this is not directly relevant to the point here.

Similarly, should the gametes or embryos be allowed to perish, or may they be used by the Authority?

An important point of difference arises in respect of consent when dealing with embryos created *in vitro* and those obtained from a woman following lavage or laparoscopy.[43] The continued storage of embryos will depend on how the embryos were 'brought into being'. With an embryo created *in vitro* following gamete donation, the embryo may not be kept in storage without the effective consent (written consent which has not been withdrawn) of *both* gamete-donors.[44] Withdrawal of the consent of either donor to the embryo's creation appears to mean that it must be allowed to perish, although this does not appear to be explicitly stated.[45]

Where the embryo has come into being in a woman's uterus and is subsequently extracted, not only may it not be used for any purpose unless *she alone* gives consent for that use, it may not be stored unless there is an effective consent *by her, and her alone*.[46] This appears to be the Government's chosen way of avoiding the litigation spawned over cryopreserved embryos.[47]

## STATUS PROVISIONS

The Bill in clauses 26–8 considers the status of the various participants in assisted-conception procedures. Clause 26 provides that a woman who has carried a child as a result of the placing in her of an embryo or sperm and eggs[48] shall be the mother of that child, whatever its genetic make-up. This provision has been inserted to overcome a difficulty created by section 27 of the Family Law Reform Act 1987, which envisaged the possibility of using genetic tests to demonstrate that a woman who had gestated and given birth to a child was not the child's genetic mother, with problematic consequences for the child's custody. There is a saving in s. 26(2) for adoption.

Clause 27 defines 'father' for the purposes of the Bill. This is one of the most complex and difficult provisions in the Bill, but also one of great importance.[49] It creates a new class of child, the (legally) 'fatherless child.' It proceeds by providing a saving for any child treated as the legitimate child of the parties to a marriage or of any person, whether by virtue of statute or common law. So, where a woman is married, clause 27(2)

provides that if she becomes pregnant following embryo transfer, or GIFT or ZIFT or following artificial insemination, her
husband is to be treated as the father of any resulting child.
However, if he can show that he did not consent to the
pregnancy, he is not to be treated as father under clause 27(2),
although he will remain the child's *presumed* father by virtue
of clause 27(6). This saves the common-law presumption of
paternity that a child is the child of a marriage, unless the
husband shows otherwise.[50] This he would have to do by way of
blood tests, or any other method of DNA testing.

Where a man is by virtue of clause 27(2) treated as a child's
father, clause 27(3) provides that no other man is to be so
regarded. Clause 27(4)(a) provides that where a donor's gametes
are used in accordance with the consents required under Sch. 3
para. 5, then the donor is not to be treated as the father of the
child. This provision is to provide 'protection' to a donor whose
sperm is used in accordance with his consent, to assist in the
establishment of a pregnancy to which a married woman's
husband has not consented. Two conclusions seem to follow.
First, that a child born in such circumstances will be one of the
new legally 'fatherless children'. Second, where sperm is used
without the effective consents given under Sch. 3. art. 5, a donor
may not be protected by clause 27(4)(a), and may indeed be
treated as the father of a child *produced without his consent*.

The second category of legally 'fatherless child' is created by
clause 27(4)(b). This provides that where an embryo is created
with a man's sperm following his death, or where a woman is
allowed access to frozen sperm (whether for the purposes of
artificial insemination or for the procedure such as GIFT) after
a man's death, then he is 'not (posthumously) to be treated as the
father of the (resulting) child'. This will be the case whether the
woman becoming pregnant uses her deceased husband's frozen
sperm in accordance with his express consent given under Sch.
3, art. 2(2)(b), or that of an unknown donor. Given that death
ends the marriage, the child will be born not only legally
fatherless, but also illegitimate, unless the woman has remarried,
in which case clause 27(2) and (6) will operate, as above.

This provision is inserted, as the *Warnock Report* recommended,
to ensure that estates can be administered with some degree of
finality[51] and to give effect to Warnock's expressed desire that

fertilization of a woman following the death of her partner (or husband as Warnock would have limited it) 'should be actively discouraged'. This they recommended because it may give rise to profound psychological problems for the child and the mother.[52] They did recommend, however, that where one of a couple who have stored an embryo died, the right to use or dispose of that embryo should pass to the survivor. Whether that is to be the case will depend on the consent given under Sch. 3 art. 2(2)(*b*) and on whether the surviving spouse is seen to have a right to demand treatment with the stored sperm.

There is one case that the clause as drafted renders complex. This is where an embryo created legitimately becomes illegitimate on its use following its genetic father's death. Where *during a man's lifetime* his sperm is used to create an embryo which is then frozen, the embryo is clearly then the legitimate offspring of the marriage. He subsequently dies, and his widow later uses the frozen embryo to establish a pregnancy. The embryo is 'used after his death' within clause 27(4)(*b*) and is legally fatherless and illegitimate. The policy behind these sections is clearly to discourage post-mortem pregnancies. But the instrument that is used is that of punishment of the child for what is seen as 'the sins of its mother'.[53] This is an odd, not to say indefensible, way of proceeding. First, it seems inconsistent with the general legislative mood of recent years which has sought to minimize or mitigate the differential statuses of children and the adults they will become based solely on the conduct of their parents.[54] And second, it seems to fly in the face of the approach taken, for example, under the Surrogacy Arrangements Act 1985. The specific reason why the surrogate and the intending parents were exempted from the criminal provisions of that Act was to give effect to Warnock's anxiety to 'avoid children being born to mothers subject to the taint of criminality'.[55] It seems unfortunate, to say the least, that the philosophy has not informed the drafting of these important status provisions.

The status provisions as presently drafted apply only to the children born to married couples. It seems that amendments will be necessary to make provision for children born to unmarried couples and perhaps also to children born into single-parent, lesbian, or homosexual households. It would be possible, of course, for such children to be left in a legal wasteland of complex intermeshing statutory and common-law provisions; but, again, that is open to the objection of visiting supposed sins of parents onto their children. In more than one sense, this Bill gives us the opportunity to determine what sort of children we want. A simple question of status should not be left to turn upon complex questions over which the child has no control.

Clause 28 provides that the legal effect of clauses 26 and 27 is to apply for all purposes, such as incest and prohibited degrees of marriage, except succession to an transmission of succession rights to dignities or titles of honour. This suite of clauses will apply only to births after the coming into force of the equivalent sections, and section 27 of the Family Reform Act 1987, which dealt with status questions of children born following AID only, will cease to have effect after the commencement of those sections.

## CONCLUSION

That a Bill has appeared finally to regulate the clinical management of infertility and prescribe the limits of embryology is to be welcomed. The extent to which this particular provision can hold in balance the countervailing weights of public and professional interests and of opposing moral claims remains to be seen. Much will only become clear once the HFEA begins to direct activity in these fields. Already, however, we have seen in the drafting of the legislation the challenges posed to the very concepts of family, and indeed society as a whole, that we address in the essay 'Is birth important?'[56] The extent to which the Bill is prepared to regress from the advances made in the status of the child in recent years by creating new categories of illegitimate children is instructive. Such bizarre proposals are the price to be paid for control and confinement of the available technology to those groupings deemed worthy of familial recognition.

Bob Lee
Derek Morgan

# NOTES

1  109 S. Ct. 3040 (1989).
2  See s. 251 Criminal Code and the Canadian Charter of Rights and Freedoms as considered in *Morgentaler* v. *R* [1988] 1 SCR 30.
3  [1987] ILRM 477.
4  *Re C (a minor) (Wardship: Medical treatment)* [1989] 2 All ER 782 CA.
5  See also Celia Wells, 'Otherwise kill me: marginal children and ethics at the edges of existence', *(infra)*.
6  [1989] 2 All ER 545 sub nom. *F* v. *West Berkshire Health Authority (Mental Health Act Commission Intervening)*.
7  See the discussion of this issue in Robert Lee and Derek Morgan, 'A lesser sacrifice? Sterilization and mentally handicapped women' *(infra)*.
8  The House of Lords suggested the problematic *Bolam* principle (*Bolam* v. *Friern HMC* [1957] 2 All ER 118).
9  *Report of the Committee of Inquiry into Human Fertilisation and Embryology (Warnock Report)* Cmnd. 9314 (London: HMSO, 1984).
10  See the Abortion (Amendment) Bill introduced by Lord Houghton of Sowerby in an attempt to forestall any amendment on time-limits for abortion via the Human Fertilisation Bill. See also the history given by Linda Clarke, 'Abortion: a rights issue?' *(infra)*.
11  Cl. 3 (2): see also cl. 4(1)(*c*), considered p. xii. All references refer to the Bill as originally printed.
12  See further John Harris, 'Should we experiment on embryos?', *(infra)*.
13  Cl. 3(4).
14  *Warnock Report*, para 11. 2–9
15  Cl. 3(3)(*b*)(*c*) and (*d*).
16  For a consideration of this area see Derek Morgan, 'Towards a political economy of reproduction', in Michael Freeman (ed.) *Medicine, Ethics and Law* (London: Sweet & Maxwell, 1987).
17  Cl. 2(1).
18  *Human Embryology: A Framework for Legislation*, Cmnd. 259 (London: HMSO, 1987) para. 27.
19  This is somewhat curious as 'treatment services' are defined as for the purpose of assisting *women* only.
20  Cls. 11(2) and 11(1) respectively.
21  Cl. 16.
22  See cl. 12 and the further discussion (pp. xvi–xviii).
23  Cl. 13(5), which also demands counselling for a man where treatment services are provided for the woman 'together with a man' (see n. 19 and discussion, p. xiv).
24  Schedule 2 art. 1(1)(*a*)(*b*) and (*c*). Cryopreservation is a procedure whereby cells are subjected to freezing in the laboratory, usually in liquid nitrogen, and subsequently thawed step-by-step for later use.
25  Schedule 2 art. 1(1)(*d*)(*e*) and (*f*).
26  That is, whether a body cell or reproductive cell.

27 Schedule 2 art. 3(3).
28 Directions may be issued under clauses 22 and 23.
29 Directions may be made by the HFEA under cl. 13(7).
30 If it is not known whether a child was born, information must be stored for at least 50 years, cl. 23(1). This area is analysed in Katherine O'Donovan '"What shall we tell the children?" Reflections on children's perspectives and the reproduction revolution' (*infra*).
31 The provisions may be retroactive: see the White Paper, paras 79–86.
32 For some detail on the background of regulation to date see Frances Price, 'Establishing guidelines: regulation and the clinical management of infertility' (*infra*).
33 Sched. 2 art. 3(8).
34 Sched. 2 art. 3(2).
35 To be prescribed by regulations under cl. 37.
36 Presented in the 1984 (Powell MP) and 1985 (Hargreaves MP) Sessions of Parliament.
37 Cl. 16(1)(*c*); but see the 'conscientious objection' provision in cl. 33, which applies to participation in any activity governed by the Bill.
38 Cf. Companies Act 1948, s. 210 referring to affairs of the Company 'being conducted' – was held inapplicable both to a one-off situation and conduct which had ceased. It seems likely this will need to be amended in Committee; otherwise the only available remedy would be a limited and precarious action for breach of statutory duty.
39 Sched. 3 arts 3(1), (2), 4(1), (2). The HFEA, by directions under art. 2(3), is empowered to provide for the coverage of matters in consents which may assist in clarifying these provisions.
40 As to the fiscal burdens see cl. 15(1), (6), (7).
41 Sched. 3 art. 2(1).
42 In the *Rios* case, parents of frozen embryos held in store were killed in a plane crash. As their Will made no provision for the fate of the embryos, the State Minister of Health had to make special provision for them: See G. P. Smith, 'Australia's frozen orphan embryos: a medical, legal and ethical dilemma' *Journal of Family Law*, vol. 24 (1985), p. 27.
43 Lavage: the recovery of the embryo by flushing the uterus; Laparoscopy: a micro-surgical technique permitting the recovery of the embryo instrumentally.
44 Sched. 3 art. 8(2).
45 But see cl. 12(*c*), 14(1)(*c*), together with Sched. 3 art. 4(1), 8(1), (2). Clarification would be welcome.
46 Sched. 3 arts. 7(1), 8(3).
47 See the Tennessee Circuit Court litigation over the ownership of cryopreserved embryos on divorce: *Davis* v. *Davis* (15 Family Law Reporter 1551 (1989)).
48 That is, so-called GIFT or ZIFT procedures.
49 In relation to this whole area generally see John Dewar, 'Fathers in Law? The case of AID' (*infra*).

50 *Gardner* v. *Gardner* (1877) 2 App Cas 723.
51 *Warnock Report* paras 10. 9 and 10. 15.
52 *Warnock Report* para 4. 4.
53 Cf. Law Commission, *Second Report on Illegitimacy* (Law Com. No. 157).
54 See particularly the Family Law Reform Act 1987.
55 *Warnock Report*, para. 8. 19.
56 Robert Lee and Derek Morgan, 'Is birth important?' *(infra)*.

# LIST OF CONTRIBUTORS

**Linda Clarke** lectures in law at the University of Essex. She is the author of a number of articles on the law relating to sex discrimination and equal pay and is currently engaged in research into the legal regulation of pornography. School of Law, University of Essex, Wivenhoe Park, Colchester, Essex CO4 3SQ.

**John Dewar** is a Lecturer in the School of Law at the University of Warwick. He has published work in the areas of family law and legal theory, and is currently writing a student textbook on *Law and the Family*, due for publication in 1989. School of Law, The University of Warwick, Coventry CV4 7AL.

**John Harris** is Reader in Applied Philosophy in the Department of Education, and Research Director, Centre for Social Ethics and Policy, University of Manchester. He is the author of *The Value of Life: An Introduction to Medical Ethics* (Routledge & Kegan Paul, 1985), and is the series editor (with Anthony Dyson) of *Social Ethics and Policy* (Routledge). Centre for Social Ethics and Policy, University of Manchester, Oxford Road, Manchester M13 9PL.

**Elizabeth Kingdom** is Lecturer in Continuing Education at the University of Liverpool. Her recent publications include 'Legal recognition of a woman's right to choose', 'Consent, coercion and consortium: the sexual politics of sterilisation', and 'The right to reproduce'. Department of Continuing Education, University of Liverpool, 19 Abercromby Square, Liverpool L69 3BX.

**Robert Lee** is Director of Education at Wilde Sapte Solicitors. He is the author of numerous articles in relation to medicine law and housing law. He is currently working on *Legal Regulation of Health Care Allocation*, a book in the Gower series of Medico-Legal issues. Department of Law, University of Lancaster, Lancaster LA1 4YN.

**Derek Morgan** is Fellow in Health Care Law, Centre for the Study of Philosophy and Health Care, an assistant editor of the *Journal of Law and Society* and a member of the Gwent Health Authority Ethics Committee. He is presently completing a book on *Surrogacy* for Gower. Centre for the Study of Philosophy and Health Care, University College Swansea, Singleton Park, Swansea SA2 8PP.

**Katherine O'Donovan** is Professor of Family Law and Legal Theory at the University of Kent and has held a visiting appointment in the Faculty of Law at the Univerity of Hong Kong since 1985. She is the author of *Sexual Divisions in Law* (Weidenfeld & Nicolson, 1985), and (with Erica Szyszchzak) of *Equality and Sex Discrimination Law* (Blackwell, 1988). Rutherford College, University of Kent, Canterbury, Kent CT2 7NP.

**Frances Price** is Senior Research Associate in the Child Care and Development Group, University of Cambridge. A medical sociologist, her research interests are in social networks of support and public interpretations of science, technology and perceptions of risk. She is currently completing a report of a DHSS-funded national study involving the parents of higher order births born in the United Kingdom, which forms one of a series of integrated surveys providing the first population-based data on the problems of those who care for such children. Child Care and Development Group, Department of Paediatrics and Social and Political Sciences Committee, University of Cambridge, Free School Lane, Cambridge CB2 3RF.

**Celia Wells** is a Lecturer in Law at Cardiff Law School and an assistant editor of the *Journal of Law and Society*. She is the co-editor of *Ellot and Wood's Casebook on Criminal Law* (4th edn, 1982) and is presently working (with Nicola Lacey and Dirk Meure) on a criminal law text and materials for the Weidenfeld & Nicolson 'Law in Context' series. Cardiff Law School, P.O. Box 427, Cardiff CF1 1XD.

# 1

## IS BIRTH IMPORTANT?

### ROBERT LEE and DEREK MORGAN

> O, wonder!
> How many goodly creatures are there here!
> How beauteous mankind is! O brave new world
> That has such people in't!
> *(The Tempest,* V. i. 181–4)

## LANGUAGE, SCIENCE, SOCIETY

Aldous Huxley's novel, *Brave New World*,[1] published in 1932, has lent its title to a wide range of disciplinary assessments, ranging from biology, physiology, and psychology, through architecture, literature, and the cinema, to physics, chemistry, and engineering. But it is with developments in the biological sciences that the fashioning of a brave new world has become most closely associated. Huxley's novel is a fabulous account of a world state in which social stability is assured by personal gratification and satisfaction based on a scientific caste system. It is reinforced by a sexual 'freedom' which flows from the abandonment of family and the incarnation of artificial reproduction, controlled by the state; human beings are graded according to pre-planned intelligence quotients, hatched in incubators and brought up in communal nurseries. The dangers of such developments have long been thought to be self-evident; the *Sunday Despatch* in 1945 warned of the spectre of artificial insemination by donor creating a super race of test-tube babies who would become guardians of atom bomb secrets. It envisaged that, 'Fathers will be chosen by eugenic experts of the United Nations. The mothers will be hand picked on their health and beauty records, family background and their achievements at school.'[2]

The essays in this book are not exclusively concerned with medical and technological advances in human reproduction. They are, however, written in the shadow of such developments. The 'revolution' in reproductive processes brings in its wake many new and difficult choices; it challenges fundamental values attaching to both individual and groups; previously accepted and understood relationships have become contested concepts. When and how much people are disturbed by things anomalous to their systems of classification is not, of course, susceptible to easy or cosy evaluation; the 'normal' and 'pathological' are cultural and historical specificities. Our understandings of molecular science, and our relationship with technology, our use of the classifications of knowledge which these disciplines urge, have hastened our notions of self and self-conception to the brink of an evolutionary surge. The institutions of value and worth, the nature and meaning of institutions which have traditionally been accorded a privileged status – maternity, paternity, motherhood, fatherhood – the concept of the family, are all implicated and questioned.

The 'reproduction revolution'[3] which is here identified is not – despite perhaps some of the more colourful imagery – a popular uprising, but a technical and technological upheaval, a diverse series of 'medical advances' which insinuate and suffuse their values more indirectly. They serve to augment the 'panoptic technology'[4] through which nation-states are concerned with the minutest details of the lives of their citizens; states become increasingly, perhaps necessarily, more implicated in the renegotiation of some of the most familiar contours of domestic, conjugal, and affective lives.[5] This assault is the more needful of close and careful analysis because the ideological weaponry which accompanies the technological apparatus is discreetly concealed behind cloaks of scientific objectivity and moral neutrality. The changing reproductive processes offer at once opportunities for liberation and for enslavement. The genesis and revelation of reproductive technology and its power biomedically to determine, manage, and control reproduction, has piloted medical science across a rubicon for which there is no return ticket. Science has finally abandoned its claims authoritatively and independently to decide and dictate the parameters of its behaviour, the direction and breadth of its approach path, and the velocity and course of its descent.

In this bewildering world, responses are none the less difficult; there are no easy answers, only troubling and demanding questions. The pace and propulsion of change strain the categories of language and thought which we have available to us, and which we use. As Elizabeth Kingdom writes in her essay here (Chapter 2), referring to recent litigation in surrogacy cases, 'it is clear that concepts such as "the real mother" and "parental rights" are in suspense'. It seems, almost, that we are condemned 'to grasp the meaning of the world of today, [by using] a language created to express the world of yesterday'.[6] Three examples will suffice to clarify this point.

First, the question of whether there can be circumstances in which it is accepted that a handicapped neonate should be allowed to die, is often translated into a drama in which pathologists argue as to the cause of the death, and lawyers dance attendance on the supposed importance of distinguishing between acts and omissions in order to ascribe culpability. The limitations of these exercises are addressed here by Celia Wells (Chapter 11).[7] Meanwhile, as Robert Lee demonstrates (Chapter 10), a similar dilemma is resolved in 'wrongful life' cases in terms of legal duty, actual breach, and resulting damage. Finally, in relation to 'new' reproductive technologies arising out of sperm or egg donation, legal debate has tended to focus on status issues in family law – illegitimacy is a core example – which serves to deflect attention away from concerns such as the physical risks and social traumas of multiple order births, and large ethical issues such as the selective reduction of multiple pregnancy human foetuses.[8] These different concerns are expressed in this collection in various ways, but particularly by Frances Price, Katherine O'Donovan and John Dewar (Chapters 3, 6 and 7 respectively).

Gena Corea has cautioned against an uncritical audience for the revolutionary heralds of these reproductive transformations:

> If we think of medicine as an institution which exists to heal us, it follows that we think of reproductive technologies as therapeutic. When we hear terms like 'treatment', 'therapeutic modality' and 'patient' in connection with test tube babies, such terms seem appropriate. The language we have available to us – in this case, the language of therapy – shapes the way we perceive reality. Yet, in attempting to grasp the new reproductive technologies, that language utterly fails us.[9]

This forms a bridge with a second level of debate: the terms by and within which legal and medical actors have spoken their parts in these social and ethical dramas. A mother is tagged a 'surrogate' without much wider analysis of what assumptions of motherhood this invokes; a claim for compensation for handicap becomes one for 'wrongful' life, implicitly lacking appeal since life itself is, surely, a 'pearl beyond price'. Similarly, embryo research translates into embryo *experimentation*, but the scientific empire strikes back with GIFT, gamete intrafallopian transfer, suggesting all the most benign motives, intentions, and practices, which simultaneously oblige the recipient to the donor.[10]

The limitations imposed by these labels reflect the limitations of language and of thought. And while they may help to narrow and focus the debate, they also shape and direct it towards certain ends and values, which then have all the appearances of being 'freely chosen' or 'natural' outcomes. But as Edward Yoxen has reminded us, the language of 'nature' and of 'the natural' are often used collusively to presume or imply a shared agreement where none really exists; the symbolism of what nature permits is extremely powerful. According to Yoxen, science *is* the transformation of nature; we select bits of the external world and call them nature; we put together models of how we think the world is and of how we think it should be, a process which each culture does differently, and we call the resulting pictures 'nature'.[11] Cultural specificities recall the changeable currency of the nature of nature; a clear but controversial example is suggested by reactions to the reports of sex-determination tests followed by abortion of female foetuses performed in the United Kingdom for Middle-eastern and Asian women who want, or are obliged and pressurized, to conform to the dominant cultural expectations and valuation of male children.[12]

Debate and discussion of reproductive technologies discloses fears which we harbour. Paradoxically, the discussion illustrates the way in which we have allowed technology to assuage many of those fears and deliver up our expectations. Reproductive technologies liberate those fears because they concern whether, when, and with whom members of our species may reproduce. The new genetics stands to re-order much of our lives; 'our sexual relations, our basic satisfactions, our kinship, our sense of meaning to life and what we have on our conscience'.[13] And yet, as Frances Price reminds us, notions of kinship are often based on assumptions which are scarcely rendered explicit; they become part of the 'natural order', 'a natural moral code relating to kinship'.[14] This bestows permanence on what may be a series of shifting and temporary alliances. It also disguises or camouflages the political and economic subterrains beneath the external surfaces of our private lives.

## PLOTTING AND PERCEIVING THE TERRAIN OF BIRTH . . .

> I opened out a copy of the *National Geographic Magazine*, and asked him to describe some pictures in it. His responses were very curious. His eyes would dart from one thing to another, picking up tiny features, individual features. . . . A striking brightness, a colour, a shape would arrest his attention and elicit comment – but in no case did he get the scene-as-a-whole. He failed to see the whole, seeing only details, which he spotted like blips on a radar screen. He never entered into relation with the picture as a whole – never faced, so to speak, its physiognomy.[15]

Sigmund Freud entitled his essay on the relationship between complex physiological phenomena and disorders of recognition and perception *Aphasia*; it is identified with the specialisms of neurology and neuropsychology. Until relatively recently, this work concentrated almost exclusively on syndromes connected with injury to the left side of the brain. The right side, or minor hemisphere, was long felt to be primitive and less important. The left hemisphere is indeed more sophisticated and specialized, associated with specific functions and powers. Classical neurology long concerned itself with the programmes and schematics of the left side, mapping and manipulating the specific difficulties which followed damage to particular portions of it. The right hemisphere has been identified as that which controls the critical and central faculty of recognizing reality and the controlling hemisphere in neurological disorders of the self.[16]

Of the very different disorders to which such damage can give rise, one, visual agnosia, is a very important and influential metaphor for the chapters which we have commissioned in this book. The quotation above, from the work of Oliver Sacks, Professor of Clinical Neurology in New York, illustrates his work with one patient who suffered from a misperception, or partial perception of visual faculty. His opthalmologist had examined his eyes closely; there was nothing wrong with them, but with the visual parts of the brain. Given a glove, Dr P. was unable to state concisely its

nature; 'A continuous surface, infolded on itself. It appears to have
five outpouchings'; or, of another object, 'About six inches in length,
a convoluted red form with a linear green attachment.'[17] The patient
had no real visual world, he saw nothing as familiar. He functioned
as a machine, with an excess of abstract and propositional thought,
but no feeling or relational experience. This metaphor may stand
for the relationship between the very different aspects of birth which
we have assembled here, and systems of ethics and systems of law.
It is a classic characteristic of law makers and law givers that
they do not, indeed, see the scene-as-a-whole; in Paul Freund's
memorable phrase, 'courts glimpse the world through the keyhole
of litigation'.[18] We do not need to follow through on all the potential
consequences of this realization here; several of the essays implicitly
argue against such a backcloth, our own on 'Sterilization of mentally
handicapped women' (Chapter 8) takes the criticism on which such
a view might trade the most extensively. The simple point, however,
is that we do not see the law as a finely tuned instrument with
which difficult and demanding operations can be successfully and
reliably performed. Rather, it is itself a piece of technology; a
resource to be tapped and consumed for particular purposes and
outcomes, none or few of which can be predicted. Literally and
metaphorically, it is a resource to be appealed to in the hope of
discovering certain types and forms of legitimation and authority.
And yet, it has increasingly become a favoured resource for a varied
constellation of consumers.

The pace of change associated with the increasingly visible and
contested corners with which this book deals is illustrated by a brief
consideration of some of the developments which have taken place
or been foreshadowed since its genesis. The United Kingdom courts
alone have been called upon to decide two separate issues relating
to surrogacy;[19] two on the sterilization of mentally handicapped
young women and two on the lawfulness of proposed abortions on
severely mentally handicapped adults;[20] one regarding the status of
a foetus which a woman wanted to abort against the wishes of its
putative father;[21] two contested cases where a hospital authority
was accused of making misguided resource-allocation decisions in
relation to young children with heart defects who had been waiting
lengthy periods for surgery;[22] two cases in which local social services
departments threatened, and one where they actively sought, to
enlist the Court's wardship jurisdiction for the 'protection' of the

6

foetus;[23] one where a neonate was taken into care because its mother was alleged to have mistreated it during gestation;[24] and one where a woman sought the courts' assistance following her removal from an infertility clinic's waiting list because of information which the clinic had obtained about her past social behaviour.[25] In addition, litigation which intimately affects the status and rights of women at work and which have a direct and often decisive impact on childbirth decisions have been reported.

In order to begin fully to colour in the ground of which legal disputes mark out only the broadest contours, to begin to see the scene as a whole, we need to recall that this same period has seen sustained parliamentary activity. This has included attempts to amend the 1967 Abortion Act[26] and the Infant Life (Preservation) Act 1929,[27] and moves to pilot through an Unborn Children (Protection) Bill.[28] Amendments secured through the Family Law Reform Act 1987 to the legal relationship between children born following AID and their genetic and social parents, are an example of the sorts of response which the legislature has already made to the 'reproductive revolution'. They are discussed in various ways by Katherine O'Donovan and John Dewar in their contributions here. And the publication by the Government of a White Paper, *Human Fertilisation and Embryology: A Framework for Legislation*,[29] its response to the [*Warnock*] *Report of the Committee of Inquiry into Human Fertilisation and Embryology*,[30] gives a glimpse of the direction in which regulation might further proceed.

Other questions have arisen about the legality of certain procedures adopted by medical practitioners. The selective reduction of multiple implanted foetuses to achieve an optimum pregnancy number is an example. The use of this technique by Professor Ian Craft has been condemned by the Voluntary Licensing Authority, which withdrew the licence it issued for Craft to undertake his clinical *in vitro* fertilization work; a file has been referred to the Director of Public Prosecutions.[31] Other ethical problems have arisen in relation to the treatment of severely handicapped neonates. Proposals for the wider use of the organs of anencephalic neonates for the purposes of donation and transplant is just one aspect of these dilemmas. Reports of the use of foetal and embryonic tissue and cells for brain cell transplant surgery have occasioned review by ethical committees of medical associations.[32] The inquiry mounted to consider the practice of

7

consultant obstetrician Wendy Savage illustrates a different concern with birth: the continuing debate about its professional capture by a medical profession increasingly dependent on technological assistance and paraphernalia.[33] It is this very technology which now poses moral and legal dilemmas not evident until the very recent past.

An atlas of these environments must chart these winds of change onto a landscape of shifting social sands. Occasionally the foreshore is buffeted with a swell of unusual, sometimes unexpected provenance and power. Technology is like one of these tides which sweep across the sands and into the rivers and streams of social and personal life, so that not even the quietest backwater remains undisturbed. This is the energy of the biotechnological transformation. One of our tasks is to plan and build; to decide whether we should conceive and construct aqueducts to channel and direct this technological flow, or tidal barrages to dam up its onsurge.

## . . . AND OF RIGHTS

What, in these shifting and changing circumstances, is the task to be expected or demanded of law; how is it to respond to moral entrepreneurs' use of the patches of light and shadow which it casts over profound and perplexing ethical dilemmas?[34] It can be used perhaps as it is traditionally understood in western, liberal democracies, as a bulwark against challenges to existing social and individual autonomies. The language of rights is frequently invoked here to express the medium through which law should and does work to guarantee or protect given forms of ordering. But this serves not only to protect, but to privilege certain ways of seeing the world and the boundaries which we use to construct our affective and productive lives. 'Rights' are sometimes seen to have an appeal as a way of protecting or facilitating certain types of conduct which would or do attract criticism or censure, or as trumping utility. Philosopher Mary Midgley has written that;

> the hope that an abstract system of rights, discovered by impartial reasoning, could directly generate a just society was a noble one. It is constantly being frustrated by the difficulty of making these rights specific enough to arbitrate conflicts of interest. Its working has been injured far more gravely by increasing insistence on

freedom of competition, a competition which multiplies and sharpens these conflicts.[35]

Additionally, these competitive rights are usually seen as a system of oppositional, hierarchical entitlements. Rights, especially in their paradigm liberal conception, are part of an individualizing, competitive system of values and not a collectivizing grid.[36] This has drawn a forceful critique, of which the core, as Alan Hunt has expressed it, is that the claim made by liberalism 'to have resolved the persistent and systematic conflict between individual and social interests through the mechanism of objective rules within a framework of procedural justice is inherently flawed'.[37] Mediation of conflicting interests offers at best only a pragmatic response to social conflict, 'which can achieve nothing other than a set of results which reflects the unequal distribution of power and resources whilst claiming to act in the name of a sct of universal social values'.[38] Mere possession of rights comes to be seen almost as some actual gain in real terms – rights bccome reified, take on a life of their own – and the pursuit and possession of rights comes to be viewed as an end in itself.[39] And when they are won, rights are discovered to bc almost completely procedural in nature; as long as you are denied something fairly, the denial is not only legitimized but legitimate. Even these pragmatic responses are questionable; 'any discussion of "rights" and "choices" assumcs a society in which there are no serious ditferences of power and authority between individuals'.[40] And, where differentials exist, the subtlety of coercion is often one of the dark patches of which an agnostic legal system is unaware or indifferent.

None the less the appeal of universal rights 'is a hypnotically arresting ideology'.[41] And to the argument concerning the substantive rather than purely procedural force of rights, Tom Campbell has responded by distinguishing two concepts which the 'core' of a right might possess. First, it might be seen as the 'absolute and indefeasible element within each right: the irreducible minimum which cannot be subject to any limitation'.[42] Alternatively,

> the core may be viewed . . . as the fundamental purpose or objective of the right in question, which forces us to think not only of the irreducible core but also of those consequential associated rights which are necessary for the realization of the central objectives of a human right.[43]

But further than this, Campbell has provided a schema of rights in which he claims that the antithetical relationship with collectivism and co-operation can be resolved. Arguing that a system of socialist rights can be the normative resolution of socialist principles, he suggests that the 'principle of distribution in accordance with need can be brought to bear on determining liberties, claim-rights and powers'.[44]

> Interpreting the need principle as having primarily to do with the allocation of pre-existing resources for the satisfaction of human needs, the characteristic type of right that it justifies is one which places obligations on those in a position to provide the wherewithal for the satisfaction of the needs of others. Such rights will be positive or affirmative rights in that they correlate with obligations that others take positive steps to meet the needs of right-holders. This assumes the rejection of the liberal assumption that, while there is a general moral requirement not to harm others, there is no equivalent requirement to assist them, even when in need.[45]

We have not attempted to provide a resolution to these conflicting approaches to rights in this essay. Nor did we ask our contributors specifically to address this point when their essays were commissioned. What is fascinating, then, is to see the different networking and patterns which have emerged in response to the sketchy brief which we did propose. As quickly becomes apparent from Elizabeth Kingdom's chapter on, the notion, utility and compromises of rights-based arguments, whatever guise they assume, is still something which can provide a fruitful and dramatic arena for thought, debate and action.

An example of the disturbing clash of rights and interests is provided by those claimed on behalf of pregnant women or those who have carried a foetus to term, and those on behalf of the foetus. This particular conflict is starkly drawn in abortion and arguments made for the recognition of antenatal duties owed by pregnant women to their foetus. This envisages that women may be involuntarily enjoined to safeguard their health, or submit to court-ordered obstetrical regimes, both according to physicians' estimations of the best interests of the foetus.[46] These gathering tensions reflect the emergence of the foetus from the shadows of moral and legal concern, and demands for its protection during the course of pregnancy; the unborn and the unbearable have come to enjoy a public presence which was until recently virtually unknown and unthinkable.[47] The courts of the United Kingdom have so far stopped short of allowing that a foetus may be made a ward of court, such that the mother may be subject to compulsory hospitalization in its best interests.[48] They have ruled, however, that a decision as to the nontreatment of a handicapped neonate reached by a parent may be challenged by health care professionals using the wardship jurisdiction,[49] and a decision reached in conjunction with parents may lead to criminal proceedings against the doctors or parents.[50]

This concentration on the emerging rights or interests of the foetus is paralleled by the attention lavished on the pre-implantation cell grouping which has become known as the embryo or pre-embryo. Edward Yoxen has suggested that an overemphasis on the status of these cells, such that the pre-embryo has achieved an independence, almost an autonomous moral status, without an appreciation of the necessary conditions for its continued potential, has begun to obscure the nature and limitations of its dependence.[51] These sorts of rights arguments are poised to become the most pressing and the most intractable of the dilemmas which the legal and moral systems will be called upon to confront in this area in the 1990s. They demonstrate that the language of rights as a privileging discourse, as well as a protective one, can serve to obscure that which is surrendered to the privilege. Thus, in the rights conflict, the foetus comes to represent an abstract individualism, 'effacing the pregnant woman and the fetus' dependence on her [and giving] the fetal image its symbolic transparency'.[52]

## IS LAW IMPORTANT?[53]

We are conscious, however, that whatever resolution is proposed to this small corner of the field, there is a wider and more profound dilemma which confronts anybody thinking about the legal system and matters such as sexuality, sexual relations, and birth. What can it deliver? Are there limitations which are inherent in any legal process which counts it out as even a bargaining chip in the negotiation of what Jeffrey Weekes has termed 'sexual identity'?

According to Weekes, 'sexual identities are fixed', in so far as possible, 'not by Nature but within defined social relations'.[54] He suggests that sexuality is constructed through a subtle blend of

11

power operations, which are expressed through the practices and apparatuses of medicine, psychology, education, and law each of which has its own specific forms and boundaries of regulation. But law is not a unitary phenomenon; it is not, as it has sometimes been portrayed, 'a seamless web'.[55] Rather, and especially when it comes to confront and regulate sexuality, it is an incoherent and incomplete kaleidoscope of fabrics, stitched together after an awkward and incomplete pattern, and then thrown loosely as a protective or distinctive covering according to the demands of the time and the tailor. It is possible to find contradictions both in law and legal practice, a distinction often overlooked, which cast doubt upon the existence or deployment of a class- or gender-based conspiracy.[56] What is important, however, is the constitutive aspect of law; not its impact, where it is necessary to distinguish between law and its effects, but the way in which it sets parameters to what is considered 'normal'.[57]

Lorraine Harding has encapsulated the dynamic of this understanding in her analysis of the relationship between law and social policy. She suggests that the changing status of children, parents and parental substitutes has been a major force in placing reproductive technologies firmly on the social agenda. She contends that uncertainty and conflict now attend parental rights and that the care, control, and upbringing of children conceived and born in the wake of the technological tide has inevitably led to demands for the recognition and regulation of the rights and interests of children.[58] And Michelle Stanworth identifies the current tensions of family life as an important dimension in the debates which are being conducted. Accelerating rates of divorce and remarriage bring 'pressing questions about claims over children directly [to] impinge on many people's lives'.[59]

## IS BIRTH IMPORTANT?

At the heart of much current debate are attempts to reinforce or strengthen traditional family relationships and to bind sex further to parenthood. In the context of social processes such as divorce and remarriage, the accompanying growth of 'blended' families and competitive stresses on interpersonal relationships, it perhaps should not be surprising that reproductive alternatives generate conflict. Perhaps the most immediate and the most pressing which demands resolution is decoding the choices which they offer or mandate for individual women, and to a lesser extent men. As Ann Oakley has suggested, reproduction has come to be recognized as one area in which women are either liberated or oppressed, either free to determine and control their own individual and collective destinies or compelled to have them chosen and directed by others.[60] It is this, she argues, which underlines the dual nature of reproductive freedom; where *involuntary* reproduction can be eliminated and *involuntary* infertility overcome. One effect of the struggle for this freedom has been to create out of maternity a battlefield not only for patriarchal but also for professional supremacy; 'motherhood is a political battleground, a contested area for control – of women's bodies, of the fortunes of families, of the obligations of community support, of the constraints on choice'.[61]

Childbirth, child rearing, and child care are perhaps more easily and readily identifiable these days as raising core issues of social justice. This helps to explain why the study of birthrights, or birth rites, may throw into relief developments, structures and practices which sustain and strengthen reproductive power and reproductive discrimination. Michelle Stanworth has rightly claimed that a study of the 'new' reproductive technologies is important because they 'crystallise issues at the heart of contemporary social and political struggles over sexuality, reproduction, gender relations and the family'.[62] What we have attempted to show in drawing together the essays in this book is that decision-making in relation to a broad spectrum of medical and legal developments clustered around birth also exhibits these tensions. In order fully, then, to address the question 'Is birth important?', we would need to know what is meant or understood by 'birth' and by the notion of importance. We should also want to ask, who wants to know and why? The chapters which follow attempt to establish some starting-points for these enquiries.

## NOTES

1 Aldous Huxley, 'Foreword', *Brave New World*, (Harmondsworth: Penguin Books, 1958), p. 8.
2 *Sunday Despatch*, 21 November 1945, quoted in Naomi Pfeffer, 'Artificial insemination, in vitro fertilisation and the stigma of infertility', in Michelle Stanworth (ed.), *Reproductive Technologies: Gender, Motherhood and Medicine* (Oxford: Polity Press, 1987), p. 93.

3 The term is taken from Peter Singer and Deane Wells, *The Reproduction Revolution: New Ways of Making Babies* (London: Oxford University Press, 1984).

4 Michel Foucault, *Discipline and Punish. The Birth of the Prison* (Harmondsworth: Penguin Books, 1977), pp. 200–8.

5 For the notions of productive and affective lives see Frances Olsen, 'The family and the market: a study of ideology and legal reform', *Harvard Law Review*, vol. 96 (1983), p. 1497.

6 Antoine de Saint-Exupéry, *Wind, Sand and Stars* (Harmondsworth: Penguin Books, 1975), pp. 39–40.

7 Notice the moralization of the issues here; the metamorphosis of language closely parallels the metamorphosis of the clinician's neonate into the emotionally closer newborn infant.

8 For references to this work see Frances Price, Chapter 3 below.

9 Gena Corea, *The Mother Machine: Reproductive Technologies from Artificial Insemination to Artificial Wombs* (New York: Harper & Row, 1985), pp. 1–2.

10 Marcel Mauss, *The Gift*, trans. I. G. Cunnison (London: Cohen & West, 1954). On the importance of these linguistic usages, see Michelle Stanworth, 'Reproductive technologies and the deconstruction of motherhood', in Stanworth, *Reproductive Technologies*, p. 10, at pp. 25–7.

11 Edward Yoxen, *Unnatural Selection: Coming to Terms with the New Genetics* (London: Heinemann, 1986), pp. 4–5.

12 *Independent*, 4 January 1988, p. 2, discussed in Derek Morgan, 'Fetal sex identification, abortion and the law', *Family Law*, vol. 18 (1988), pp. 355–9.

13 Yoxen, *Unnatural Selection*, p. 5.

14 See below, p. 47.

15 Oliver Sacks, *The Man Who Mistook his Wife for a Hat* (London: Picador, 1986), p. 9.

16 Sacks, *Man Who Mistook*, pp. 1–8.

17 A rose, by any other name.

18 Quoted in P. Thomas, 'Have the judges done too much?' *Time*, 22 January 1979, p. 91.

19 *Re P (Minors) (Surrogacy)* [1987] 2 F.L.R. 314; *Re an Adoption Application (Surrogacy)* [1987] 2 All E.R. 826.

20 *Re B (A Minor) (Wardship: Sterilisation)* [1987] 2 All E.R. 206, *Re T. T. v. T, Times*, [1988] 1 All E.R. 613; and on abortion, see *Re X, Times*, 4 June 1987 and the case cited in *The Law Magazine*, 29 May 1987.

21 *C* v. *S* [1987] 2 W.L.R. 1108.

22 *Ex parte Walker, Independent*, 25 November 1987, p. 27; *Ex parte Collier, Independent*, 7 January 1988, p. 1.

23 *Re F., Independent*, 19 January 1988, p. 3, *Guardian*, 18 January 1988, p. 1; see further Derek Morgan, 'Judges on delivery', *Journal of Social Welfare Law* (1988), pp. 197–203.

24 *D* v. *Berkshire County Council* [1987] 1 All E.R. 20, on which see Jane Fortin, 'Legal protection for the unborn child', *Modern Law Review*, vol. 51 (1988) p. 54.

25 *R* v. *Ethical Committee of St Mary's Hospital ex parte Harriott* (1988), *Family Law* vol. 18 (1988), pp. 165–6.
26 See Linda Clarke, Chapter 9 below.
27 *House of Lords' Select Committee Report: Infant Life (Preservation) Bill* (London: HMSO, 1988); see *Times*, 16 February 1988, p. 4.
28 See its various formulations, 1985, 1986, 1987 (London: HMSO).
29 Cm 259 (London: HMSO, 1987).
30 Cmnd 9314 (London: HMSO, 1984), reprinted with a new introduction by Mary Warnock as *A Question of Life* (Oxford: Basil Blackwell, 1985).
31 See the discussion by John Keown, *New Law Journal*, vol. 137 (1987), pp. 1165–6.
32 *Independent*, 22 February 1988, p. 3; Diana Brahams, 'Transplantation, the fetus and the law', *New Law Journal*, vol. 138 (1988), pp. 91–3. See also George Annas, 'From Canada with love: anencephalic newborns as organ donors?' *Hastings Center Report*, vol. 17 (1987), p. 36.
33 Wendy Savage, *A Savage Inquiry: Who Controls Childbirth?* (London: Virago, 1986).
34 For the notion of a moral entrepreneur see Howard Becker, *The Outsiders* (New York: Free Press, 1963), ch. 8.
35 *London Review of Books*, 7 June 1984, p. 12.
36 Allan Hutchinson and Patrick Monahan, ' "The rights stuff." Roberto Unger and beyond', *Texas Law Review*, vol. 62 (1984), p. 1477.
37 Alan Hunt, 'The theory of critical legal studies', *Oxford Journal of Legal Studies*, vol. 6 (1986), p. 1, at p. 5.
38 ibid.
39 See the discussion in Hutchinson and Monahan, ' "Rights' stuff" '.
40 Corea, *Mother Machine*, p. 3.
41 Tom Campbell, 'Introduction: Realising human rights', in Tom Campbell, David Goldberg, Sheila McLean, and Tom Mullen (eds), *Human Rights: From Rhetoric to Reality* (Oxford: Basil Blackwell, 1986), p. 1.
42 ibid., p. 10.
43 ibid., p. 11.
44 Tom Campbell, *The Left and Rights: A Conceptual Analysis of the Idea of Socialist Rights* (London: Routledge & Kegan Paul, 1983), p. 142. For the standard presentation and analysis of claim rights, liberties and powers, see W. H. Hohfeld, *Fundamental Legal Conceptions* (New Haven, Conn.: Yale University Press, 1919).
45 Campbell, *Left and Rights*, p. 143.
46 For an analysis of these developments in the United States, see Veronika Kolder, Janet Gallagher, and Michael Parsons, 'Court ordered obstetrical interventions', *New England Journal of Medicine*, vol. 316 (1987), p. 1192, and the discussion in Dawn Johnsen, 'The creation of fetal rights: conflicts with women's constitutional rights to liberty, privacy and equal protection', *Yale Law Journal* vol. 95 (1986), p. 599.
47 For the dynamics involved here see the brilliant analysis by Rosalind Pollack Petchesky, 'Foetal images: the power of visual culture in the politics of reproduction', in Stanworth, *Reproductive Technologies*,

pp. 57–80; and Christine Overall, ' "Pluck a fetus from its womb": a critique of current attitudes toward the embryo/fetus', *University of Western Ontario Law Review*, vol. 24 (1986), pp. 1–14.

48 *Re F*, discussed in Morgan, 'Judges on delivery'.
49 *Re B (A Minor) (Wardship: Medical Treatment)* [1981] 1 W.L.R. 1421, at p. 1421.
50 *R.* v. *Arthur, Times*, 4–5 November 1981.
51 Edward Yoxen, 'Human embryo research: a cause for concern?', paper presented at the British Sociological Association Conference, Leeds, April 1987, p. 29.
52 Petchesky, 'Foetal images', p. 63.
53 See John Griffiths, 'Is law important?', *New York University Law Review*, vol. 54 (1979), p. 351 for an extended discussion on the limited instrumental importance of law.
54 Jeffrey Weekes, *Sexuality and Its Discontents* (London: Routledge & Kegan Paul, 1985), p. 181.
55 Patrick Devlin, *Law and the Enforcement of Morals* (London: Oxford University Press, 1968), p. 38.
56 Julia Brophy and Carol Smart, 'Locating law; a discussion of the place of law in feminist politics', in Julia Brophy and Carol Smart (eds), *Women-in-Law: Explorations in Law, Family and Sexuality* (London: Routledge & Kegan Paul, 1985), p. 17.
57 ibid., p. 1.
58 Lorraine Harding, 'The debate on surrogate motherhood: the current situation, some arguments and issues; questions facing law and policy', *Journal of Social Welfare Law* (1987), p. 37, at pp. 44–5.
59 Stanworth, 'Deconstruction of motherhood', pp. 19–22.
60 Ann Oakley, *Subject Women*, (London: Fontana, 1985), pp. 189–90.
61 Ann Oakley, *Captured Womb* (Oxford: Blackwell, 1984), p. 254.
62 Stanworth, 'Introduction', *Reproductive Technologies*, p. 4.

# 2

# BIRTHRIGHTS: EQUAL OR SPECIAL?

*ELIZABETH KINGDOM*

Both in the United States and in the United Kingdom, feminists have been concerned at the inability of the concept of equal rights to address the realities of women's unequal treatment.[1] In general, their concern has not been to attack the achievements of equal rights campaigners. Rather, what is involved is a well-documented awareness that the ideology of equal rights has severe limitations for feminist politics, limitations stemming from its failure to recognize the implications of significant differences and divisions between females and males, between men and women. This line of argument can be, and has been, pursued in a variety of legal contexts, but it has peculiar appeal where reproduction in general and childbirth in particular are at issue. Here, the argument continues, is an obvious case where the differences between men and women, notably but not exclusively in relation to the capacity to give birth, point to the need for legislation which accords special rights to women.

In this chapter, I first present examples of the equal rights strategy. Through that presentation, three concepts of equality are identified. Explicitly or implicitly, these different concepts are employed both by supporters of the equal rights strategy and by those feminists who, for one reason or another, have doubts about equal rights legislation.

Secondly, I describe an alternative strategy. It is introduced by its supporters as a solution to the problem of equality and it emphasizes the justice of special rights for women. I criticize this strategy on two main grounds. First, in so far as the shift from an equal rights strategy to a special rights strategy involves an appeal to biological sex differences, it has some familiar and some new

17

risks for women. It should on that account be treated with caution by feminists. The second criticism starts with the observation that supporters of the shift to the special rights strategy themselves acknowledge that there is no criterion for the identification of a difference between men and women which is sufficient for the constitution of a special right for women. My criticism is that this acknowledgement is far from innocent. On the contrary, it is typically informed by a battery of references to 'real' sex differences, to 'the human family', to the fact that the human species is 'sexed', to 'our wonder at the talents and perspective of the other sex', and so on.

My objection here is not that conventional values are being asserted. (Who, at the end of the day, has not wondered at the talents and perspective of the other sex?) My objection is that these conventional values are asserted at precisely the point in the special rights strategy where what is called for is a reappraisal not just of the equal rights strategy, nor just of the special rights strategy, but of the use of either strategy. Briefly, if it can be shown that the equal rights strategy poses serious problems for feminist politics, and if it can also be shown that the special rights strategy, far from solving those problems, merely redescribes them, then a strong case can be made for avoiding both strategies. In practice, it may not always be possible to avoid them, because the terms of political dispute are not always a matter of choice. For example, there are periodic calls for the introduction of a bill of rights in this country. If such a campaign started to gain political ground, feminists would almost certainly have to engage in some form of equal rights/special rights debate. Even then, the greater part of their political energies would be better placed scrutinizing any small print and calculating the likely effects of such a bill on existing legislation and institutions. It would be more useful to argue for statutory provisions, exclusionary requirements, codes of practice, exemptions, appeals procedures, and monitoring organizations, their standards and functions, than to get caught up in irresolvable wrangles about rights.

## THE EQUAL RIGHTS STRATEGY

In encounters between feminist politics and legislation in the USA and in the UK over the last twenty years or so, the concepts of equality and of equal rights have had a complex public life. In the first part of this section, I present arguments which have been typically the support of women's struggles for equal rights through the courts. In the second part, I outline the main reasons why that strategy has met with scepticism, disillusion and even hostility from politically experienced individuals and organizations forming part of the women's movement, whether or not they would describe themselves as feminist.

In 1972, the century-old history of women's struggles in the USA for equality before the law came to a head when Congress sent the ERA (Equal Rights Amendment) to the states for ratification. Whereas the Fourteenth Amendment included an equal protection clause under which the Supreme Court had designated race and nationality 'suspect classifications' for discriminatory practices, no court had unanimously declared sex an impermissible classification.[2] To remedy this, the ERA was to eliminate differential legal treatment of the sexes. If ratified, the ERA would apply not to purely private action but to governmental and state action, for example in the areas of employment and family law and in statutory controls over education, prostitution, and jury service.[3]

Writing in 1973, Karen DeCrow, then president of NOW (National Organization for Women), had reason for optimism when thirty of the necessary thirty-eight states had ratified the amendment, including California where victory had not been seen as likely. Significantly, she uses the active future tense to point out that although debate about the ERA frequently turns on the matter of public bathrooms it is on women's employment that the ERA will have most effect. She cites two major objections frequently made to the ERA in this context – first, that women will be forced to work overtime or lose their jobs and, second, that women will lose some significant existing advantages, such as being allowed to retire earlier than men. She replies that state protective laws should apply not only to women but to all workers. She uses a similar appeal to equality in her discussion of the effect of the ERA on domestic relations law. While opponents of the ERA argue that it will deprive women of rights of support from husbands, DeCrow argues that it could be used to require that the spouses in divided families contribute equally *within their means* to the support of children. She suggests that a corollary of this would be the requirement that the spouse with custody of children, typically the woman, should be no worse off than the other spouse and that, in consequence, the position of divorced women with children will improve overall.

Immediately after that discussion, and of particular interest in any discussion of rights surrounding childbirth, DeCrow tackles the question of the ERA's effect on maternity benefits. She mentions that special maternity benefit laws are virtually non-existent and she also claims that the ERA will not prohibit such laws. These assertions are clearly designed to fend off any objections that the ERA would itself have the effect of permitting discrimination on grounds of sex, either through state legislation proposing special maternity benefits where none exists or through state legislation making them unlawful where they do exist. She recognizes, however, that, whichever way a state might try to legislate, a further argument is needed to deal with the view that there is something unique about pregnancy and childbirth which justifies making an exception to the general principle of equal treatment for men and women in all areas of social life.

DeCrow's argument, briefly, is that, 'Since men do not bear children, a law which applies to pregnancy and childbirth and which refers only to women is not making a sex classification'.[4] The implication would seem to be that a law is not discriminatory in an unlawful way, in the sense of contravening the amended Constitution, if it seeks to allocate benefits to a category of persons which, as a matter of fact, can be filled by women only or by men only. Similarly, a law is discriminatory in an unlawful way if it refers to a category of persons which can be filled by men or by women and if it seeks to allocate benefits to men only or to women only. To develop these points, DeCrow cites Mary Eastwood:

singling out childbirth for special treatment does not discriminate on the basis of sex even though the law refers only to women because men cannot give birth. But if in referring to childbirth the law goes beyond to spheres other than the reproductive differences between men and women (*e.g.* employment), the law must treat women who give birth the same as men are treated in respect to the area of regulated employment (*e.g.*, absence from work for temporary disability). . . . Similarly, women and girls could not be discriminated against in pursuing education because of childbirth. The expulsion or segregation of girls in public schools who have become mothers, but not boys who have become fathers, would be inconsistent with the Equal Rights Amendment. Just as laws prohibiting women from working for certain periods before (or after) childbirth regulate women's employment, not the childbirth, exclusion of pregnant girls from public schools regulates their education, not their pregnancy.[5]

The precise legal implications of this type of reasoning would clearly depend on how the distinction between the law's treatment of 'the reproductive difference' and the law's 'going beyond' that were to be drawn. In the event, it was not possible to test the effect of the ERA on state legislation in these respects, because the ERA was not ratified but defeated in 1982.

For British readers, Eastwood's reasoning is instructive as evidence of the commitment to project the principle of equality into as many areas of social life as possible. It is also instructive as an argument against the widely held view that a law is itself discriminatory on grounds of sex if it allocates benefits to a category of persons which can be filled by men only or by women only. To be more precise, Eastwood's reasoning can be used in defence of the provision of the Equal Pay Act 1970, s 6(1)(h) that a woman can be given 'special treatment' in relation to birth or expected birth of a child. Perhaps even more usefully, it can be used as an example of reasoning which is committed to the concept of equality and which is unencumbered with the ideology of comparability that has been such a problem for women who engage with the British equality legislation. One of the most frequently cited examples of that ideology is *Turley* v. *Allders Department Stores Ltd* in which the EAT (Employment Appeal Tribunal) decided that Ms Turley could be lawfully dismissed for pregnancy. It argued that, since she was no longer simply a woman but a woman carrying a child and since there could be no comparison with a masculine equivalent, there could be no less favourable treatment.[6] As a result of the Turley decision, among others, Catherine Scorer and Ann Sedley argued for an amendment to the Act. This is that the words 'special treatment' be replaced by 'more favourable treatment'.[7] It is clear that this proposed amendment raises the whole question of the relationship between equal rights and special rights, between equal treatment and special treatment. Before moving on to the discussion of that issue, however, one or two comments are necessary about the type of reaction there has been to the equal rights strategy in the USA and the UK.

Whether informed by optimism or apprehension, much of the literature surrounding the ERA in the 1970s was necessarily speculative and all of it in the mid-1980s is retrospective. A useful account is given by Hester Eisenstein. She suggests that the second-wave feminism of the 1970s aimed at the minimizing of gender differences, that the defeat of the ERA symbolized how far women were from achieving parity with men in respect of rights, and that recent feminist theory has moved to a celebration of female difference. In some versions of this woman-centred programme, she suggests, 'the concept of the social construction of gender was replaced by a claim to the intrinsic moral superiority of women'.[8]

In the UK there has been some support for the ideology of female superiority, but reaction to the British equality legislation has for the most part concentrated on the shortcomings of the legislation itself. The two Acts – the Equal Pay Act 1970 and the Sex Discrimination Act 1975 – have come under sustained scrutiny and criticism. For example, soon after the Equal Pay Act became effective, even its supporters in the women's movement argued that the concept of equal pay for equal work could make no impact on women's average earnings so long as successful awards depended on demonstrating comparability between men's and women's work, often in industries where employers and unions have been adept at segregating work according to sex, either historically or in deliberate response to the new Act. It remains to be seen how effective the Equal Pay (Amendment) Regulations 1983 (S.I. 1983 No. 1794) will be with their introduction of the concept of equal pay for work of equal value.[9] Again, the National Council for Civil Liberties Rights for Women Unit argued for substantial amendments to the two Acts in 1977 and in 1983. The burden of their argument has been for the amalgamation of the two Acts.[10] The need for this rationalization has had further support from the Equal Opportunities Commission.[11] Its case is in turn supported by the recent passing of the Sex Discrimination Act 1986, dealing with matters such as overtime restrictions and night work which have obvious implications for equal pay and contractual matters in the area of employment.[12] And another example of tension and conflict was noted in 1978 by Albie Sachs and Joan Hoff Wilson. They make the point that while the principle of gender equality is expressed in the anti-discrimination legislation it is denied in much social security legislation.[13] They also refer to the position taken by the Rights for Women Unit on protective legislation:

They favour the use of exemptions to cover cases of women without family responsibilities, urge the extension to men of protection against special hazards, and generally call for the creation of a comprehensive system of social support for parents and genuine equality at work as a pre-condition for repeal of the laws. The Unit concedes that there are strong arguments the other way, in particular that differentiation in one area of the law leads to inequality in another.[14]

In much the same spirit, Jean Coussins argued that 'Rather than to promote and enforce equal pay, the Act was . . . designed, and has been used, to control and delay it.'[15]

Explicitly or implicitly, these commentaries make use of three concepts of equality:

- the moral principle of gender equality;
- formal legal equality, as it might be defined in Acts;
- substantive equality, as found in economic, domestic, financial, political or other relations between men and women.

A characteristic way of relating all these concepts can be found in the writing of Susan Atkins and Brenda Hoggett as they discuss, first, the removal of married women's legal disabilities and, second, the attempt of the 1970s legislation to prevent discrimination on grounds of sex, marital status, or pregnancy:

But behind this thin veneer of formal equality lay the structural inequality produced by the relegation of most married women to their separate sphere . . . . But the process [sc. of anti-discrimination] is far from complete. Nor do we find that the values underlying modern legislation are inevitably translated into action by the courts and other agencies.[16]

But, in terms of these three concepts of equality, four different responses to the problem of equality and equality legislation can be identified.

First, no matter how deep the scepticism and disillusion with equality legislation, the equal rights strategy continues to exercise appeal. The moral principle of gender equality, so it could be

argued, has been badly served, whether by poorly drafted legislation, whether by that enacted legislation's weakness in comparison
with other areas of law, whether through the sexism of the judiciary,
or through lack of political will on the part of employers and unions.
What is needed, on this argument, is continued pressure for legislative reform, better funding of agencies such as the EOC to improve
enforcement, and constant publicity for the potential of the laws in
making society more just. Second, other feminists have opted for
analyses and strategies which they see as more radical. These feminists, as Carol Smart and Julia Brophy point out, are not concerned
'to achieve formal legal equality. This is primarily because much
of the work has been done, but it is also because there is now little
faith that formal equality will provide substantive equality.'[17] Such
feminists prefer to put their political energies in struggles outside
the sphere of law, for example in setting up rape crisis centres,
rather than engaging directly with what they see as bastions of
male power and privilege. Third, Smart and Brophy themselves
acknowledge the discrepancy between substantive and legal equality
but what distinguishes their position from the second is that they
resist the notion of law as a unified bastion of male power and
privilege. Instead, they insist that the law must not be 'read' as
gender-neutral and that 'it is important to distinguish between the
law and the *effects* of law and legal processes in order to identify
the contradictions which allow space for change'.[18] I have argued
for a version of this position in the specific context of abortion
legislation.[19] These three positions all emphasize the gap between
formal legal equality and substantive equality and they propose
remedies through a variety of legal and peri-legal strategies. In
contrast, and this is the fourth position, supporters of the special
rights strategy see the problem of equality as a problem with
prevailing analyses of the moral principle of gender equality. The
remedy, it is argued, lies in the redefinition of that moral principle
in terms of a combination of equal rights and special rights, a
combination which must find expression in legislation.

## THE SPECIAL RIGHTS STRATEGY

In the first part of this section I summarize arguments presented
in support of a shift from the equal rights strategy to a special rights
strategy. In the second part I point to a danger which this shift

holds for feminist politics and also to its supporters' failure to pursue the logic of the shift to the point where the strategy has to be rejected.

Since the special rights strategy emanates from dissatisfaction with prevailing analyses of the moral principle of gender equality, it is not surprising that it is moral philosophers who have given most attention so far to the need to redefine the principle. The clearest and best-known position is that of the American philosopher, Elizabeth Wolgast, in *Equality and the Rights of Women*[20] and I shall treat her work as representative of the special rights strategy. Of special interest to the present paper is the way in which Wolgast pursues her philosophical arguments on to the terrain of law. British readers might find the framework of the American Constitution too obtrusive for Wolgast's analysis to be instructive in this country. On the other hand, Section 1 of the ERA was drafted in very abstract terms, just as abstract as the moral values of equality and anti-discrimination which heralded the British equality legislation and which it is supposed to embody. Both in the USA and in the UK, then, legal and peri-legal struggles and disputes have been about the precise legal meanings to be attributed to 'equality', either by the courts or by any interested parties.

Wolgast's opening remarks throw down a challenge to the assumption that equal treatment is a remedy for injustice. Her view is that men and women are not the same in all respects: they have natural sex differences and naturally different sex roles. She identifies two unacceptable results of ignoring these facts and of continuing to argue for women's rights on the basis of their equality with men. First, women are encouraged to stress those qualities they do share with men and to develop their different natures, concerns, and perspectives. Second, the model of equality 'does not give a credible place to such a basic social form as the human family'.[21]

Wolgast does not reject the concept of equality. Indeed, she acknowledges that 'some rights should obviously be equal'. She cites as an example the case where an Idaho law was challenged in the Supreme Court because 'it provided that when two persons of different sexes had comparable claims to be appointed administrator of an estate, the male candidate should be chosen over the female'.[22] The Supreme Court ruled that the appellant, a woman, should be entitled to the same treatment as a man and that her

25

qualification as administrator should not include her sex. Wolgast supports this ruling on the grounds that nothing intrinsic to being a woman entails that women are unqualified to administer an estate. For Wolgast, the Idaho law is a clear example of sex discrimination in a context where 'Justice should be blind.'²³ She means that, in the case of equal rights, no attention should be paid to the distinguishing characteristics of individuals; rather, people have these rights anonymously, as a presumption, and as if individuals were substitutable for each other. In contrast, Wolgast proposes, special rights depend on individual differences, on accidents or fortune, or on other features that distinguish people. Examples she gives include the right of a blind person to use a white cane, the right of a veteran to burial at public expense, and the right of a fatherless child to public support. A key example is the special right of women to maternity benefits. It is worth noting that at this point Wolgast cursorily rejects the discourse of benefits or privileges as an alternative to the discourse of special rights. Her grounds are first that when people use the phrase 'women's rights' they commonly mean benefits such as maternity leave and second that her terminology of special rights merely follows that established practice.

Armed with the distinction between equal and special rights, Wolgast turns to law to see how the two rights and their respective justifications are related. The section in which she discusses the ERA opens with the remark that, 'Where the differences of sex is [*sic*] relevant to a right, say, in the case of a right to maternity leave or medical coverage for pregnancy, claims to equal rights can interfere with rational ways of arguing.'²⁴ She gives as examples the types of reasoning described earlier in this paper. Here are two of Wolgast's quotations from the Senate Hearings on the ERA. The first is from a response by Myra Harmon, then president of the National Federation of Business and Professional Women's Clubs, to Senator Bayh's question about laws governing maternity benefits and criminal assault against women. The second is from a response by Aileen Hernandez, then president of NOW, to a similar question from Senator Bayh:

It seems to me that these are special aspects of our life and would require special laws. For instance, the maternity laws are provided to help the extension of the human race and not [just women] . . . If a man could bear children he would be under the same law as a woman is.

Maternity benefits are not a sex benefit. They are medical benefits for some women who are about to become mothers, and motherhood, it seems to me, is a different kind of concept and a legitimate benefit.[25]

Faced with what she calls comical reasoning, Wolgast replies that the more that women are encouraged to make their case in terms of equality the less they can make sense of a great deal of their everyday life. The use of the concept of special rights restores meaning to women's, and especially married women's, ordinary experiences by permitting women's differences from men to be properly acknowledged, both in laws and in institutions.

Clearly, the identification of these differences is crucial to Wolgast's argument, and to that end, in her chapter devoted to arguing that humans belong to a two sexed species, she develops the concept of women as 'primary parents'. This means that they are the ones who bear children and who, it is reasonable to argue, should learn something about child care. The concept of primary parenthood is used to combat feminist ideals of androgyny and feminist distinctions between mere biology and sexual reproduction on the one hand and the social construction of gender on the other. Wolgast cites evidence from research into the sex and social roles of other species and from psychological researches of Eleanor Maccoby and C. N. Jacklin to support her claim that 'concrete differences exist between the sexes besides the reproductive ones'.[26] Precisely what these differences are is a complicated matter, Wolgast opines, and in order to avoid stereotyping she advocates a piecemeal approach to the matter of choosing sex roles. I shall return to this point later.

In presenting these arguments, Wolgast is most sympathetic to the position adopted by the British moral philosopher, Mary Midgley.[27] Returning the compliment, Mary Midgley and Judith Hughes give strong support to Wolgast's attack on the ERA and its supporters.[28] Like Wolgast, Midgley and Hughes believe that 'starting from a total commitment to an equality principle can lead us into silly situations like talking about pregnant men'.[29] They can, however, follow the reasoning why feminists have used the equality principle – to curb the time-honoured elision between women's

27

being different because of their biology and their being deviant because of it. Their considered assessment, on the other hand, is that it is no longer necessary to combat that hierarchical view of the world which gives pride of place to the human male, since nobody who wishes to be taken seriously would nowadays dare to advance such a theory.

All feminists would like to think that this historical judgment is sound; scarcely any think it is. Even so, feminists would agree with Midgley and Hughes that women have been disadvantageously defined in terms of their biological sex differences from men. Again, while some feminists might politely assent to their propositions that 'Some differences are real',[30] others are likely to voice strong scepticism about the intellectual advances intimated by that proposition. For the difficulty with the type of position taken by Wolgast, Midgley, and Hughes is not that they are unsympathetic to a number of feminist views. There is, in any case, no convergence of feminist views in these matters. Rather, the difficulty is with the attempt by Wolgast, Midgley, and Hughes to reclaim biology for the characterization of relations between men and women, to rescue it from its bad reputation of supporting and colluding in a concept of women as inferior to men, and to reinvest it with the moral values of the stable and caring relationship to be found between men, women, and children in the human family.

Two points are pertinent here. First, this endeavour is identical in structure with radical feminists' and political-lesbian feminists' reclamation of biology for the celebration of female superiority; as for content, the difference is only one of the moral values to be reinvested in biology. It would be worth making this point if only to give the lie to the persistent claim that feminists invariably favour an androgynous society geared to the needs and interests of men. But the comparison has a further significance. Radical feminists have never thought that the biological sciences were an uncontested academic discipline in which the pursuit of the truth and the facts could be immune from ideological constructions of what it is to be a mother/wife/woman, a father/husband/man, a boy-child/girl-child/sibling, or whatever, especially where such biological/ideological analyses are incorporated, however variously or indirectly into the practices of medicine or law. In contrast, and this is the second point, Wolgast and Midgley and Hughes appear to think that their appeal to the biological sciences is both a matter of common sense and an inquiry capable of yielding 'the facts' about 'the sex difference'.[31] Further, Midgley and Hughes insist that just because some areas of knowledge, such as genetics, have 'been put to bad use', that is no excuse for ignoring them. 'If certain facts are dangerous, the remedy is, as usual, not suppression but more facts.'[32]

What is immediately striking about this confidence in the capacity of the biological sciences to deliver undisputed truths about the common-sense categories of men and women is that it is made in the contexts first of sexual reproduction and secondly of appropriate legislation. Yet it is in precisely these contexts that, at least since 1978, the date when the first child was born as a result of *in vitro* fertilization, there have had to be the most radical reappraisals of what exactly is meant by terms such as 'mother', 'offspring', 'parenthood', 'family', and so on. There is no shortage of examples, either of the extent to which current research in the sphere of human reproductive technology is forcing new concepts of the limits of human biology, or of the ensuing uncertainties produced by unprecedented legal actions. Even so, it is worth mentioning three of the issues currently given media prominence.

First, in the light of remarks by Wolgast, Midgley, and Hughes quoted above, it has to be said that talk about pregnant men will not go away simply because it has been described as comical or silly. One serious weekly magazine, two television programmes and a popular magazine gave coverage in 1986 to the views of various consultants and scientists about a woman who conceived a few days before having a hysterectomy and whose child, now 7 years old, was delivered from her abdomen by Caesarian section.[33] This phenomenon raises the possibility, bruited by various consultants and scientists that a man could carry a baby, and there is no doubt that the possibility of male pregnancy is taken very seriously, at least by some men. However repugnant or incomprehensible the idea may be to most people, the 'successful' outcome of any such experimentation would give curious substance to Harmon's position on maternity benefits quoted above.

More familiar in the field of new reproductive technology is the practice of surrogate parenting where a child is carried by one woman on the understanding that it be transferred to another after birth. It is clear from the opening paragraph on surrogacy in the *Warnock Report* that the practices making a surrogate pregnancy possible – artificial insemination and *in vitro* fertilization – have to be matched by new terminology: the carrying mother, the commissioning mother, the genetic mother, the commissioning father, the genetic father, the male partner of the carrying mother, and so on.[34] The legal implications of these various relationships and statuses are far from clear. As *Warnock* points out, questions of inheritance, citizenship, claims for wrongful death and, I would add, claims for wrongful life, are all likely to be affected by any decision as to whether the commissioning mother or the carrying mother should have custody of the child in any dispute. In the United Kingdom, the High Court rejected the claim of a commissioning father in a disputed custody case.[35] The Supreme Court of New Jersey, in an important American test case, reversed in part the decision of the lower court judge. The Supreme Court held a surrogacy contract between Mary Beth Whitehead and William Stern contrary to public policy. They refused to overturn the lower court's order in favour of the father's claim to custody, however, but did award the child's mother visitation rights. The case had been brought against the carrying mother for refusing to give up the 9-month-old daughter. There are many legal complications in this case – whether the contract was invalid through violation of a New Jersey law banning baby-selling, whether the commissioning parents are guilty of fraud in claiming the commissioning mother to be infertile, and whether adoption principles can govern surrogacy arrangements.[36] Whatever the eventual legal outcome of this and similar cases, however, it is clear that concepts such as 'the real mother' and 'parental rights' are in suspense.

While those concepts are in suspense, a new concept is proposed in another debate surrounding artificial insemination and surrogacy – the 'right to genetic information' and the 'right to control genetic inheritance'. In September 1985 Andrew Veitch reported that the Infertility Services Ethical Committee of a District Health Authority refused to give a widow an operation of artificial insemination using the deep-frozen sperm of her dead husband. This was in spite of the fact that before he died the husband had been warned that his treatment for cancer might leave him infertile and in spite of the fact that he had left both a written and a video-taped request for artificial insemination for his widow. The hospital committee said that the husband had no legal dominion over his genes and that the wife had no legal right to receive them. (According to the

*Liverpool Echo*, the hospital took the view that living human tissue cannot belong to anybody!)[37] Consistent with that view, the hospital also refused the treatment to the widow's sister, who subsequently volunteered to be a surrogate mother. In contrast, Veitch refers to the views of Robert Jansen, an Australian gynaecologist. Jansen has argued that although society has no obligation to use reproductive technology to fulfil the desires of dying patients to preserve their genetic potential, none the less, 'because the implied motive in leaving stored semen behind after death is the wish for it to be used to secure offspring, an explicit or testamentary wish for passage of inheritance rights during the reproductive life of the wife should, if she wants it that way, be allowed'. This view is then redescribed by Veitch in terms of the widow's right to the genetic information contained in her dead husband's sperm and the husband's right to control his genetic inheritance. He concludes that for the sake of future generations, it may be that we need a Genetic Protection Bill.[38]

Cases such as Veitch describes have not yet come to court in the United Kingdom.[39] If comparable cases were to be the subject of legal action, however, feminists would find themselves faced with an increasingly familiar sort of dilemma. On the one hand, there is sympathy for the childless widow and for the helpless sister-in-law. On the other hand, the notion of a right to control genetic inheritance has to be seen as an alarming extension – beyond death – of rights based on biological relations between fathers and children. In this respect, feminists should recall the remarks of the FLSG (Family Law Subgroup) of Rights of Women in their discussion of the liberal-sounding proposal that the status of illegitimacy should be removed from law and that any child should be linked to a father as if that child were the child of a married father:

> We felt that the drift of this legislation . . . was, in fact, very anti-women because it was suggesting that a child could only have a proper status if it was linked to a man . . . we wanted a recognition of alternative ways of having legal relationships between parents and children . . . . We also felt it was important in some cases to acknowledge and formalise the relationship between non-parents and children, and to take more seriously social relations rather than always putting such a high premium on biological relations.[40]

The phrase 'in some cases' is significant. Alert to the complex ways in which both the biological sciences and current law are making the concept of parenthood problematic, feminists involved in legal studies and in legal struggles are increasingly taking the position that there is no single principle from which to derive feminist politics in law.[41]

At this point, one might expect moral philosophers to complain about such unprincipled opportunism, especially a moral philosopher like Wolgast who has gone to the trouble of producing a distinction between equal rights and special rights to tackle just these sorts of social complexities. It comes as a surprise, then, to find Wolgast herself advocating a 'case-by-case' approach. She arrives at this position in the crucial chapter on Gender and the Law. We have already seen that she grants that there are cases where men and women should have equal rights, such as those connected with jobs and promotions. What she also argues, however, is that there is no general principle of equality from which such cases can be derived, since their various justifications are not all the same. Quite consistently with this position, Wolgast goes on to make the point that there is no one rationale either for equal rights or for special rights. And in case the reader is in any doubt, she stresses that, 'For some issues the biological and reproductive differences of the sexes play a crucial part, but in others these have to be carefully ignored.'[42] In a word, rights ought to be equal when they ought to be equal and special when they ought to be special.

The vacuity of the distinction between equal rights and special rights could, of course, be surmised from any attempt to apply the distinction. In the *Baby M* case in New Jersey, for example, the adult parties would not be eligible for equal treatment on Wolgast's analysis and the two women could not have equal rights as between each other, because although they are both women their circumstances are crucially different. Further, even if a case could be made for giving each category – carrying mothers and commissioning mothers – special rights, appeal would still have to be made to some independent principle in order to arrive at a decision as to which category of special rights should have priority over the other. Wolgast might appeal to her concept of primary parenting, but, since she herself wants to blur the distinction between childbirth and child care,[43] both carrying mothers and commissioning mothers could claim to be primary parents and therefore to have identical special rights. Wolgast offers no other independent principle with which that dispute could be settled. Indeed, any such independent principle would present a prima facia conflict with Wolgast's claim that there is no general principle for settling rights disputes.

What remains to be considered is why, having pushed her analysis to the point where she rules out the possibility of general criteria for the settling of the equal rights/special rights question, Wolgast should not have realized that the concept of special rights, far from being a solution to the problem of equality, is no more than a redescription of it: people ought to be treated equally except in cases where they ought to be treated specially. One answer to this question may be that Wolgast's continued use of the distinction between equal and special rights makes it easier to treat all these complex issues as if they were entirely questions of jurisprudence, of philosophy. In those areas of enquiry, there is no pressing need to produce draft legislation or to engage in analysis of the social effects of legislation. If that were the reason, then feminists could quite reasonably leave such debates to the philosophers, hoping all the while that smart barristers will not pick up useful bits of rhetoric.

But the appropriation of the socio-legal issues of new reproductive techniques by jurisprudence or by philosophy still leaves unexplained the continued use of the distinction between equal and special rights when it is demonstrably vacuous. It is unexplained because within jurisprudence and philosophy there is a strong tradition of dismissing rights discourse as being incapable of determining legislation. Faced with the inadequacy of the equal rights/special rights distinction to the determination of legislation, one might expect the whole discourse of rights to be seen as suspect and as a discourse which might sensibly be abandoned.

The proposal to dispense with the discourse of rights does not usually meet with easy assent. Resistance is typically based on two positions, both pragmatic. The first is that feminists are understandably uneasy about walking down from the high ground of moral rights and on to the slopes of what they, and their opponents, see as *ad hoc* and unprincipled struggle. The second is that an alternative vocabulary has not been developed. In reply to the second position, I would point to the established use of the highly developed discourse of competences, exemptions, qualifying conditions, disabilities and their removal, status definitions, favourable treatment, and so on. This is, of course, precisely the discourse explicitly rejected by Wolgast. It is also the discourse used by Scorer and Sedley to make their numerous recommendations for amending the equality laws, without once having recourse to rights discourse. Some feminists, speaking from the first position of resistance, may none the less want to gloss such recommendations with rights discourse, remaining unpersuaded of its dangerous vagaries. It is beyond the range of this chapter, however, to argue for the systematic rejection of rights discourse.[44] My main aim has been to contribute to this book on birthrights the recommendation that, whatever the shortcomings of the equal rights strategy as incapable of meeting the complexities of female and male differences, those shortcomings are not remedied by an appeal to special rights.

## NOTES

1 The emphasis in this chapter is initially more on American than on British sources. This is because the existence of the American Constitution and the politics of the Equal Rights Amendment put into sharp focus the debate about equal rights and special rights. On the other hand, at the European Conference on Critical Legal Studies in April 1986 in London, the special theme was 'Feminist Perspectives on Law'. Speaker after speaker in informal discussion expressed doubts about using the discourse of equal rights for feminist politics, and occasionally the question of an alternative to it was posed in terms of the discourse of special rights. This chapter is a contribution to that debate. It developed out of remarks which I made as Recorder for a session in which M. L. P. Loenen commented on Elizabeth H. Wolgast's *Equality and the Rights of Women* (London: Cornell University Press, 1980). In her as yet unpublished paper, Loenen sought to defend the principle of equality from Wolgast's misinterpretation of it. My remarks were to the effect that, whether or not Loenen can make her case, the debate is pitched at a philosophical level which permits neither its own solution nor the formulation of feminist policy in relation to legal issues.

   I very much appreciate the help of Barry Hindess in making useful comments on the first draft and of Christine Bennett and Linda Pepper in alerting me to some relevant materials.
2 Albie Sachs and Joan Hoff Wilson, *Sexism and the Law* (Oxford: Martin Robertson, 1978), pp. 212ff.
3 The Equal Rights Amendment is as follows:

   Section 1. Equality of rights under the law shall not be denied or abridged by the United States or by any State on account of sex.
   Section 2. The Congress shall have the power to enforce, by appropriate legislation, the provisions of this article.

Section 3. This amendment shall take effect two years after the date of ratification.

The article used by supporters and opponents of the ERA as the authoritative source of interpretation of its effects is Barbara A. Brown, Thomas I. Emerson, Gail Falk, and Ann E. Freeman, 'The Equal Rights Amendment: a constitutional basis for equal rights for women' *Yale Law Journal*, vol. 80, no. 5 (1971), pp. 871–995.

4 Karen DeCrow, *Sexist Justice* (New York: Vintage Books, 1975), p. 312.

5 Mary Eastwood, *Job-Related Maternity Benefits* (London: Citizens' Advisory Council on the Status of Women, 1970).

6 *Turley* v. *Allders Departmental Stores Ltd.* [1980] I.C.R. 299; see also *Brown* v. *Stockton-on-Tees B.C.* [1988] 2 W.L.R. 935.

7 Catherine Scorer and Ann Sedley, *Amending the Equality Laws* (London: National Council for Civil Liberties, 1983), p. 14.

8 Hester Eisenstein, *Contemporary Feminist Thought* (London: Allen & Unwin, 1984), pp. 140–1.

9 Michael Rubenstein, *Equal Pay for Work of Equal Value*, (London: Macmillan, 1984). This is a thorough introduction of the regulations and their implications. In the first case under the regulations, the female applicant, a shipyard canteen worker, initially had her case dismissed when seeking parity with male painters and fitters see *Hayward* v. *Cammell Laird Shipbuilders Ltd* [1987] 2 All E.R. 344; a second case, *Pickstone* v. *Freemans Ltd*, succeeded but only because the Court of Appeal applied EEC law. The court found that there could be 'no remedy under national legislation' and that 'the decision was likely to involve formidable industrial and commercial inconvenience'. But see now *Hayward* [1988] 2 All E.R. 257 and *Pickstone* v. *Freemans Ltd*, [1988]. 2 All E.R. 803, respectively reversing and amending these restrictive judgements.

10 Scorer and Sedley, *Amending the Equality Laws*, pp. 7ff.

11 Equal Opportunities Commission, *Legislating for Change: Review of the Sex Discrimination Legislation* (Manchester: EOC, 1986).

12 For an introduction to the new Act, see '*Equal Opportunities Review* clause-by-clause guide to the Sex Discrimination Act 1986', *Equal Opportunities Review*, no. 11, January/February 1987.

13 Sachs and Wilson, *Sexism and the Law*, p. 205.

14 ibid.

15 Jean Coussins, 'Equality for women', *Marxism Today*, January 1980, p. 8.

16 Susan Atkins and Brenda Hoggett, *Women and the Law* (Oxford: Basil Blackwell, 1984), p. 4.

17 Carol Smart and Julia Brophy, 'Locating law', in Carol Smart and Julia Brophy (eds), *Women in Law* (London: Routledge & Kegan Paul, 1984), p. 15.

18 Smart and Brophy, 'Locating law', p. 17.

19 Elizabeth Kingdom, 'Legal recognition of a woman's right to choose', in Smart and Brophy, *Women in Law*, pp. 146ff.

20  Wolgast, *Equality*.
21  ibid., p. 155.
22  *Reed* v. *Reed*, 404, U.S. 1971, cited in Wolgast, *Equality*, p. 78.
23  Wolgast, *Equality*, p. 49.
24  ibid., pp. 87–8.
25  Quotations taken from Catherine Stimpson (ed.), *Women and the 'Equal Rights Amendment'* Senate Subcommittee Hearings on the Constitutional Amendment, 91st Congress, (New York: Bowker, in conjunction with the Congressional Information Service, Washington, DC, 1972), p. 26, and cited in Wolgast, *Equality*, p. 92.
26  Wolgast, *Equality* p. 126.
27  Mary Midgley, *Beast and Man: the Roots of Human Nature* (Ithaca, NY: Cornell University Press, 1978).
28  Mary Midgley and Judith Hughes, *Women's Choices* (London: Weidenfeld & Nicolson, 1983), pp. 158ff.
29  ibid., p. 162.
30  ibid., p. 164.
31  Wolgast, *Equality*, pp. 125ff, and Midgley and Hughes, *Women's Choices*, p. 187.
32  Midgley and Hughes, *Women's Choices*, p. 187.
33  Women's Reproductive Rights Information Centre, *Newsletter*, October 1986.
34  *Report of the Committee of Inquiry into Human Fertilisation and Embryology*, (*Warnock Report*), Cmnd. 9314 (London: HMSO, 1984), p. 42.
35  *Re P (Minors) (Surrogacy)* [1987] 2 F.L.R. 314.
36  *In Re Baby M*, 217 N.J. Sup. 313, 525 A.(2d) 1128 (1987) (Superior Court); 109 N.J. 396, 537 A.(2d) 1227 (1988) (Supreme Court, New Jersey).
37  *Liverpool Echo*, 19 May 1986.
38  Andrew Veitch, *Guardian*, 25 September 1985; Rios embryos, discussed in G. Smith, 'Australia's frozen "orphan" embryos: a medical, legal and ethical dilemma', *Journal of Family Law*, vol. 24 (1985), p. 27.
39  But see Douglas Cuisine, 'Artificial insemination with the husband's semen after death', *Journal of Medical Ethics*, vol. 3 (1977), pp. 163–5.
40  Family Law Subgroup, 'Campaigning around family law: politics and practice', in Smart and Brophy, *Women in Law*, pp. 194–5.
41  See, for example, Smart and Brophy, 'Locating law', pp. 16ff, and Kingdom, 'Legal recognition', pp. 146–7.
42  Wolgast, *Equality*, p. 87.
43  This point is further explored by Derek Morgan in Chapter 4 below.
44  See, for example, Mark Cousins, 'Mens rea: a note of sexual difference, criminology and the law', in Pat Carlen and Mike Collison (eds), *Radical Issues in Criminology* (Oxford: Martin Robertson, 1980); Paul Hirst, 'Law, socialism and rights', in Carlen and Collison, *Radical Issues*; Elizabeth Kingdom, 'Legal recognition', and Elizabeth Kingdom, 'Consent, coercion and consortium: the sexual politics of sterilisation', *Journal of Law and Society*, vol. 12, no. 1 (1985), p. 19.

# 3

# ESTABLISHING GUIDELINES: REGULATION AND THE CLINICAL MANAGEMENT OF INFERTILITY

*FRANCES PRICE*

## INTRODUCTION

Professional self-regulation in the clinical management of infertility has become subject to critical scrutiny, even by those within the field. Existing guidelines have been flouted and there is a growing demand for greater social and ethical accountability. Yoxen refers to an 'unstable sense of concern'.[1] Specific anxieties about practices in the field of medically assisted reproduction now have put pressure on the government to legislate. The drafters of the few statutes in UK law which relate to obstetric practice did not envisage the emergence of the new technologies of pre-natal intervention.

Until relatively recently the idea that law has a place in regulating any field in medicine was novel. Medical law has been undeveloped, except in relation to medical malpractice.[2] In a wider context, a strong case has been made that trust both in science and the regulation of scientists has declined since the late seventies.[3] Public discussion about the status of professions and their accountability has also increased. The implications of this broad shift in credibility are likely to be far-reaching.

Knowledge of the process of human reproduction, cell biology and early embryology has advanced rapidly in recent years. Complex monitored techniques, such as *in vitro* fertilization and embryo transfer (IVF and ET) and more recently gamete intrafallopian transfer (GIFT) and zygote intrafallopian transfer (ZIFT) have been developed to provide innovatory clinical services in reproductive medicine.[4]

There is close collaboration between clinicians and scientists. Practitioners acknowledge that, together with the psycho-social objective of alleviating childlessness, there are the scientific objectives of improving the techniques of IVF and its analogues, exploring early embryo development, the causes of human infertility and the development of pre-implantation diagnosis of genetic disorders. However the procedures raise fundamental ethical questions about the control of human reproduction and the grounds for limiting clinical freedom. There is controversy and public interest.[5] Action to monitor and control scientific and clinical procedures involving human gametes and embryos has been on various agendas, professional and public, national and international, for some considerable time.[6]

The first legislation in the world 'relating to the regulation of certain procedures for the alleviation of infertility, or to assist conception' was the Australian State of Victoria's Infertility (Medical Procedures) Act 1984: based on the recommendations of the Waller Committee. The Act was proclaimed in August 1986.[7] A regulatory hiatus, by comparison, has prevailed in the United Kingdom. The debate about the nature of the action to be taken, which gathered momentum at the time of the *Warnock Report*, was stimulated afresh by the publication in 1986 of the Department of Health and Social Security's consultation document, *Legislation on Human Infertility Services and Embryo Research*.[8]

A majority of the respondents to this document favoured statutory regulation, advocating the establishment of an independent Statutory Licensing Authority (SLA) as a monitoring body with discretionary powers over research and clinical practice.

The issue of regulation acquired a new urgency in the face of challenges to the legitimacy of the review body, the Voluntary Licensing Authority (VLA). This body was set up jointly by the Royal College of Obstetricians and Gynaecologists and the Medical Research Council in 1985 following *Warnock*. Under the original remit from the sponsoring bodies the Authority was required 'to review work in centres undertaking IVF and research involving human pre-embryos'.[9] Charged with the responsibility of licensing, of constructing interim guidelines and of monitoring, the lay, clinical, and scientific membership of the VLA now total eighteen.

Only work, clinical or experimental, which has already been vetted by a local Ethics Committee is countenanced and the VLA has no power to enforce its guidelines beyond withdrawal of its licence. This regulatory authority without 'teeth' was always intended to be a temporary measure whilst legislation was awaited.

However, views about good practice in the field of assisted reproduction differ. Squabbles between clinicians have surfaced in public and been amplified in the media. Some clinicians regard the VLA guidelines as a threat to their freedom of clinical judgment. On three issues in particular the VLA's authority has been challenged; how many embryos or eggs to transfer; selective foeticide on grounds of number; and egg donation by close relatives. All three have been at the forefront of controversy about practices in the field and have received significant media coverage. Such developments give substance to the growing recognition that the contested issues are not solely matters of clinical judgment: they pose pressing moral dilemmas that extend beyond the doctor-patient dyad. The VLA is unable to settle conflicts of value without some dialogue between the public, or rather various 'publics', doctors, and scientists.

These three issues provide striking examples of the problems of professional self-regulation in this field and are the focus of discussion in the second part of this chapter. At the outset, however, it is important to outline the context in which these challenges have arisen.

## INFERTILITY AND IVF

The birth in July 1978 of Louise Brown, the first baby conceived outside her mother's body, was widely hailed as both a scientific wonder and a medical breakthrough for the infertile. Leach observed in Annex 3 to the *First Report* of the VLA in 1986:

> Ever since that time [i.e. the time of Louise Brown's birth] *in vitro fertilization* has been sporadically in the news and is often confused in people's minds with quite different issues, such as surrogacy. Meanwhile, medical and scientific professionals, with the Government's help, have been debating the real issues.[10]

Despite the volume of associated literature expressing a broad spectrum of moral, ethical, and legal concerns, each does not indicate that there might be ambiguity as to what are the 'real' issues.

Human reproduction is remarkably inefficient but, despite this, most women who attempt to do so conceive within a year. Should pregnancy not result, as is the case for an estimated one in six of the reproductive population, the infertility services in the United Kingdom are woefully inadequate and, where available, of limited effectiveness.[11] Historically accorded a low status in medicine[12] the investigation and management of infertility have changed greatly since the introduction of IVF. There are new methods of follicular stimulation, of control of the follicular phase and the cryopreservation of gametes and embryos, and new developments associated with the management of conditions such as endometriosis or ideopathic infertility, where one or both oviducts are intact. Nevertheless, monitoring of practice and its effectiveness remain an issue. Reliable data on the number of patients treated, the outcomes and costs of the various treatments are difficult to find. The IVF specialists Fishel and Webster contend that in the absence of statutory powers clinics are not likely 'to be honest about their successes'.[13]

The major clinical risks of these procedures for the woman are ectopic pregnancy and multiple pregnancy, which may result in late miscarriage, prematurity and neonatal mortality.[14] Other factors, such as maternal age, frequent nulliparity, the context of sterility and factors associated with the IVF technique, in combination Cohen suggests, put at high risk such clinical pregnancies as are established.

Only a small literature exists on the biological issues surrounding children conceived by *in vitro* fertilization and embryo transfer. In a review of possible factors which could lead to an increase in the incidence of congenital abnormalities to above the level taken to be normal, Biggers[15] lists four: the induction of chromosomal aberrations: an increase in the rate of fertilization by abnormal spermatozoa; the induction of point (single gene) mutations; and the actions of physical and chemical teratogens. Both Angell and his co-workers[16] and Edwards[17] have pointed to chromosomal imbalance as the causative factor in the estimated high frequency of embryo loss occurring shortly before or after implantation *in vivo*. The significance of these concerns is yet to be established. The number of births following IVF is as yet insufficient to determine if the risk of congenital malformation is increased after IVF.[18]

Further data are needed to ascertain whether spina bifida, transposition, and possibly other malformations, occur more often than usual. In the United Kingdom, following the emphasis by the *Warnock Report* on the need for follow-up studies of these children and for a centrally maintained register of such births, the British Medical Research Council has set up an In-Vitro Fertilization Register to determine whether such children differ from the population as a whole, especially with regard to congenital malformations.[19]

## WHERE TO DRAW THE LINE?:
## THREE PROBLEMATIC INSTANCES

The guidelines are intended to set the minimum acceptable standards required and to offer a basis on which local ethical committees can agree their own house rules.[20]

The original VLA guidelines were based on those already in use by several expert groups. Recommendations made by the *Warnock Report* by a working party of the Medical Research Council and by the ethics committee of the Royal College of Obstetricians and Gynaecologists were also influential. Pronounced 'not sufficiently comprehensive' after a year the guidelines have subsequently been revised.[21] Developments in three areas in particular were addressed. First, new techniques, analogues of IVF, were in clinical use: GIFT, peritoneal oocyte and sperm transfer (POST) and vaginal intraperitoneal sperm transfer (VISPER). Second, the effects, for all concerned, of the multiple pregnancies following IVF and ET were a source of anxiety to the Authority, including 'the additional burden such effects may cause to fall on our already over-stretched NHS neonatal units and social and welfare services'.[22] Finally the VLA had received reports of particular requests for and particular cases of donation of eggs for fertilization and transfer to another woman. The consensus view among the membership was that 'there are relationships within which the practice would be inadvisable'.[23] Thus, in the Second Report of the VLA in 1987, certain of the original guidelines were amended and expanded and several new ones added. Certain practices were censured as a matter of public policy. The new guidelines were however regarded by some practitioners as a challenge to clinical judgment. Control by 'diktat' was a phrase publicly employed by more than one obstetrician critical of

41

the non-statutory VLA's new guidelines.[24] Three of the contentious issues are considered here.

### Multiple egg and embryo transfer: Guideline 12

Many clinics practising IVF and ET and GIFT have achieved both high rates of oocyte recovery and of fertilization. But, although cleavage of such embryos is satisfactory, the rates of implantation remain low. The vigour of research and the considerable publicity surrounding births following IVF and ET and GIFT belies the low success rate in establishing clinical pregnancies.

Any IVF clinic will aim to achieve as high an incidence of pregnancy as possible. In the early 1980s Biggers predicted that the pregnancy rate in IVF would increase with the number of embryos replaced, and early reports from IVF centres worldwide apparently supported his prediction.[25] Certainly such data encouraged the transfer of three, four, five or six embryos in clinical practice. By the time of the Third World Congress on IVF and ET in 1984, fifty-eight teams of IVF specialists had contributed to an international pooling of results: the overall pregnancy rate after embryo replacement was related to the number of embryos replaced and was 9.7, 14.7, 19.4 and 23.8 per cent respectively for the replacement of one, two, three or four embryos.[26]

In 1987 a spate of letters in professional journals and in newspapers in the United Kingdom called attention to the contentious issue of how many eggs or embryos should be transferred in GIFT or after IVF, and on the risks and consequences of multiple births.[27] A multiple pregnancy rate of 34.5 per cent after the transfer of three or more embryos was reported in a small series in one centre in Nottingham.[28] Moreover IVF centres worldwide have reported an enhanced multiple pregnancy rate where larger numbers of embryos are transferred.[29]

The extra perinatal stresses widely associated with a twin pregnancy are heightened in a triplet, quadruplet, or higher order multiple pregnancy. Such 'grand' multiple pregnancies are at risk of maternal and foetal morbidity and mortality. The complications of prematurity and placental insufficiency may make the infants particularly vulnerable when, as is likely, they are pre-term and of low birthweight. Many will require neonatal intensive care. Although more of these children now survive, the multiple birth mortality rates have not declined at the same rate as have singleton mortality rates.[30] If they do survive the neonatal period their care-takers' face extraordinary demands in relation to the provision of food, nurturance and physical care. Little is known, however, about how parents cope or the extent to which they can obtain help and support.[31]

Multiple embryo transfer received the attention of neonatal paedi-atricians at national and international conferences from 1986 onwards: the incidence of and neonatal and community provision for higher order multiple birth children has become of increasing concern. The unusual demands made on behalf of these children are not only on the health services but also on social services, which are already stretched as a consequence of the implementation of welfare policies transferring care to the community,

More clinical data are now available. IVF centres throughout the world are achieving greater levels of success at initiating preg-nancies with the transfer of no more than three embryos. It is evident that the percentage of women who become pregnant does not greatly increase if more than three or four embryos are trans-ferred, although the magnitude of any consequent multiple preg-nancy does increase.[32] The risks of such pregnancies and the neonatal and long-term complications are widely acknowledged. Beyond this, promising developments in cryopreservation tech-niques have been reported and there is evidence that the transfer-ence of a single embryo in the IVF cycle, the others being frozen for transfer in subsequent cycles may enhance the efficacy of IVF and ET.[33]

On the issue of multiple transfer, the VLA's decision to act to limit the number of eggs and embryos transferred was backed by scientific and clinical data. In the May 1987 Second Report of the VLA, Guideline 12 was a new instruction:

(12) Consideration must be given to ensuring that whilst a woman has the best chance of achieving a pregnancy the risks of a large multiple pregnancy occurring are minimized. For this reason:

(a) if the IVF procedure is used no more than three pre-embryos should be transferred in any one cycle, unless there are exceptional clinical reasons when up to four pre-embryos may be replaced per cycle,

(b) if the GIFT procedure is used no more than three or exceptionally four eggs should be introduced to the fallopian tubes.[34]

At one licensed centre the medical team would not give a written undertaking that they would adhere to this guideline. They argued for the flexibility to continue their clinical practice of transferring up to twelve embryos.[35]In September 1987, faced with this refusal from one of thirty licensed centres, the VLA had no option but to withdraw their licence of approval.[36] The Authority remain adamant about guideline 12.

### Selective foeticide: an additional issue in relation to Guideline 12

The practice of partial termination by foeticide of a multifoetal pregnancy in the first trimester rests on advances both in obstetric ultrasonography and prenatal diagnosis. This tailoring of multi-parity received adverse publicity in 1987 as an apparent loophole in the law on abortion. No VLA guideline makes explicit reference to the procedure: it features in the Second Report as an additional issue in relation to the newly introduced Guideline 12:

> It would be improper deliberately to introduce more than four pre-embryos to the uterus and then, should a large multiple pregnancy result, to reduce the number of live embryos other than for legitimate clinical reasons such as malformation or ectopic pregnancy.[37]

The Chairman of the VLA, Dame Mary Donaldson, made it clear in a letter to *New Scientist* that the Authority regards selective foeticide after a multiple egg transfer in a GIFT procedure and multiple embryo transfer in an IVF procedure as unacceptable and unethical.[38]

Selective foeticide following diagnosis of twins discordant for severe abnormality or for genetic anomaly is a technique which has been employed in the United States for over a decade[39] and in the United Kingdom for more than five years.[40] The first published report of termination in a higher order multiple pregnancy in the first trimester was in 1986: a quintuplet gestation in Holland was reduced to a twin gestation which continued to spontaneous term labour and the birth of two healthy females.[41] This multiple foeticide, the quintuplet case subsequently reported in the UK by Rodeck[42] and the forty-two selective foeticide cases in France involving two sets of sextuplets, ten quadruplets, eighteen triplets and twelve twins reported by Salat-Baroux and his colleagues[43] were justified on grounds of the number, not the abnormality, of the foetuses. The surviving three foetuses, in a selective foeticide case in Germany involving twelve foetuses, were delivered at 34 weeks gestation.[44] Different techniques may be adopted. One or more foetuses may be exsanguinated or aspirated. Alternatively the amniotic sac may be injected with potassium chloride.

Lawyers and medical ethicists are wrestling with the issues raised by this procedure.[45] The question arises of whether or not selective foeticide is permitted by the law relating to abortion.[46] In the United Kingdom the few clinicians practising selective foeticide to date have not carried out the procedure under the criteria laid down by the 1967 Abortion Act. Their view is that there is no abortion or miscarriage and no termination of pregnancy occurs or is intended. Whether or not selective foeticide falls within section 58 of the 1861 Offences Against the Person Act has not been tested in the courts. There are different views. Legal advice received by those who employ the procedure, practitioners such as Craft at the Humana Hospital Wellington in London, is that the procedure is not an abortion, because the foetuses are not expelled from the body at the time of the procedure and the pregnancy is not terminated. Licensed practitioners were advised, however, at a VLA meeting in November 1987 that, to avoid possible prosecution if they engage in selective foeticide, they should abide by the 1967 Act.

On this issue the VLA are faced with a dilemma of an undoubtedly major legal dimension. The ethical and social dimensions, however, are of similar magnitude. Even with the knowledge that the clinical prognosis for a higher order multiple birth is likely to be poor, selective foeticide in such cases is a difficult option for the woman involved. Here is a challenge to the meaning of motherhood.[47] The clinician must decide which foetuses to leave and which to aspirate or exsanguinate. Brahams cautions, 'obviously if selective reduction is performed on grounds of preferred sex, the procedure becomes open to increased censure.'[48] The long-term consequences of such tailored multiparity for both parent and resultant child are, as yet, unknown. The VLA have neither the remit nor the funds to initiate follow-up studies.

## Egg donation by known donors: Guideline 13(j)

Should the VLA, and subsequently the SLA, endorse medical participation in the initiation of pregnancies using gametes from known donors: close relatives, in particular sisters, and close friends? There is a divergence of opinion. In the absence of any informed debate about the wisdom of the practice, clinicians have used relatives for sperm and egg donation in IVF and GIFT procedures.[49] Press reports suggest that the perception of any ensuing risk to those involved is low. But the wider social implications, not only for the individuals concerned, have not been examined. One woman who accepted eggs donated from her sister remarked: 'With my sister's eggs we are continuing the family's bloodline – at least there is still that connection with my parents and grandparents.'[50] The high value placed on genetic inheritance is often advanced as sufficient explanation: that women feel secure in the knowledge that the eggs donated to them come from 'within the family', thus 'keeping it in the family gene pool'. Such facilitation, when available, is presented as the obvious remedy.

Egg donation, for some couples, 'provides the only chance of their having a child which the woman can carry to term, and which is the genetic child of her husband'. This is the argument for egg donation which was considered by the *Warnock Report*. It found such a donation to be ethically acceptable 'where the donor has been properly counselled and is fully aware of the risks'. Reference is made to possible physical risks for the egg donor 'from the actual removal of the eggs'. Egg donation requires the donor to undergo surgical intervention.

Techniques for the cryopreservation of human oocytes were not developed when the *Warnock Report* was published.[51] Difficulties in egg collection and storage were believed to provide adequate grounds to make an exception to the principle of donor anonymity 'where the egg was donated by a sister or close friend'. The rationale was not spelt out, but the Committee advocated that 'particularly careful counselling for all concerned would be necessary'.

In May 1987, at a meeting held at the Royal College of Obstetricians and Gynaecologists, clinicians from one centre in London reported that babies had been born to three women each of whom had been the recipient of eggs donated by a sister. The Second Report of the VLA published subsequent to this meeting, advised that egg donors should be, and should remain, anonymous. 'There are relationships within which the practice would be inadvisable', the Authority considered.[52] However, the terms of the Guideline 13(j) did not forbid the use of known donors:

> Egg donors should remain anonymous and for this reason donations for clinical purposes from any close relative should be avoided.[53]

Some leading clinicians in the field argue strongly for relatives, and particularly sisters, to be able to donate eggs for use in both *in vitro* fertilization and embryo transfer, and gamete intrafallopian transfer. There is a shortage of donated eggs and fears that women will be offered money to donate eggs. More than facilitation is at stake here, however. There is a range of highly significant issues. Possibly they are interrelated.

First, the facilitation takes place only with the surgical intervention of clinicians. The practice is thereby in the public domain and influences views of the options available. If there is evidence that women seem 'happier with known donors'[54] will gamete donation by relatives become the preferred option, and thence normative, in infertility cases in which gamete donation is judged by the clinician to be appropriate?

Before any authoritative statement is produced, the term 'known donor' needs to be critically examined, and safeguards made against powerful appeals by professionals or by a potential recipient. Some potential donors may consider themselves always under an obligation to particular individuals, whilst others are free of such influence and able to refuse. Stage in life course and degree of dependence may be pervasive influences, particularly when intergenerational donation of gametes is proposed.

Second, general discussions about kinship are often premised on assumptions which are the more significant for seldom being rendered explicit. Ideas about the 'naturalness' of relationships with kin, and about a natural moral code relating to kinship, convey powerful images that can bestow a sense of permanence on what, for various reasons, may well be a transient state of affairs. Such ideas may encourage also the idea that relationships with kin are somehow quite apart from political and economic structures.

Assumptions about the 'naturalness' of particular relationships between kin influence estimations of what is to be regarded as feasible and what responsible behaviour by those located 'in a family'. Concern and obligation, expressed in mutual aid, are associated with kinship in numerous anthropological and sociological studies undertaken in the United Kingdom.[55] Such aid relationships have however no public identity. No principle of organization can be identified. There is scope for selectivity. Recognition of kin may be precarious and intermittent. Social conventions permit quite considerable variations. Relationships with relatives are constantly being renegotiated and mutual aid between them is bounded in significant ways which have been the focus of recent research.[56]

Third, will a perception of relatedness to a potential recipient entail an obligation on a potential donor to donate? Moreover, will such an obligation to donate extend beyond the donation to an obligation to provide care, in greater measure than might otherwise be the case? Or may a donor, who might in other circumstances have provided care and support to the recipient relative and her child(ren), withdraw or distance herself? Perhaps the latter is more likely?

Fourth, the *Warnock* recommendation was that the egg donor should have no rights or obligations in respect of the child. There is, however, an extensive literature which charts the significance of relatives in the provision of support and aid in child care.[57] Possible adverse consequences of the donation for the donor and recipient and resultant children require sensitive study: what might be the likely consequences, for instance, if the outcome is not what the donor and/or recipient envisages: e.g. medical complications, handicap, multiple birth? Where there is handicap Glendinning has emphasized the extent of 'unshared care' even 'within the family'.[58] There is a need also to consider the way in which notions like risk and risk perception are employed in discussions.[59]

What are the social conditions conducive to gamete donation by known donors and under what circumstances is such a donation contra-indicated? These and other issues only anthropological, sociological, psychological, and perhaps historical research can illuminate. The presumption seems to be that the transfer is between a relative or friend living in a separate household but, by the nature of the close relationship, the donor remains a continuing presence in the life of the recipient and her child(ren) – an eventuality which usually rules out adoption in the United Kingdom. Moreover the donation is apparently seen in terms of a diffuse altruism: 'a lovely gift'. The possibility of the expression of reciprocity in the relationship have not featured in reports of discussions of such donations. The preference for sibling relationships in egg donation may be that such relationships, particularly between sisters, are presumed to rest on a fundamental equality of status that is unlikely to lead to future material claims.

Those in the limelight on this issue seem reluctant to acknowledge the authority of, or to seek expert advice from, those who are neither scientists nor clinicians: anthropologists, sociologists, and historians for instance. The controversy turns on what is to count as 'evidence'. Only in the closing months of 1987 were worries expressed that forthcoming legislation might endorse the practice by default, and in the absence of proper research.

## STATUTORY REGULATION

Challenges to the VLA's authority on these three issues: how many embryos or eggs to transfer; selective foeticide on grounds of number; and egg donation by known donors; widely reported in the press, on television and in the letters pages of the leading medical journals, do nothing to detract from a heightened concern that professional self-regulation by means of a non-statutory review body is not satisfactory.

In the field of reproductive medicine the focus, in the main, has been on biology and on achieving a successful outcome in terms of establishing a pregnancy. The psychological and social aspects of the management of infertility have not been entirely neglected but have featured in ethical committee discussions concerning selection of couples for treatment, rather than in discussions either of the psycho-social aspects of the experience of a procedure, or the broader social and political consequences of the development and outcome of practices in the field. Many dispute that the contested issues are just matters of clinical judgment. So novel is the combination of conditions and reproductive choices which have developed that there is not yet any systematic appraisal of the consequences. To accommodate not only conflicting expert evidence but also critical forms of 'non-expert' knowledge and different value premises, those who make decisions about a technology and who make reappraisals of its development confront social and political issues. Non-medical observations and judgments are highly significant, particularly in relation to the awareness and identification of problems concerning the new technologies of prenatal intervention.

Clinicians acknowledge that they are 'testing the water' and the law is a blunt instrument in all this. But the view that the proper mechanism for regulation and control must be a statutory authority is reflected in the proposed legislation published in November 1987 in the White Paper *Human Fertilisation and Embryology; A Framework for Legislation.*[60] Here the need 'to regulate and monitor practice in relation to those sensitive areas which raise fundamental ethical questions', which was the principle behind the recommendations in the *Warnock Report*,[61] is reaffirmed and explicitly interpreted as extending beyond professional concerns about efficacy and safety. Clinicians and their scientific colleagues have no 'special' social responsibility, nor have they any special skills to make ethical and social decisions. The clinical management of infertility is now on the public policy agenda.

## NOTES

1 E. Yoxen, *Unnatural Selection?: Coming to Terms with the New Genetics* (London: Heinemann, 1986), p. 3.

2 I. Kennedy, 'A survey of the year I: the doctor–patient relationship', in P. Byrne (ed.), *Rights and Wrongs in Medicine: King's College Studies 1985–6* (London: King's Fund, 1986).

3 D. Nelkin, *Science as Intellectual Property. Who Controls Research?* (London: Collier Macmillan, 1984); Royal Society, *The Public Understanding of Science* (London: Royal Society, 1985).

4 S. Fishel and E. M. Symonds (eds), *In Vitro Fertilization: Past, Present, Future* (Oxford: IRL Press, 1986); H. W. Jones, G. S. Jones, G. D. Hodgen, and Z. Rosenwaks (eds), *In Vitro Fertilization: Norfolk* (Baltimore: Williams & Wilkins, 1986); R. H. Asch, O. R. Ellsworth, J. P. Balmaceda, and P. C. Wong, 'Pregnancy after translaparoscopic gamete intrafallopian transfer', *Lancet* (1984), ii, pp. 1034–5.

5 G. Bock and M. O'Connor (eds), *Human Embryo Research: Yes or No?* (London: CIBA, 1986); M. Stanworth (ed.), *Reproductive Technologies: Gender, Motherhood and Medicine* (Oxford: Polity Press, 1987).

6 M. Warnock, *A Question of Life: the Warnock Report on Human Fertilisation and Embryology* (Oxford: Basil Blackwell, 1985); Council of Europe, Ad hoc Committee of Experts on Progress in the Biomedical Sciences, *Provisional Principles on the Techniques of Human Artificial Procreation* (Strasbourg Council of Europe, 1986); M. Stacey, 'The manipulation of the birth process', Research Implications Paper presented at Feb. 1988 meeting of the WHO European Advisory Committee for Health Resources.

7 L. Waller, 'New law for laboratory life' *Law, Medicine and Health Care*, vol. 14 (1987), p. 121.

8 Department of Health and Social Security, *Legislation on Human Infertility Services and Embryo Research: a Consultative Paper*, Cm 46 (London: HMSO, 1986).

9 Voluntary Licensing Authority (Joint Medical Research Council/Royal College of Obstetricians and Gynaecologists), *The First Report of the Voluntary Licensing Authority for Human 'In Vitro' Fertilisation and Embryology* (London: VLA, 1986).

10 P. Leach, 'Human in vitro fertilization', in *The First Report of the Voluntary Licensing Authority for Human 'In Vitro' Fertilisation and Embryology*, p. 40.

11 D. Mathieson, *Infertility Services in the NHS: What's Going On?*, A Report prepared for Frank Dobson, MP, House of Commons, 1986; R. J. Lilford and M. E. Dalton, 'Effectiveness of treatment for infertility', *British Medical Journal*, vol. 295 (18 July 1987), pp. 155–6; R. Winston and R. Margara, 'Effectiveness of treatment for infertility', *British Medical Journal*, vol. 295 (5 September 1987), p. 608.

12 N. Pfeffer, 'Artificial insemination, in-vitro fertilisation and the stigma of infertility', in Stanworth (ed.), *Reproductive Technologies*, pp. 81–97.

13 S. Fishel and J. Webster, 'IVF and associated techniques: whom can we believe?', *Lancet* (1987), ii, p. 273.

14 H. Cohen, 'Pregnancy, abortion and birth after in vitro fertilization', in Fishel and Symonds, *In Vitro Fertilization*, pp. 135–46.

15 J. D. Biggers, 'In vitro fertilization and embryo transfer in human beings', *New England Journal of Medicine*, vol. 34 (1981), pp. 336–42.

16 R. R. Angell, R. J. Aitken, P. F. A. van Look, M. A. Lumsden, and A. A. Templeton, 'Chromosome, abnormality in human embryos after in vitro fertilization', *Nature*, vol. 303 (1983), pp. 36–8.

17 R. G. Edwards, 'Chromosomal abnormalities in human embryos', *Nature*, vol. 303 (1983), p. 283.

18 P. A. L. Lancaster, 'Congenital malformation after in vitro fertilization', *Lancet* (1987), ii, pp. 1392–3. Analysis of data from the register of IVF and GIFT pregnancies in Australia and New Zealand indicates a greater than expected prevalence of spina bifida and transposition of the great vessels. The probablity is low that the increased number of infants with these two types of congenital malformation occurred by chance. But as yet there is insufficient data.

19 See also D. N. Mushin, M. C. Barreda-Hansen, and J. C. Spensley, 'In vitro fertilization children: early psychosocial development', *Journal of In Vitro Fertilization and Embryo Transfer* (1986), no. 3, p. 247; F. Wirth, N. Morin, D. Johnson, M. Frank, H. Presberg, V. Vanderwater, and J. Mills, 'Follow-up study of children born as a result of IVF', paper given at the Fifth World Congress on In Vitro Fertilization and Embryo Transfer, Norfolk, Virginia (1987).

20 VLA, *First Report* (1986), p. 8.

21 Voluntary Licensing Authority (Joint Medical Research Council/Royal College of Obstetricians and Gynaecologists), *The Second Report of the*

*Voluntary Licensing Authority for Human 'In Vitro' Fertilisation and Embryology* (London: VLA, 1987).

22 VLA, *Second Report*, p. 1.

23 VLA, *Second Report*, p. 8.

24 W. Savage, 'A nest of aunts?' (letter), *Guardian*, 13 May 1987. I. Craft, P. Brinsden, E. Simons, and P. Lewis, 'Concern over multiple births' (letters), *Observer*, 22 November 1987.

25 J. D. Biggers, 'IVF and embryology transfer in human beings', S. J. Muasher, A. Wilkins, J. E. Garcia, Z. Rosenwaks, and H. W. H. Jones, 'Benefits and risks of multiple transfer with in vitro fertilization', *Lancet* (1984), i, p. 570; see also J. Webster, 'Embryo replacement', in Fishel and Symonds, *In Vitro Fertilization*, p. 128.

26 M. Seppala, 'The World Collaborative Report of In Vitro Fertilization and Embryo Replacement: current state of the art in 1984', in M. Seppala and R. G. Edwards (eds), *In Vitro Fertilization and Embryo Transfer*, Annal of the New York Academy of Sciences, vol. 442 (1985), pp. 558–63.

27 I. Craft, P. R. Brindsen, and E. G. Simons, 'Voluntary licensing and IVF/ET', *Lancet* (1987), i, p. 1148; D. C. Anderson, 'Licensing work on IVF and related procedures', *Lancet* (1987) i, p. 1373; M. Richards and F. Price, 'Licensing work on IVF and related procedures', *Lancet* (1987), i, pp. 1373–4; I. Craft, P. Brindsen, and E. G. Simons, 'How many oocytes/embryos should be transferred?', *Lancet* (1987), ii, p. 109; P. A. L. Lancaster, 'How many oocytes/embryos should be transferred?', *Lancet* (1987), ii, p. 109.

28 Fishel and Webster, 'IVF and associated techniques'.

29 See Lancaster, 'How many oocytes/embryos should be transferred?', p. 110; S. J. Muasher and J. E. Garcia 'Pregnancy and its outcome', in H. W. Jones *et al.* (eds), *In Vitro Fertilisations*, p. 245.

30 B. Botting, I. MacDonald Davies and A. MacFarlane, 'Recent trends in the incidence of multiple births and associated mortality', *Archives of Diseases in Childhood*, vol. 62 (1987) p. 941.

31 F. V. Price, 'The risk of high multiparity with IVF/ET', in *Birth: Issues in Perinatal Care and Education*, vol. 15 (1988), pp. 157–63.

32 R. W. Shaw, 'In vitro fertilization', paper given to the Meeting for Ethical Committees for IVF Centres, RCOG, London, June 1987.

33 J. Testart, B. Lassalle, J. Belaisch-Allart, R. Forman, A. Hazout, M. Volante, and M. D. Frydman, 'Human embryo viability related to freezing and thawing procedures', *American Journal of Obstetrics and Gynecology*, vol. 157 (1987), pp. 68–71.

34 VLA *Second Report* (1987), p. 35.

35 In a climate in which there was no published data from the Humana team on the numbers transferred, rumours flourished of the transfer of up to fifteen embryos. Members of the team complained in a letter to the British Medical Journal of misrepresentation and 'trial by television'; I. Craft, P. Brindsen, E. Simons, and P. Lewis, 'The fertility debate and the media', *British Medical Journal*, vol. 295 (31 October 1987), p. 1134.

36 Ian Craft, the director of the Humana's infertility unit, has kept a high

profile throughout this much publicized dispute. He continues to assert publicly that the VLA has 'moved the goals', that clinical freedom is at stake and that the VLA guidelines must be 'flexible'. See J. Laurance, 'The test-tube dilemma', *New Society*, vol. 82, no. 1296, pp. 19–20.

37 VLA, *Second Report*, p. 8.

38 M. Donaldson, 'Early embryos' (letter), *New Scientist*, 9 July 1987, p. 64.

39 A. Aberg, F. Mitelman, M. Cantz, and J. Gehler, 'Cardiac puncture of fetus with Hurler's disease avoiding abortion of unaffected co-twin', *Lancet* (1978), ii, p. 990.

40 C. H. Rodeck, R. S. Mibastion, J. Abramowicz, and S. Campbell, 'Selective feticide of the affected twin by fetoscopic air embolism', *Prenatal Diagnosis* (1982), no. 2, p. 189.

41 H. H. H. Kanhai, E. J. C. Van Rijssel, R. J. Meerman, and J. Bennebroek Gravenhorst, 'Selective terminations in quintuplet pregnancy during first trimester', *Lancet* (1986), i, p. 1447.

42 C. Rodeck, 'The twin fetus', paper given at a Symposium on Multiple Births at the Institute of Obstectrics and Gynaecology, University of London, 1986.

43 J. Salat-Baroux, J. Aknin, and J. M. Antoine, 'The management of multiple pregnancies after IVF', paper presented at the Third Meeting of the European Society of Human Reproduction and Embryology, Cambridge, UK, 1987.

44 M. Breckwoldt, F. Geisthovel, J. Neulen, and H. Schillinger, 'Management of multiple (12) conceptions after ovulation induction: case report', paper presented at the Third Meeting of the European Society of Human Reproduction and Embryology, Cambridge, UK, 1987.

45 O. Gillie, 'Test tube baby hospital denies abortion claim', *Independent*, 10 March 1987, p. 5; see also A. Ferriman, 'Better we have just one baby than none', *Observer* 1 November 1987, p. 6.

46 J. Keown, 'Selective reduction of multiple pregnancy', *New Law Journal*, vol. 137 (1987), pp. 1165–6; D. Brahams, 'Assisted reproduction and selective reduction of pregnancy', *Lancet* (1987), ii, pp. 1409–10.

47 B. K. Rothman, 'The products of conception: the social context of reproductive choices', *Journal of Medical Ethics*, vol. 11 (1985), pp. 188–92.

48 Brahams, 'Assisted reproduction'.

49 A. Veitch, 'Three become mothers with eggs from sisters', *Guardian* 5 April 1987, p. 3; L. Fraser, 'Sisters share test tube joy of twin girls', *Mail on Sunday*, 8 November 1987, p. 17.

50 C. Steven, 'Test-tube sisters', *Independent*, 29 September 1987, p. 13.

51 Human oocyte cryopreservation was first developed as a technique in Victoria, Australia in 1985. See A. Trounson, 'Submission to the Senate Select Committee on the Human Embryo Experimentation Bill 1985', *Senate Official Report* (Hansard) (1986); see also C. Chen 'Pregnancy after human oocyte cryopreservation', *Lancet* (1986), i, p. 884.

52 VLA, *Second Report*, p. 8.

53 VLA, *Second Report*, Annex 1, p. 35.

54 *Lancet*, 'Egg donation by relatives', *Lancet* (1987), ii, p. 1163.

55 See for instance G. Allen *Sociology of Friendship and Kinship* (London: Allen & Unwin, 1979); S. Wallman, *Eight London Households* (London: Tavistock, 1984).
56 J. Finch, *Duty Bound* (Oxford: Polity Press, forthcoming 1989).
57 See for example M. Hill, *Sharing Child Care in Early Parenthood* (London: Routledge & Kegan Paul, 1987).
58 C. Glendinning, *Unshared Care* (London: Routledge & Kegan Paul, 1983).
59 M. Douglas, *Risk: Acceptability According to the Social Sciences* (London: Routledge & Kegan Paul, 1986).
60 Department of Health and Social Security, *Human Fertilisation and Embryology: A Framework for Legislation*, Cm 259 (London: HMSO, 1987).
61 DHSS *Human Fertilisation and Embryology*.

# 4

# SURROGACY:
# AN INTRODUCTORY ESSAY

## *DEREK MORGAN*

Surrogacy has appeared at the eye of the storm surrounding assisted reproduction. The lightning rod for the controversy which has engulfed it in the United Kingdom was the well publicized case of *Re A Baby*, the 'Baby Cotton' case in January 1985.[1] Even though it does not *necessarily* demand the most technologically sophisticated contribution to conception, nor is it presently thought to be the most statistically significant response to infertility, surrogacy has become the whipping post for the moral backlash against what is seen as the brave new world of technological rationality and scientific finality. It is seen to cut clearly into fundamental values; to disturb cherished ideals of personal integrity, family life, and national security. It is identified as a time bomb primed to explode in the course of the 'reproduction revolution'.[2]

In this essay I want to suggest an alternative understanding of surrogacy, one which sees it as a by-product of the industry which has created the nuclear family. On this view, it may be characterized as highly volatile matter resulting from the fusion of personal desire, psychological drive, and societal demand or imperative. I want to suggest the necessary accommodation of surrogacy as a reproductive alternative. But I want to do this understanding and recognizing the potential which surrogacy holds for economic exploitation, moral confusion, and psychological harm; whether for surrogate mothers, surrogate-born children or their prospective parents.

Issues such as childbirth, child rearing, and child care are more easily seen and readily identifiable today as raising core issues of social justice. This perspective helps to explain why the study of surrogacy may throw into relief other developments and help to reveal patriarchal structures and practices which help to sustain and strengthen reproductive domination; Freeman has suggested that surrogacy may present us with an opportunity to challenge unacceptable features of medical and social work imperialism.[3] Michelle Stanworth recommends the study of the 'new' reproductive technologies because they are controversial, and controversial because 'they crystallize issues at the heart of contemporary social and political struggles over sexuality, reproduction, gender relations and the family'.[4] Surrogacy parallels some of these concerns. Even if characterized as a mere side-show at the margins of the moral jamboree which reproductive technologies herald, surrogacy may be able to illuminate something about the nature of the whole which the bright lights of the major attractions, such as embryo transfer and experimentation, *in vitro* fertilization, sex determination and preselection, occlude or distort. Particularly, the crepuscular images of value and worth predicated in the surrogacy story challenge our understanding of the 'natural' and the 'brave new' worlds, and the values which inhere in each. To study surrogacy involves an appreciation of critical family law and social policy; an understanding of the social construction of fertility and infertility and the deconstruction of the limits and possibilities of reproductive technology.

## THE LANGUAGE OF SURROGACY

By surrogacy, which I use as a shorthand for surrogate motherhood, I mean an understanding or agreement by which a woman – the surrogate mother – agrees to bear a child for another person or couple. Of course, this popular understanding immediately encounters the objection that it is the person – I will assume for the present purposes a woman – who takes and rears the child rather than she who gives birth who is properly the surrogate. The woman giving birth is *the* mother, not the surrogate. This consideration is not lightly dismissed as semantic felicity; rather it raises an important issue.

Bernard Dickens has joined the complainants who would regard my understanding of surrogate motherhood as a misnomer. He has castigated it as one which is;

> now probably irrevocable. . . . The gestating woman is not, of course, a deputy or substitute mother, but is a genuine and

56

authentic mother to the child she bears. . . . The description of
the gestational mother as a surrogate is journalistic in origin, and
is based on the uncritical presumption that genuine parenthood
is exclusively genetic and intrafamilial, so that a woman who
assists a couple to have a child that is genetically that of one or
both partners by gestating it is engaging in secondary or non-
authentic parenthood. Once it is recognized, however, that the
functions of motherhood are divisible into the genetic, the
gestational and the social or psychological, it becomes clear that
a woman engaging in this practice is primarily involved in
gestational motherhood, which in most cases to date also entails
her genetic motherhood.[5]

This opinion appears to be based on two misunderstandings, one
of them primary, and the second consequent on accepting the divisibility of functions in relation to birth, as suggested by Goldstein,
Freud and Solnit.[6]

First, Dickens proceeds on the assumption that there is an exact
parallel between our understanding of motherhood and our understanding of maternity. The distinction urged between stages or
experiences of motherhood, as Goldstein suggests, is to recognize
that the surrogate is not, in fact, a surrogate for motherhood, but
for maternity.[7] It is, indeed, more consistent with Dickens's argument that the gestational woman be regarded as the real mother
and the commissioning woman as the surrogate if we draw *no*
distinction between different forms of procreative functions.[8] What
is involved is the uncritical assumption that pregnancy is the only
fit state of preparation for the role of caring and nurturing a young
child and providing it with a loving and caring environment in
which to grow up. (The corollary which shadows this, of course, is
that the eventual birth of a child is the only fit purpose for which
a pregnancy might intentionally or unwittingly be established.)

A number of different issues are being collapsed here, and for a
number of different reasons. They rest on acceptance of the legal
presumption that *mater est quam gestatio demonstrat;* the mother of a
child is the one who gives birth to it. That is a *presumption* which,
in most cases, I think we would want to defend and retain. As
Juliette Zipper and Selma Sevenhuijsen have argued, it is one of a
number of protective elements in family law for women:

[the rule] is a legal confirmation of the 'right' of a woman to keep a child which she bore . . . . This protection counts in . . . cases of surrogacy, when a woman changes her mind and wishes to keep the child. If *mater semper certa est* were to be abolished, women could be brought before court about their legal and real relationship to their child. . . . Maintaining this rule creates a situation in which there will be legal problems only where a surrogate mother wants to give her child away, but the intended parent(s) will not accept it.[9]

Building on this approach, Mason and McCall Smith[10] argue that 'no genetic niceties should obscure the fact that these are the essential features of motherhood'. This assumes we have, for all purposes, an agreed understanding and definition of motherhood, and that that definition serves as well for legal purposes as it does for social purposes. That this prescriptive analysis causes difficult problems for surrogacy is illustrated in litigated cases where a dispute has arisen between a surrogate mother who has changed her mind about surrendering the baby on birth and the commissioning parents who want to force through the deal. The two most notorious examples here are the American case of *In Re the Matter of Baby M*[11] and the contemporaneous English case of *Re P.*[12] However, literally throwing the baby out with the bath water is not a sensible or constructive approach to resolving difficult and contested issues which surrogacy throws up. Notice that the point which I am presently concerned with is not that which goes to the resolution of disputed custody questions between the surrogate and the commissioning parents, but the apparently more theoretical and semantic felicity of who should 'properly' be called the 'surrogate mother'.

The tenets which support these approaches to surrogacy are reflected in the *Warnock Report*'s repeated argument that surrogacy distorts the relationship between gestational mother and the child, and that the surrogate in allowing herself to become pregnant with the intention deliberately of surrendering the child on birth demonstrates 'the wrong way to approach pregnancy'.[13] The correct way of becoming pregnant and approaching pregnancy is implicitly intimated as being with the intention of keeping the child. Nothing is offered on the fact that the intention may subsequently change, by deciding to have an abortion, or rejecting the child on birth. Or that it may do so by allowing the child to be fostered or adopted because of countervailing circumstances. Nothing is suggested as to why the time and circumstances of forming the intention to keep or surrender the child are decisive, nor why it is decisively established that forming that intention *prior* to conception, as in surrogacy, rather than at any other time is likely to be more damaging to the surrogate, whose interests are properly of major concern here. A similar argument is adduced in support, with respect to the surrogate-born child, 'whose bonds with the carrying mother, regardless of genetic connections are held to be strong, and whose welfare must be considered to be of paramount importance'.[14]

The nature of the mother–child bond preceding and during pregnancy is accepted as unproblematic; but it is not.[15] Andrea Stumpf has articulated the consequences of this uncertainty and confusion for the debate about surrogacy most clearly. Drawing distinctions between four different phases of procreation, the initiating stage, the preparation stage, the gestation stage and the child raising stage, she argues that the full process of birthing is not a simple biological linearity, and that the procreative process itself should be taken as a new starting point for understanding and analysing reproductive technologies, of which surrogacy might here be thought of as one.[16] Following this, the fact that an infertile woman has no genetic or gestational link to the child, does not mean that she has no *procreative role* in its birth or that she has no *procreative intent* in assuming the child as her progeny.[17] This intent and link is, of course, strengthened where the surrogate mother is implanted with an embryo which is genetically that of the woman who wishes to raise the child and her partner or a donor.[18] Stumpf suggests that the importance of this analysis is that it recognizes that in surrogacy the divisibility of procreative tasks is the essence of the practice. It is a recognition that

> The psychological dimension of procreation precedes and transcends the biology of procreation. Motherhood can be a product of both mental and physical conception; reductionist modes of legal reasoning have ignored this fullness. The significance of induced postpartum maternal behaviour is debated and evidence of psychological bonding is not sufficiently clear to give automatic rise to automatic rights.[19]

What ensues from this, according to Stumpf, is that 'we really have no definition of "mother" in our law books . . . . "Mother" was believed to have been so basic that no definition was

59

needed . . . . The legal definition of "mother" has traditionally carried an unshakable presumption: She was the one from whose womb the child came.'[20] Two things may now cause complications for these assumptions; recognition of the divisibility of procreative roles and, allied with this, the very niceties of genetic make-up which Mason and McCall Smith are anxious for us to gloss over. Shaking the unshakeable exposes choices which we have to make, and which we have always previously made by denying the existence of choice.

I am sensitive to the objection that challenging the assumption that maternity invariably connotes motherhood has dangerous Aristotelian or Thomistic undercurrents; that in surrogacy there is the danger of viewing the surrogate merely as 'the vessel for a man's seed . . . merely [supplying] the matter which the active male formed and moulded into a human being . . . [serving] as the passive incubator of [male] seed'.[21]

Those objections would be very forceful if there were no circumstances under which they could be countered or rebutted. However, the assumptions underlying the 'protective' aspects of the rule *mater est quam gestatio demonstrat* as discussed may give rise to social and psychological difficulties for women who do want to act as surrogates. Such women may have no intention of becoming or being pregnant for the purposes of rearing the child themselves and may have no desire to be regarded as the mother. This semantic debate, then, reflects a tension between these protective elements of family law, originally introduced for purposes far removed from those in which they are now being prayed in aid and challenged in ways which were quite unforeseen even in the recent past,[22] and their use as judgmental social norms against which surrogacy is played out: if the rule is that the mother of the child is the woman who gives birth to it, *how could she give it away?*[23] In averting to this descriptive controversy, I want only to alert to the argument that seeing the woman who gives birth to the child as the surrogate is not an uncontested notion, and to suggest that there are conclusions which appear to flow more comfortably from such a description. It is an example of the use and elision of language to appear to make one set of circumstances more natural, thereby less objectionable, therefore commanding support among right-thinking people.

## THE NATURE OF SURROGACY

To recall, I take surrogacy to mean that a surrogate agrees before she becomes pregnant that she will on the birth of the child she carries throughout her pregnancy, hand that child to the couple with whom she has made the surrogate agreement. This appreciation of the nature of surrogacy leaves some questions unanswered and begs some questions. Some of these need to be identified here.

The initial question is how the surrogate becomes pregnant. There are at least four straightforward possibilities. First, the surrogate could become pregnant following sexual intercourse with the man of the couple who are to look after the child or through the use of artificial insemination with his sperm, having had no prior relationship, legal or emotional, with him or his partner. Secondly, the surrogate could become pregnant through AID using the sperm of another man. In these first two cases the surrogate would make a *genetic* contribution to the resulting baby, her genes would constitute one half of the resulting child's make-up.

Third, she could be the recipient of an embryo implanted into her womb. The surrogate here would have no necessary genetic relationship with any resulting child. The egg could be that of a woman who has some gynaecological complication which makes pregnancy medically undesirable or impossible but which does not prevent the production of eggs in her fallopian tubes, or it could be contributed by a third-party, anonymous egg donor. It could, of course, be an egg from the surrogate herself. The fertilizing sperm could be that of the infertile woman's own partner or of a donor, or of the surrogate's partner. The embryo could be produced following sexual intercourse between the competent partners and lavage of the fertilized egg, or after the egg of the woman has been fertilized *in vitro* with the sperm of her own partner, or an anonymous donor. The complete embryo could be a donated embryo, having no genetic connection with the surrogate or the woman or the man of the infertile couple, or it could be related to one or two of that trio.[24] Similarly, the surrogate may be related to one or both partners of the infertile couple, or to neither. But unless she contributes the egg for fertilization, she has no primary genetic relationship with the foetus she then carries. Of course, if she is the sister or other blood relative of the egg or embryo donor she may share some of their genetic characteristics. Unlike the first two possibilities, some variants of which call for no use of technological resources, any variant on this third option calls for highly sophisticated medical technology and highly specialized medical skills.

Finally, the surrogate could become pregnant following sexual intercourse with her own partner, or with a partner of her own choosing, the conceptive intention being that on birth the child should be regarded as the child of some other identified couple. One of these people may, of course, be the surrogate's sister or some close friend. In this case, the activity is markedly low technology.

A second series of questions is for whom the surrogate becomes pregnant. Each of the four cases outlined above proceeds on a number of assumptions. For example, it has been implicitly assumed that the couple wanting the surrogate to bear a child for them is a heterosexual couple, rather than a lesbian couple or a homosexual couple. Secondly, that it is a couple, rather than a woman or man living on her or his own who desires a child. Third, that there is some medical complication which makes it undesirable for a woman to bear a child herself. The possibility that a woman might not wish to undergo the pain, discomfort and inconvenience of pregnancy and childbirth whether for reasons of career, or vanity or otherwise, has not yet been identified.

Most of the uses and possibilities of surrogacy which are commonly discussed involve the commissioning of a surrogate by a heterosexual couple, and indeed usually a married heterosexual couple, of which the wife is infertile or sterile. It is worth emphasizing that I use that here as a model only for the immediate purpose of simplicity of exposition and argument; the value of holding the discourse within heterosexual confines outweighs the necessary losses and distortions thereby produced.[25]

A third vector along which the base point questions might be tracked involves considerations of who may become pregnant for whom. There are two different types of problem involved here. The first concerns the physical, emotional, psychological, and financial health of the surrogate prior to the conception; are these of any legitimate concern to the commissioning couple, such that they can screen potential surrogates for desirable physical characteristics and acceptable health regimes? Can the surrogacy contract impose negative or positive obligations on the surrogate during the course of pregnancy, in order to reduce any risks to the surrogate and the foetus during the course of pregnancy?[26] Are there any rights which the surrogate may not alienate?[27] Secondly, there is the question of the surrogate-commissioning woman/man relationship. Is it more desirable that the relationship be established and maintained solely at arms length, with the participants' identities known only to a third party? Or is it preferable, as is sometimes suggested, that if surrogacy is to take place, it should only be between close friends or sisters?[28] Finally, what of two stories which broke in the media in early October 1987. In the first, a 17-year-old woman in Lancashire, England, had just given birth to a child for her own mother. The mother had been unable to conceive the child she desired in a new marriage.[29] In a second report, a 48-year-old woman had given birth in a Johannesburg, South Africa, hospital to triplets. The intended mother of the children was her daughter, who had had her womb removed following the delivery of her first child.[30] These two examples show graphically the moral and legal webs which can be woven with surrogacy. A woman gives birth to her own sister, or to her own grandchildren. If, in each case, the child was to be regarded as the child of the gestational and not what Stumpf calls the 'psychological mother', how is the legal and familial relationship between the child(ren) and her to be construed, and with what consequences?

Other questions include whether the compact between the surrogate and the commissioning couple should be formal or informal, commercial or altruistic. I am silent here on what effect those alternatives should have on the status of the arrangement judged from a legal or moral point of view. I have not addressed what should be the effect of a change of mind by the surrogate before or after the birth. Further variations envisage a change of mind or circumstances by the commissioning couple before the birth, or the effect of the birth of a handicapped neonate whom they reject. These conundrums serve to illustrate the breadth of the spectrum of difficult and perplexing choices which surrogacy discloses.

## AN IMPRESSIONISTIC HISTORY OF SURROGACY

If charting the nature of surrogacy presents a hostile and unwelcoming environment, accounting for its emergence and energy is an equally puzzling task. Most accounts of surrogacy's antecedents relate the story of Sar'ai, Abram, and Hagar as an Old Testament illustration of the antiquity of the phenomenon.[31] Most fail then to go on to relate the unhappy denouement of that reproductive experiment,[32] or advance the similar examples of Rachel, Jacob, and Bilhah, and Leah, Jacob, and Zilpah,[33] or point out that the surrogates in question in each of these adventures were household servants and therefore in a rather awkward position should the question of their reproductive autonomy have been raised. An example of rather differently motivated surrogacy arrangements appears in the fourteenth-century Japanese text, *The Confessions of Lady Nijo*.[34] While a child, Nijo was forced to become the concubine of a retired emperor. Her book tells of the devices which she adopted on a number of occasions to conceal from the patriarch pregnancies which he had not fathered. It recounts her despair over the realization of having to give birth to the babies in secret and to hand them over to others to bring up. Finally, Zipper and Sevenhuijsen adduce the fictional use in 1929 by Dutch feminist Emmy van Lokhorst of positive images of an informal surrogacy arrangement to suggest that these compacts may have been known in the Netherlands and other European countries.[35]

Despite such random examples, it is very difficult to discover whether or in what shape the practice of surrogacy survived into the Middle Ages, although many people appear prepared to assume that it did. Anthropological parallels are equally difficult to pin down. In the area of the eastern Orthodox Church, surrogate motherhood is reported from the beginning of the twentieth century, and in the borderlands between Christianity and Islam. For example, in Montenegro, Jiri Haderka asserts that it was the custom that an infertile woman would herself bring to her husband another wife who could have children. It was then up to the original wife whether she stayed in the house in addition to the surrogate, or whether she left the household altogether.[36] Similarly, Lorraine Harding recalls that it has been suggested that in some African societies it would be quite usual for a woman to have a baby for her sister, but gives no supporting reference.[37] This, of course, is a very difficult picture to focus. We cannot impose our westernized notions of familization and child rearing on cultures and societies in which, for example, the child's relationship with its extended family is emphasized and regarded as more important than its relationship with either its genetic father or its gestational mother. In many traditional African and Indian societies the biological family unit is deliberately superseded by the extended family through enforced and lengthy periods of separation, such that 'children are not born at the whim of the parents, but in response to a broader pressure from the whole group'.[38] That children born to one woman are raised by another or group of others does not, of itself, establish a surrogacy relationship at all; even if it did, it is not clear what conclusions we might want or be able to draw from that. There may be much to suggest that we should confine our study of the phenomenon to westernized societies, and to modern ones at that. A further reason for doing this would be that it is those societies, now, which are worrying about surrogacy and its presumed effects. The lessons of history and anthropology may have only limited guidance to offer in explaining and understanding surrogacy and in assisting in the task of establishing normative responses to it.

Reported litigation from westernized societies is, until the last ten years, perhaps surprisingly rare. We might now describe the mid-nineteenth-century Canadian case of *R* v. *Armstrong*[39] as a surrogacy arrangement. It involved a dispute following the birth of an illegitimate child to a woman who had agreed to transfer all claims and rights in respect of the child to its acknowledged father. The common law then regarded the father of an illegitimate child as a complete stranger to the child and its mother, even though she could have obtained an affiliation order against the father requiring him to pay her maintenance on behalf of the child. The Court refused the woman's application for habeas corpus on behalf of the child from the physical custody of the father. It said that where the father had obtained the child by agreement with and by the assent of the mother, without force or fraud, it would not intervene to revoke their compact.

This isolated case apart, it is difficult to discern any surrogacy cases, properly so called, which have been publicly aired in the courts and attracted the attentions of the reporters. The incidence of arrangements for the surrogate birth of a child is more numerous in the recent past, and the reasons for that are worthy of consideration. First, however, it is important to try to construct a perspective within which to view the state of our current knowledge.

# CONTEMPORARY ESTIMATES OF THE INCIDENCE OF SURROGACY

In the late twentieth century, when the practice and problems of surrogacy have slowly begun more openly to emerge in the west, estimating its extent and incidence is still remarkably difficult. This is despite the assertion that 'there is plenty of anecdotal evidence of women who grow children for their infertile sisters'.[40] The reasons for this are not, I think, too difficult to gauge. It is not an activity which has yet attracted a high degree of moral approval and the threat of official obstruction or institutional intransigence remains. Public acceptance is best described as muted; a survey conducted by *Woman* magazine amongst its readers revealed that 90 per cent of their respondents would never consider using a surrogate mother, and 60 per cent felt that the practice should be prohibited altogether.[41] In debate on the Surrogacy Bill 1985, Secretary of State Norman Fowler indicated that over 90 per cent of the comments received by the government following the publication of the *Warnock Report* had been hostile to commercial surrogacy.[42] And in the methodologically more secure *British Social Attitudes: The 1986 Report*, only 46 per cent of respondents thought that surrogacy should be a lawful option to an infertile couple. This was even where the pregnancy was established through artificial insemination of an unpaid surrogate who had agreed to bear the child for a couple, and following medical advice and counselling. When the payment of the surrogate was raised, the percentage of respondents still in favour of surrogacy fell to 27 per cent.[43] Amongst participants in an Australian IVF programme, however, 78 per cent of the respondents thought that surrogacy was an acceptable infertility treatment, but only if the parents could not have their children in any other way. Ninety-three per cent of those same patients thought the use of surrogates for 'convenience' unacceptable.[44] The Council of the British Medical Association has declared its opposition to surrogacy. It was felt wrong to deprive a child of one of its natural parents and that there were no circumstances in which it would be possible to guarantee the interests of the child. The Association's members rejected this advice, however, and have voted only against the involvement of members until guidelines are established.[45]

Against such a background of fairly unrestrained popular hostility, I suspect that any survey of surrogacy will under-report its true incidence. Two estimates from the United States of America enable us to obtain an impressionistic picture of the extent of acknowledged or open surrogacies there. They also offer a sidelight on the extent to which surrogacy is growing as a reproductive alternative. Gena Corea,[46] writing in May 1983, put the probable number of surrogate-born children since 1976 at between 75 and 100. More recently, a feature article in the national weekly magazine *Time* for 19 January 1987 quoted Michigan attorney Noel Keane, whose practice now includes a large degree of surrogacy contracting, estimating a figure of 500 births since 1976. Sixty-five of those births were in 1986, most of them arranged through the dozen or so surrogate centres which have been established across the United States. If we assume that as national and local press publicity bring the successes and failures of surrogacy more to the attention of potential parents and surrogates, and that the figures for the later years 1983–6 are likely, therefore, to outweigh those for 1976–9 or 1979–83, then it seems plausible to suggest that Corea's figure for 1983 was an understandable underestimate. Keane's higher figure is likely to be a result both of more people being prepared to contemplate surrogacy arrangements each year, and of more people who have in the past ten years participated in a surrogacy arrangement now being prepared to acknowledge it.[47]

The task of charting surrogacy arrangements in the United Kingdom is no less the subject of conjecture and hypothesis. Here again, 'there is a commonly held belief that inter-familial surrogacy is historically a reasonably common practice',[48] but putting a human face to the mask which surrogacy participants wear is hazardous and fraught with methodological uncertainty. However, a number of definite surrogate contracts or compacts can be clearly identified. Using what might be called primary sources, such as the reported judgments of contested legal disputes, informal reporting of surrogacy arrangements recorded by local social services departments or academic commentators acting on social service contacts, newspaper reporting of known surrogacy agreements and the experiences of surrogates and the parents with whom they were in contact, it is possible to construct a fairly accurate picture of known, definite surrogacy arrangements. All these provide fairly secure and reliable sources from which an initial outline of the picture can be painted onto what is otherwise a very sparse canvas. Less sure lines can then be traced from what might be called secondary and less easily verifiable sources. For example, following the birth to them of a child, surrogate mothers report receiving a great deal of correspondence from other potential surrogates or infertile couples. The same is true of couples who have had a child born to them by a surrogate. In each case, it is possible to use their reports of compacts firmly established to suggest the existence of further surrogacy arrangements. Also in this second category fall the comments made by local authority social workers where they have suspected but have not been able affirmatively to identify a surrogacy arrangement.

Using these distinctions, and 1976 again as a starting-point, it is possible to report 29 cases which fall into the first category.[49] In the second category, surrogates' folk knowledge produces an additional 7 cases and suspicions of local authorities' social services departments at least another 7. That produces a total of 43. It is, of course, possible that between categories one and two there has been some unverifiable double counting; that possibility, although I think that for various reasons it is a very slender one, arises in 5 cases. In other words, the cautious observer would state that there have been between 29 definite, 38 probable and 43 possible cases of *known* surrogacy arrangements in the United Kingdom since 1976. These figures under-report, possibly substantially, the actual incidences of surrogacy, even in the relatively recent past. The responses to a letter which I sent in March 1987 to Directors of Social Service Departments – not necessarily the best-placed point of entry – in the United Kingdom reveal a consistent pattern of suspected surrogacy.

One hundred and thirty-three requests for information on known or suspected surrogacy arrangements were sent to Directors. These covered the English and Welsh County Councils, the Metropolitan Districts, London Boroughs, Scottish Regions, the four Health and Social Services Boards in Northern Ireland and the relevant administrative headquarters of the Isles of Scilly. By August 1988 I had received ninety-nine replies,[50] a response rate of 74.4 per cent. Of these responses, seven (7.1 per cent) reported a Council policy decision to make no responses to researcher's requests for information; three (3.1 per cent) were preliminary replies with fuller responses pending, seventy-one (71.7 per cent) indicated that they had no direct experience of surrogacy arrangements and eighteen (18.2 per cent) Social Service Departments indicated firm knowledge amongst the Council's staff, of at least one such arrangement or circumstances in which this was strongly suspected. From the latter two categories, however, came a variety of replies from which it is possible affirmatively to conclude that surrogacy arrangements have a firmly established lineage in the United Kingdom, and that the practice, if not widespread, has been an acknowledged but subterranean reproductive alternative for some time. A random selection of those replies will substantiate this point:

> Social Workers in the Department and the Social Workers in the Adoption Unit know that it takes place but we have no specific examples.

> So far as I am aware, surrogacy has been an established practice for some time. I suspect that by and large such arrangements never came the way of the authorities as the child would be regarded as the child of the 'adoptive' parents. You will, of course, be aware that in Asian cultures particularly, there is a strong and accepted emphasis on surrogacy as a means of providing a family for an involuntarily childless couple.

> We have a suspicion that a very limited amount of internal family surrogacy has occurred. Rumours appear occasionally that 'she had a baby for her sister who can't have any'. To the best of my knowledge there has never been any real proof.

> We have come across 'Non Agency Adoption placements' where we suspect the pregnancy was planned to be the child of other parents – invariably relatives of the pregnant woman. My speculation is that, within families, this is not uncommon but whether money changes hands I do not know. Within this sphere of work we particularly note how many Asian families adopt relatives from overseas. I have also interviewed several childless adoptors who, since publicity gave surrogacy an understood name, tell me that they very seriously considered surrogacy as an alternative to a 'home grown' baby. In cases I know of, it was usually the female applicant's sister who was to be the surrogate parent. However, there was one situation where the male applicant – the infertile partner – was intending to use his brother to fertilize the female applicant (somehow without the brother knowing! – the applicant was a GP).

> I have been informed by social work staff throughout this Board's

area that surrogacy has occurred for some time at an informal level within extended families. Although this is speculative it does appear that in some rural communities, especially those which are isolated, the carrying of a child for another member of the family has been known to happen. More common was the practice of a local doctor or nurse knowing of an unwanted child and arranging a placement with a childless couple.

Against these observations, however, might be placed that of the Director of Social Services for a Metropolitan Borough in the North of England:

The breakdown of those arrangements reported recently and the disappointment of 'potential parents' seems to weigh heavily against surrogacy as a realistic alternative to the more clear and respectable image of the methods previously mentioned, to combat infertility and childlessness . . . surrogacy does not with the majority appear to be number one on the list of strategies to overcome childlessness within the B—— area.

Nevertheless, I think it is safe to conclude that surrogacy is seen as an alternative form of assisted reproduction for some couples or individuals, and possible even to speculate that its incidence will continue to grow in the coming years. The United Kingdom government's announced intention in the White Paper *Human Fertilisation and Embryology: A Framework for Legislation*[51] not criminally to prohibit all forms of surrogacy may well encourage some people who would have been uneasy about engagement in criminal activity to seek to use or work as a surrogate. The proposal for legislation seeks to do nothing which will facilitate the operation of non-commercial, charitable or self-help and support groups, such as the recently formed COTS group, Childlessness Overcome Through Surrogacy,[52] and also provides that the surrogate contract will be declared to be unenforceable.[53] In this sense, the government have chosen to treat the surrogacy contract and the surrogate and participating parents as gamblers in a wagering contract, in which the bargaining chips will be moral pressure and financial inducement, the risks, emotional vulnerability, psychological distress, and familial uncertainty. As the English courts are presently advised, the tables are stacked in favour of the surrogate in the event of a dispute as to the eventual custody of the child(ren) born following the surrogacy.[54] The malleability of the welfare principle by which the courts are guided, the 'best interests of the child' cannot be said always to guarantee this outcome.[55] Whether this is a laudible state of affairs and what the likely or possible consequences of it are do not concern me here;[56] indeed the 'disputed custody' case is *the* single most difficult problem, the judgment of Solomon question, in the whole of surrogacy law. For the present, I am content to speculate that the publicity which has been accorded to surrogacy in the past few years has *legitimated* its use by people who might previously have considered it and then discounted it, or by those to whom the thought of asking another woman, whether within or without the family group, had not previously occurred.

## THE VISIBILITY OF SURROGACY: GIVING IT AN UNDERSTOOD NAME

I want finally to make some observations on the public discovery of the surrogate mother, and the reasons for and results of her contemporary visibility. I do not want to suggest that there can be assigned one causal agent in the manifestation of surrogacy, although the publicity attendant on the birth in 1985 of 'Baby Cotton' gave an impetus to its gathering materialization which otherwise it would not have enjoyed in the United Kingdom. Indeed, Cotton's case was at least the eighth since 1978 which even the casual observer of national and local British newspapers would have been able to identify.[57] Rather, it is the blending of elements which have combined to produce the chemistry of surrogacy which are more noteworthy. There are, I think, three major reasons why surrogacy now attracts the attention that it does. First, there have been significant shifts in our understandings of fertility and infertility, both at a scientific and social level, and this has had an effect on the *demand* for surrogacy. Secondly, different and controversial approaches to overcoming childlessness have produced an attenuation in the officially sanctioned attitude towards surrogacy; there is a sense in which, even if it is not seen as desirable in itself, it can be understood as the lesser of a number of competing evils, having an effect on the *acceptability* of surrogacy. Finally, I think that an increasing individuation of life, and a parallel familization of political life, is leading to changes at what are best described as the ideological level, a level which perceives surrogacy as resulting from the social and individual lives we construct for ourselves. In other words there is a metamorphosis in the *construction* of surrogacy.

## The demand for surrogacy

The increasing demand for 'treatments' for conditions diagnosed as infertility is spawned by and producing a new and revitalized understanding of the existence and the *construction* of infertility; 'fertility is never just "fertility alone", there is no pure biology in the socialised world'.[58] At the level of 'pure biology', however, the incidence of infertility, understood as the inability to procreate as desired, accompanies and results from a steady rise in its real and acknowledged incidence. Ironically, this is in part a product of chemical attempts to control fertility as a means of contraception, as well as of diet, stress, and general health routines. It is intimately linked with what Judith Daniluk, Arthur Leader, and Patrick Taylor have called 'a parenthood mystique', in which 'reproduction [is seen as] a necessary criterion for personal fulfillment, social acceptance, religious membership, sexual identity, and psychological adjustment'.[59] Estimates suggest that of those attempting to become biological parents, one in six (17 per cent) experience problems with their fertility, although the figure of one in ten is thought by some to portray more accurately the incidence of long-term, 'incurable' infertility.[60] The former figure is used often to speak of those who experience difficulties of reproduction or conception, rather than inability, but the problem is still there. Access to 'expert medical care' suggests that between 50 and 60 per cent of couples (notice there is something of a coyness in speaking of *individuals* with fertility problems or difficulties) who experience infertility can be helped (i.e. medically or surgically) to overcome their infertility, although for many couples the turn to medical care is after years of unsuccessful attempts to secure a pregnancy, often involving severe emotional and sometimes financial cost.[61] Periods of emotional disequilibrium associated with infertility give rise to what has been called 'the crisis of infertility'.[62] In turn, this may result in frustration, anxiety, and stress, having adverse impacts on the self-esteem, self-image, psychological well-being, marital relationship and sexual satisfaction and functioning of one or both people affected by the infertility.[63]

Naomi Pfeffer has forcefully challenged the adequacy of this

72

assessment. Desperation, she has argued, is only one of a potential range of emotions which 'the infertile' do or may be expected to manifest. Not all such emotions are negative, and desperation 'may not be a result of the condition of infertility but of the insensitive and humiliating treatment sometimes received at the hands of medical and other authorities.'[64] A graphic example of this is illustrated in my own research. A couple who had for many years been trying to adopt a child, and who were removed from the local social services adoption list following the voluntary hospitalization of the man for an alcohol-related condition, sought to appeal against their removal from the list. In responding, the officer dealing with the case attempted to offer some solace:

> Many people . . . do not have children and still enjoy happy and satisfying lives . . . . I can only suggest that you develop your interests as much as possible in all your other activites and talents. Animals of course are a great substitute and not so demanding as children and work is also, along with time, a great healer.

Advances in reproductive and medical technology have indeed rendered the possibility of alleviating or overcoming some of these infertilities more realistic. But this can presently be achieved only at significant financial cost, the 'success rates' are low, and the invasiveness of some of the surgical techniques barbaric. While the *Warnock Report* deplored the low status still accorded infertility practice within medical specialisms, and urged remedial action,[65] a cost not so frequently or publicly recognized is the increased burden placed on those who *are* infertile; the stigma of infertility is compounded by its public visibility. This itself compounds the demand for successful treatment, for which the 'low tech' form, surrogacy, can claim a remarkably high success rate in comparison with other forms of 'reproductive technology'. Less visible with other reproductive technologies are the facts of surgical assistance which, when it does come, is often expensive, invasive, and although not usually advertised as such, experimental or hazardous.[66]

A second reason why infertility has been highlighted is due to the decline in new-born babies available for adoption. Figures produced by the UK Office of Population Censuses and Surveys suggest a 55 per cent decline in the number of adoptions since 1976, with the biggest numerical drop among adopted babies. In 1976 over

1,500 children under 6 months of age were adopted, all but 52 of whom were recorded as illegitimate. In 1986, only 472 babies were placed for adoption, of whom all but 16 were recorded as illegitimate. The Editor of the British Agencies for Adoption and Fostering *Adoption and Fostering Journal* said that adoption is now very much 'a service for children with special needs' and not a service for infertile couples.[67]

This shortage is particularly acute in respect of white, healthy neonates. The reasons for this decline are commonly linked to the more easy availability of contraception and its more specific tailoring to the needs of individuals concerned; the availability of abortion, and a gradual movement in attitude which has occurred in favour of legal abortion for reasons of preference and a smaller shift in the same direction for reasons of health.[68] Finally, changes in attitudes to single parent/motherhood and the availability of at least minimal welfare payments make this at least a possibility for women who want to keep their babies rather than to feel they have no alternative but to make them available for adoption. This is, of course, allied with the role of women in society generally and the view and expectations of them, and them alone as mothers.[69]

The result of these shifts, however, has been to augment the stigma of infertility with allegations of racial and handicap prejudice against those who remain involuntarily childless in the face of black, coloured, or handicapped neonates being available for adoption. A similar motivation lies behind suggestions which propose that pregnant women who are considering an abortion be counselled or even paid to carry their foetus to term in order to make the newborn child available for adoption by a childless couple.[70] This 'lottery' approach to infertility resolution and to the very real problems of handicap, disability and prejudice, all of which are serious and pernicious problems confronting modern British society, cannot be underestimated; but to suggest that they can easily be resolved by matching the involuntarily infertile childless person or couple with the involuntarily disabled, non-parented child insults and undervalues both. Rather, it is a cheap and convenient way to alleviate guilt rather than discrimination, helping us to overcome two difficult and very different social problems by the quick fix of alloying the selfishness of the infertile with the plight of the helpless, the abandoned, rejected or destitute. And it will not serve as a response for either; indeed, it is possible to suggest that it might even store up greater social discontent and trouble if the already burdened infertile are used as the waste bin into which to tip the marginal children which white, whole society would rather forget about, than to have to confront the awkward question which hard-to-place coloured, black or physically disabled children present; why are they hard to place?

## The desirability of surrogacy

The second reason for the contemporary emergence of the surrogate mother has to do with what I think is the glacial movement of 'official' attitudes to efforts to overcome involuntary childlessness. This gradual metamorphosis, sometimes so muted as to be imperceptible, is itself the function of a number of variables. The radical decline in traditional ways of supplementing a family unable to have its own children, such as through adoption, has had a number of dramatic effects. Infertile couples have turned to a variety of agencies and outlets in an attempt to secure a child. This has encouraged, among other things, illegal market trade in young children, often across national boundaries. Similar motivations lie behind proposals for the payment of women contemplating abortion of unwanted pregnancies to keep the foetus and make it available for adoption on birth, the massive growth of reproductive technology and interest in it, and surrogacy.[71] Compared with some of these practices, the unofficially sanctioned, the area of private morality which is 'not the law's business'[72] stretches more easily to encompass surrogacy than it does, for example, to include international trading in children. And although some argue that there is no distinction between the two, that both amount to child selling, the possibility of being able to draw a firm and clear line between these different forms of activity convinces many legislatures, I think, that the softly-softly option in relation to surrogacy is the lesser of a number of evils.

Additionally, these advances in reproductive technology are perceived as having brought with them a major advance over adoption.[73] Artificial insemination, *in vitro* fertilization, and gamete transfer techniques such as egg or embryo donation are enabling at least some couples to have a child which is genetically related to one or occasionally both members of a couple who would previously have remained involuntarily childless in the face of what has been called the 'adoption famine'.[74]

The final reason for this attenuation of 'official' attitudes to reproductive choices which include surrogacy is that I think it is possible to discern increasing resilience to and questioning of the moral authority exercised by spiritual and theological leaders who have to face only the moral and legal shadows of reproductive dilemmas and not their sometimes painful and ignominious manifestations. Although this is at the level of speculation for the time being, it may be possible to discern a relative weakening of the moral authority of the position of the Church of England and a waning of the *practical* authority of the Church of Rome, such that cultural attitudes towards children and childbirth and infertility cannot be fitted easily within the assumptions made by these 'official' discourses. In the same way, then, that Keith Thomas has identified the decline of magic with the rise of religious sentiment in the sixteenth and seventeenth centuries,[75] so the propulsion and promise of reproductive technology has continued to unseat the reverence for divine inspiration and control of 'natural' cycles of life. This has brought with it counter-charges that the scientific transmutation of nature is being conducted by those who would play gods.[76]

The most recent condemnation of surrogacy offered by the *Instruction on Respect for Human Life in its Origin and on the Dignity of Procreation*, the response of the Roman Catholic's Congregation for the Doctrine of the Faith,[77] bases its consideration of assisted reproductive techniques and procedures within the framework of the sanctity of Christian marriage and a critical reception of technological and scientific advancement;

> It would on the one hand be illusory to claim that scientific research and its applications are morally neutral; on the other hand one cannot derive criteria for guidance from mere technical efficiency, from research's possible usefulness to some at the expense of others, or, worse still, from prevailing ideologies.[78]

There is much in this which will appeal to a sense of humane critique of scientific imperialism and technological theology. It recalls Rabelais's aphorism that 'science without conscience is the ruin of the soul'.[79] Not surprisingly the conclusion of the Roman Catholic Church follows closely on this point the response to the *Warnock Report* by the Church of England Board of Social Responsi-

bility Working Party paper on Human Fertilization and Embryology, *Personal Origins*.[80] Looking to some fundamental tenets against
which to judge the wider thrust of the reproduction revolution, the
Board cautioned that they had been 'continually aware of the
danger of adapting our ethics to scientific advances'.[81]

While public policy and private morality have long conjoined in
viewing the treatment of human infants as chattels, a consumption
item for the wealthy or educated western middle classes,[82] the available evidence points the other way in practice.[83] And yet there is a
fundamental distinction between child selling and the endanger-
ment of the familial institution, under whatever religious creed it is
being promoted.

The argument that surrogacy represents an objective failure to
meet the obligations of maternal love, of conjugal fidelity, and of
responsible motherhood and that it offends the dignity and the right
of the child to be conceived, carried in the womb, brought into the
world and raised by its own parents fails to balance the fact of non-
existence against that of surrogate-born birth.

With the exception of the developmental effects on the surrogate-
born child, on which we yet know too little, the evidence does not
establish the fears of theological nightmare. In such circumstances
I suspect the waning influence of these spiritual pronouncements
as a bench-mark for societies. This is mirrored in the relaxation
with which some, perhaps many followers of the Churches of
England and Rome, approach the ordering of their personal, reproductive, and affective lives. This mutation links with the third type
of direction in which I think it is possible to identify the contemporary focus on surrogacy.

### The construction of surrogacy

This hypothesis traces a realignment of forces at an ideological or
political level which have resulted in the increasing familization of
political life at much the same time that different forces have assisted
in the emergence of family members as individual atoms. The
reaction of the nucleii of these two forces has generated the
re-individualization of family and social life. So, in the same way
that the fission of social, economic, and ideological forces produced
the nuclear family, or the ideology of it, the tensions of living
in this energized environment are themselves responsible for the

77

bombardment of political life with familial concerns. This is, then, the sense in which, as I ventured earlier, surrogacy is a by-product of the nuclear family which has thrown its field so strongly around our affective and productive relations. One clear result of this is that the completeness or wholeness of existence is threatened in the face of involuntary childlessness. As Nikolas Rose has appositely put it, what unifies the 'family machine' is not the solutions posed to the problem of living a healthy, well-adjusted and fulfilled life, raising happy children and forming satisfying relationships, rather:

> it is the terrain established by the problem itself. Domestic, conjugal and parental conduct is increasingly regulated not by obedience compelled by the threat of sanction but through the activation of individual guilt, personal anxiety and private disappointment.[84]

It is in part as a result of this that reproductive autonomy includes not only the elimination of involuntary reproduction but also the overcoming of involuntary infertility.[85] In concert with this is a mood of individuation, which encourages the respect of each and every member of the social unit to be safeguarded. The second realization of this individuation is that children have emerged from the shadows of adult life as persons whose interests must be regarded, and whose interests cannot unproblematically be assumed to be coincident with those whom they most closely share the physical space of their affective lives. It is for this reason, if no other, that the numerical insignificance of surrogate arrangements – if that assumption can be sustained – cannot be used to excuse us from a social responsibility to consider seriously the reproductive options which surrogacy offers for adults and the resulting children. While the reproduction revolution may have shattered the conventional wisdom of domestic and familial relationships and mandates that we address issues such as who stands in what relationship to whom or what and on what basis, it has had, as far as surrogate-born children are concerned, one particular result. Whereas in the past surrogacy may have been a reproductive option for some people, the watchword would have been secrecy and discretion. Nowadays, the emergence of the 'best interests of the child' as a welfare criterion makes it 'impossible now simply to allow and accept an arrangement between adults, worked out for their own convenience, which involves the transfer of children'.[86] In other words, we have not only *created* the surrogate-born children, we have made their public appearance more necessary and inevitable.

## NOTES

I owe a debt to Lorraine Harding, Bob Lee, and Celia Wells for commenting on an earlier draft of this essay. This note poorly repays it.

1 [1985] F.L.R. 846, and see Kim Cotton and Denise Winn, *Baby Cotton: For Love and Money* (London: Dorling Kindersley, 1985).
2 The term is taken from Peter Singer and Deane Wells, *The Reproduction Revolution: New Ways of Making Babies* (London: Oxford University Press, 1984).
3 Michael Freeman, 'After Warnock – whither the law?', *Current Legal Problems* (1986), p. 33, at 47.
4 Michelle Stanworth, *Reproductive Technologies: Gender, Motherhood and Medicine* (Oxford: Polity Press, 1987), p. 4.
5 Bernard Dickens, 'Legal aspects of surrogate motherhood: practices and proposals', paper presented at the UK National Committee of Comparative Law 1987 Colloquium, 'Legal Regulation of Reproductive Medicine', Cambridge, UK, 15–17 September 1987, p. 1.
6 J. Goldstein, A. Freud, and A. Solnit, *Beyond the Best Interests of the Child* (London: Burnett Books, 1973).
7 I was alerted to this important distinction, overlooked by many commentators, in correspondence from Miriam David, July 1985.
8 For a interesting attempt to build on these divisions, see Andrea Stumpf, 'Redefining mother: a legal matrix for new reproductive technologies', *Yale Law Journal*, vol. 96 (1986), p. 187, discussed below.
9 Juliette Zipper and Selma Sevenhuijsen, 'Surrogacy: feminist notions of motherhood reconsidered', in Stanworth, *Reproductive Technologies*, p. 118, at 129.
10 J. K. Mason and R. A. McCall Smith, *Law and Medical Ethics*, 2nd edn (London: Butterworth, 1987), p. 57.
11 217 N.J. Sup 313, 525 A. (2d) 1128 (1987) (Superior Court); 109 N.J. 396, 537 A. (2d) 1227 (1988) (Supreme Court, New Jersey).
12 *Re P. (Minors) (Surrogacy)*, [1987] 2 F.L.R. 314.
13 *Report of the Committee of Inquiry into Human Fertilisation and Embryology (Warnock Report)*, Cmnd 9314 (London: HMSO, 1984), para. 8.11.
14 ibid.
15 Nancy Chodorov, *The Reproduction of Mothering* (Berkeley: University of California Press, 1978), p. 29, 'conclusions about the biological basis of parenting can only be speculative'. And see Zipper and Sevenhuijsen, 'Surrogacy', p. 126.
16 Stumpf, 'Redefining Mother', pp. 192–207.
17 ibid., p. 190, n. 12.
18 Edgar Page, 'Donation surrogacy and adoption', *Journal of Applied Philosophy*, vol. 2, no. 2 (1985), pp. 161–72.

19 Stumpf, 'Redefining mother', p. 194, n. 26. Naomi Pfeffer, 'Artificial insemination, in vitro fertilisation and the stigma of infertility', in Stanworth, *Reproductive Technologies* makes the point that 'The decision to embark on parenthood, to undertake a major change in social status, antedates the attempt to conceive, particularly today when more effective means of fertility control are available. The decision is a result of the processes that are shaped by social and historical forces the impact of which are shared by the fertile and infertile alike; there is nothing peculiar about the motivation for parenthood of those who *later* find themselves infertile' (p. 83; emphasis added).

20 Stumpf, 'Redefining mother', p. 187, n. 1.

21 Gena Corea, *The Mother Machine: Reproductive Technologies from Artificial Insemination to Artificial Wombs* (New York: Harper & Row, 1985), p. 221, and see Genevieve Lloyd, *The Man of Reason* (London: Methuen, 1984), pp. 36–7.

22 e.g. *C* v. *S* [1987] 1 Q.B. 1230; Zipper and Sevenhuijsen, 'Surrogacy', p. 130.

23 Germaine Greer, *Sex and Destiny: the Politics of Human Fertility* (London: Picador, 1985), p. 12, n. 13.

24 Such embryos could be the result of an unconnected *in vitro* fertilization programme where 'spare' embryos are maintained for later use, and it transpires that they are not required by the woman from whom they were originally recovered.

25 In the United States, reports of surrogates carrying, or being asked to carry, pregnancies for homosexual males or for single males are reported in Noel Keane and Dennis Breo, *The Surrogate Mother* (New York: Everest House, 1983).

26 For examples of such conditions, see Keane and Breo, *Surrogate Mother*, pp. 275–305, and *Sunday Times*, 13 January 1985, p. 15. The contract in the disputed American case of *In re Baby M* provided that the surrogate, Mary Beth Whitehead, would attempt conception by artificial insemination, upon conception carry the child to term and then deliver and surrender the child to its genetic father, William Stern and his wife, Elizabeth, renouncing all parental rights acknowledging this to be in the child's best interests. In addition, the surrogate agreed to assume the risks of pregnancy and childbirth and not of her own volition to abort the pregnancy, and submit to a psychiatric evaluation and an amniocentesis test, which would be followed by an abortion if the test indicated a genetic or congenital abnormality in the foetus.

27 For a discussion of this issue see Note, 'Rumplestiltskin revisited: the inalienable rights of surrogate mothers', *Harvard Law Review*, vol. 99 (1986), pp. 1936–55.

28 This suggestion was made by Health Minister Kenneth Clarke in Standing Committee debate on the Surrogacy Arrangements Act 1985; *Official Report, House of Commons, Standing Committee B*, 25 April 1985, col. 7. See also Singer and Wells, *The Reproduction Revolution*, p. 124 for details of the Crozier case in France of a woman who carried a baby for her infertile twin sister: *The Guardian*, 29 September 1984, *Times*, 23

November 1984, p. 11, *Woman*, 2 June 1984, p. 21, and the BBC *Day to Day* programme, 13 January 1987, for comparable English examples. On egg donation between sisters, see *Independent*, 29 September 1987, p. 13.

29 *Star*, 1 October 1987, pp. 1, 2.

30 *Mail on Sunday*, 4 October 1987, pp. 1–4.

31 *Genesis* 16:1–16.

32 ibid., 21:9–14.

33 ibid., 30:1–13.

34 Karen Brazell, (trans.), *The Confessions of Lady Nijo* (New York: Doubleday 1973). I derived this example from Sissela Bok, *Secrets: On the Ethics of Concealment and Revelation* (London: Oxford University Press, 1984), p. 22, and see pp. 289–90, n. 9.

35 Zipper and Sevenhuijsen, 'Surrogacy', p. 123.

36 Jiri Haderka, 'Surrogate motherhood especially from the legal point of view', paper presented to the 7th World Congress on Medical Law, Gent, 18–22 August 1985, vol. I, p. 152, at p. 154, n. 17.

37 Lorraine Harding, 'The debate on surrogate motherhood: the current situation, some arguments and issues; questions facing law and policy', *Journal of Social Welfare Law* (1987), p. 54, n. 3.

38 Greer, *Sex and Destiny*, p. 421, n. 24. And see Jack Goody, *The Development of the Family and Marriage in Europe* (Cambridge: Cambridge University Press, 1983), pp. 153–6; Alan Macfarlane, *Marriage and Love in England: Modes of Reproduction 1300–1840* (Oxford: Basil Blackwell, 1986) pp. 51–78.

39 [1850] PR 6; 3 English and Empire Digest (1960 edn).

40 Editorial, *Nature*, vol. 313, 10 January 1985, p. 83; Dickens, 'Legal aspects' writes that 'Anecdotal evidence is ubiquitous that friends, sisters, cousins and others related in a familial and/or social way to wives in infertile unions act as surrogate mothers through artificial insemination . . . within particular ethnic populations in Canada's larger cities, sisters or cousins of wives unable to bear children would be artificially inseminated through the husbands, usually with no medical or nursing aid. They would go to hospital under the wives' names and health insurance numbers and, on giving birth, register the wives as the mothers. On leaving hospital, they would surrender the children to the couples . . . The practice had produced no record of harmful or disruptive effects on the participants.'

41 *Woman*, September 1984, 12 January 1985. The survey responses of over 3,000 women were adjusted for age and regional representation and weighted to ensure no over-representation of religious groups, 'infertile' women, etc.

42 *Official Report, House of Commons*, vol. 77, col. 23.

43 Roger Jowell, Sharon Witherspoon, and Lindsay Brook (eds), *British Social Attitudes: The 1986 Report* (Aldershot: Gower/Social and Community Planning Research, 1986), pp. 157–8 and Table 9.8.

44 Patsy Littlejohn, 'IVF patients and their attitudes to ethical issues.

Replies to a questionnaire', reproduced in Singer and Wells, *The Repro-duction Revolution*, pp. 234–47, esp. q. 6, pp. 246–7.

45  *Guardian*, 8 May 1987, p. 3. *Times*, 1 July 1987.

46  Corea, *The Mother Machine*, p. 214.

47  Alexander Capron, 'AID, embryo research and surrogate motherhood: public policy and the constitution', paper presented at the UK National Committee of Comparative Law 1987 Colloquium, 'Legal Regulation of Reproductive Medicine', Cambridge, UK, 15–17 September 1987, p. 7, suggests that 'it is estimated that 500–1,000 births have occurred to surrogate mothers in the United States', but gives no supporting reference.

48  Respondent to questionnaire; see below, text accompanying note 50.

49  This figure comprises four known litigated cases, one television appear-ance by a surrogate not included in any other figure, thirteen definite positive responses from local authority social services departments, seven 'newspaper report' surrogacies (*Daily Star*, 8 January 1985, p. 2; *Woman*, 2 June 1984, p. 21; *Times*, 23 November 1984, p. 11) and four known cases reported by Moira Wright, (*Family Law*, vol. 16 (1986), p. 109, at p. 110).

50  By what factor this would have to be discounted in order to produce anything approximating the 'true' level of surrogate births, even since 1976, is too speculative to contemplate here. I know from my own contacts that the figures given here are an underestimate; as yet they are the only ones which I can confidently verify. Dr Jack Glatt of the Hammersmith Hospital, London, remarked to the *Sunday Times*, that 'I wouldn't know whether it's five babies a year in this country or 500' (13 January 1985, p. 15). According to Warnock Committee member, Professor Malcolm Macnaughton, past president of the Royal College of Obstetricians and Gynaecologists, 'You cannot stop surrogacy – it has been going on for years and will continue', *Daily Telegraph*, 11 January 1985, p. 11.

51  Cm 259 (London: HMSO, November, 1987) paras 64–75.

52  I am grateful to Gena Dodd and Kim Cotton for supplying me with information on this group.

53  Cm 259, para. 73.

54  *A* v. *C* [1985] F.L.R. 445, 449; *Re P. (Minors) (Surrogacy)* [1987] 2 F.L.R. 314.

55  Carol Smart, writing in the context of divorce litigation, has called the confused notions of morality and sexuality with which the interpretation of this doctrine is infused little more than sloganism through which a form of social discipline can be exerted on errant family members. Lawyers *qua* lawyers have no realistic method of conceptualizing what the 'best interests of children' might be; Carol Smart, *The Ties That Bind; Law, Marriage and the Reproduction of Patriarchal Relations* (London: Routledge & Kegan Paul, 1984), pp. 120–7, 163.

56  I deal with this and other legal issues which surrogacy throws up in *Surrogacy and the Moral Economy* (Aldershot: Gower, forthcoming, 1989).

57  Briefly, these are the cases of *A* v. *C*: the 'Kirsty Steven' case, discussed

in Kirsty Steven and Emma Dally, *Surrogate Mother. One Woman's Story* (London: Century Publishing, 1985), the adoption application in which was heard by the High Court in 1987, *Adoption Application no. A.A. 212/86*, *Times*, 11 March 1987; Mary Stewart, see *Social Work Today*, vol. 16, no. 15, 10 December 1984, pp. 14–15 and *Daily Record*, various issues, 1984–7; Rita Parker, see various issues of the *Nottingham Evening News*, December 1981–January 1982, *Times*, 5 December 1981; Kashmini and Saraya Minerva, see Liz Hodgkinson, 'The women who breed babies for £1 an hour – the English angle', *Woman*, 2 June 1984, p. 21; Glenda and Jacki Eason, and Nicholas Timmins, 'Why I am having a baby for my sister', *Times* 23 November 1984, p. 11, which also details another anonymous case where a woman had a baby for her sister who needed emergency breast cancer surgery; and the 'Cotton' case itself. The *Daily Mail*, 28 September 1984, p. 20, reports the reputed surrogacy compact between Anne Ward and Anne Anderson which broke down when Paul Ward left his wife to live with Anderson, who had been acting as the surrogate. Although I have counted arrangements such as the Parker case and *In Re P* where the children were not eventually transferred on birth, I have excluded the Ward/Anderson case from my count.

58 Barbara Sichtermann, *Femininity: the Politics of the Personal*, trans. John Whitlam (Oxford: Polity Press, 1983, 1986 edn), p. 63.
59 Judith Daniluk, Arthur Leader, and Patrick Taylor, 'The psychological sequelae of infertility', in Judith H. Gold (ed.), *The Psychiatric Implications of Menstruation* (Washington, DC: American Psychiatric Press, 1985), p. 75, at p. 77.
60 Daniluk *et al.*, 'Psychological sequelae', p. 77 and notes; National Center for Health Statistics,(December 1982) *Vital and Health Statistics* sec. 23# 11, at 13–16, 32.
61 Daniluk *et al.*, 'Psychological sequelae', pp. 78–9.
62 ibid.
63 ibid.
64 Pfeffer, 'Artificial insemination', p. 82.
65 *Warnock Report*, paras 2.14–18.
66 This point is made by many feminist writers; see, for example, the work of Renate Duelli Klein, 'What's new about the "new" reproductive technologies?' in G. Corea, R. Duelli Klein, J. Hanmer, H. B. Holmes, B. Hoskins, M. Kishwar, J. Raymond, R. Rowland, and R. Steinbacher, *Man-Made Women: How New Reproductive Technologies Affect Women* (London: Hutchinson, 1985), pp. 64–73, and 'IVF: for whose benefit – at whose expense?', paper presented at the European Conference of Critical Legal Studies, , 'Feminist Perspectives on Law', London, 3–5 April 1986.
67 *Guardian* 12 August 1987, p. 2.
68 Jowell *et al.*, *British Social Attitudes: the 1986 Report*, p. 155.
69 Ann Dally, *Inventing Motherhood: the Consequences of an Ideal* (London: Burnett Books, 1982), *passim*.
70 Elizabeth Landes and Richard Posner 'The economics of the baby

shortage', *Journal of Legal Studies*, vol. 7 (1978), p. 323; and see Posner, 'Adoption and market theory: the regulation of the market in adoptions', *Boston University Law Review*, vol. 67 (1987), p. 59, for an expansion and defence of this view, and Jane Maslow Cohen, 'Adoption and market theory: Posner, pluralism, pessimism', *Boston University Law Review*, vol. 67 (1987), p. 105, for a vigorous and critical response.

71 See, for example, J. R. S. Pritchard, 'A market for babies', *University of Toronto Law Journal*, vol. 24, (1984), p. 341.

72 This memorable phrase was coined by the *Wolfenden Report on Homosexual Offences and Prostitution*, Cmnd 247 (London: HMSO, 1957) to inform its conclusions on the role of legal regulation in the areas there under review. I have attempted to trace the parallels between the Wolfenden and Warnock Reports in 'Who to be or not to be: the surrogacy story', *Modern Law Review*, vol. 49 (1986), p. 358, at 366–8.

73 Harding, 'Debate on surrogate motherhood', p. 42, gives the statistics which chart the decline in the number of annual adoptions.

74 ibid., pp. 42–3.

75 Keith Thomas, *Religion and the Decline of Magic: Studies in Popular Beliefs in Sixteenth and Seventeenth Century England* (Harmondsworth: Penguin Books, 1973), *passim*, but esp. pp. 209–51, 785–800.

76 For early expressions of this, see *Artificial Human Insemination*. The Report of a Commission Appointed by His Grace the Archbishop of Canterbury (London: SPCK, 1948); Gerald Leach, *The Biocrats: Implications of Medical Progress* (Harmondsworth: Penguin Books, 1972).

77 London: Catholic Truth Society (1987).

78 *Instruction on Respect for Human Life*, p. 7.

79 Rabelais, *Gargantua et Pantagruel*, trans. J. M. Cohen (Harmondsworth: Penguin Books, 1955), Book II, ch. VII.

80 Board of Social Responsibility, *Personal Origins: the Report of a Working Party on Human Fertilisation and Embryology* (London: CIO Publishing, 1985).

81 *Personal Origins*, para. 44.

82 Greer, *Sex and Destiny*, p. 22.

83 For example, J. R. S. Pritchard, 'Market for babies'; *Guardian*, 7 January 1988, p. 8.

84 Nikolas Rose, 'Beyond the public/private division: law, power and the family', in Peter Fitzpatrick and Alan Hunt (eds), *Critical Legal Studies* (Oxford: Basil Blackwell, 1987), p. 61, at p. 71.

85 Ann Oakley, *Subject Women* (London: Fontana, 1985), pp. 189–90.

86 Harding, 'Debate on surrogate motherhood', p. 45; Oakley, *Subject Women*, p. 214.

# 5

## SHOULD WE EXPERIMENT ON EMBRYOS?

*JOHN HARRIS*

The question as to whether or not we should experiment on embryos won't go away. At the time of writing this essay it has just been asked for a third time by the government. On the first occasion the government commissioned the Warnock Committee to provide an answer. This answer was duly provided in July 1984[1] and has been hotly debated ever since. The question was re-posed by the Department of Health and Social Security in the form of a consultation paper published in December 1986, and for the third time in the draft 'alternative' clauses in the government's White Paper published in November 1987.[2]

Even when we do finally have legislation the debate will continue, for this is not the sort of question that is susceptible of a final answer. The reasons why this is so will be one of the conclusions of this chapter. First, however, it is as well to be clear about two issues. They are: what is meant by 'experimenting' on embryos and why is such experimentation thought desirable?

### WHY EXPERIMENT ON EMBRYOS?

#### What do we mean by experiment?

I shall not try to define the word 'experiment'. What is at issue when we ask the question 'should we experiment on embryos?' is: should embryos be studied and used by us? This covers everything from merely examining an *in vitro* embryo under the microscope to see that it is normal with a view to subsequent implantation in its mother's uterus, to using tissue from embryos for transplant or grafting, and thus killing the embryo. Now of course we can draw

85

distinctions here, and it would be possible to argue that studying embryos without damaging them is permissible, whereas more invasive or more lethal experimentation is not. Those who might be tempted to draw this distinction should be aware that it would have been impossible to arrive at the stage at which we are able to look non-invasively at embryos without having first, *inter alia*, flattened and killed many of them in order to study them. However, most of the projected benefits from studying and using embryos and embryonic tissue depend upon doing more than merely looking at viable[3] embryos, and we cannot arrive at a realistic view of why we might want to experiment on and use embryos, without a sense of the good that might thereby be achieved.

### *What might we gain from experiments?*

First, what we have gained is many hundreds of live, wanted, babies that would not otherwise have existed; hope has been offered to countless infertile people and a whole range of possibilities that we will now consider briefly, have been opened up. Some of these possibilities are still some way off and may of course never be realized. However, they certainly won't be realized without embryo experimentation, and it is important to have some sense of what might be on the cards, of what legislating against embryo experimentation might cost us.

I shall assume that most people are by now familiar with what is presently possible, the techniques of *in vitro* fertilization, freezing and thawing embryos, surrogacy and so on.[4] We must now consider what may be possible in the reasonably proximate future. By that I mean within the next twenty years or so.

R. G. Edwards, the pioneer of *in vitro* embryology, has noted that:

Identifying embryos with genetic abnormalities would offer an alternative to amniocentesis during the second trimester of pregnancy, and the 'abortion *in vitro*', of a defective preimplantation embryo . . . would be infinitely preferable to abortion *in vivo* at twenty weeks of pregnancy or thereabouts as the results of amniocentesis are obtained. It would also be less traumatic for parents and doctor to type several embryos and replace or store those that are normal rather than having the threat of a mid-term abortion looming over each successive pregnancy.[5]

Using the same techniques, embryos could be 'sexed' and thus screened for sex-linked disorders. There are also very good indications that embryo or foetal cells, tissue, and even organs, might be used for repair and transplants to adults. Edwards is also optimistic that 'pancreatic cells may be used to repair diabetes and cultured skin cells grafted to repair lesions. . . . Human amniotic epithelial cells . . . could be useful in repairing inherited enzyme defects in recipient children and adults'.[6] Moreover there are indications that 'kidney cells may be transplanted into the human brain in order to cure illnesses such as Parkinson's disease' and that 'myocardial tissue . . . should be obtained from embryos growing *in vitro* without great difficulty,'[7] and could well be used by cardiologists to repair the major vessels of the heart.

Edwards reported very recently that work was far advanced on mouse embryos which would, if repeated in human embryos, provide a very good chance of reversing radiation damage of the sort caused at Chernobyl.[8]

We do not of course know how many of these possibilities will become actualities. Nor of course how many promising avenues for research using embryos will open up. We do however know that none of them is likely to be realized without embryo experimentation.

## Heroes, chimeras, and Centaurs

The dramatic nature of the possibilities opened up by *in vitro* embryology – possibilities of solving many of the rejection problems of organ and tissue transplants, of curing infertility, of perfecting risk-free contraception, of removing genetic disabilities in embryos, of finding ways of restoring irradiated tissue, shows immediately why the question of the legitimacy of embryo experimentation is unlikely to be finally solved. There are always likely to be projected uses for embryos which are so compelling as to cause us to re-think any decision we take to ban or limit embryo experiments. On the other hand, the possibility of any license to use embryos for scientific research being misused is also going to remain with us. The spectre of the creation of *chimeras*, no longer simply mythic beasts but in their modern incarnation literally half sheep and half goat, remind us that we might also create *Centaurs*, creatures which will be combinations of human beings and other species.

*In vitro* embryology will enable us to help improve human beings, to create beings more like heroes, but it also will enable us to create chimeras and centaurs. This is why the question of the legitimacy of experiments with and use of human embryos is likely to remain controversial, whatever we decide at any particular moment. This is not I think a grave problem. What we must always do is decide what research on, or experiments with, or use of, embryos is permissible. To suggest, as I shall shortly do, that embryo research is in principle permissible, is not of course to say that anything at all may be done to or with embryos. We must always, and always carefully, examine any proposed research protocol to see whether it is justified given what is proposed, what might thereby be achieved, the probability of its success and the costs of undertaking the work; including of course the moral costs and benefits.

We must now address the question: why not experiment on embryos? But before examining some of the answers that might be given to this question we must look briefly at the issue of abortion.

## ABORTION

The Warnock Committee set its collective face firmly against any reconsideration of the abortion issue. They doubtless felt that discussion of abortion would only fog the issue of experimentation and that abortion was an issue which had frequently been debated in the past and on which this society had already established legislation which enjoyed widespread support. I very much sympathize with *Warnock*'s reluctance to seize this nettle unnecessarily, but I fear it cannot be avoided. In any event I do not want to avoid it, for the rights and wrongs of abortion can be used in a way which allows us to short-circuit an otherwise protracted discussion of the moral status of the embryo.

I have set out at length elsewhere my account of the moral status of the embyro,[9] in the light of which clear answers as to the legitimacy of experimentation on embryos appear. However, any society which has taken the view that abortion is legitimate up to 28 weeks gestation[10] on the ground of safeguarding the health of the mother, must approve of embryo experimentation on the parallel grounds that this is necessary to safeguard the health of the community and of present and future individuals. Unless, that is, some more fundamental objection to embryo experimentation *per se* can be adduced.

At the moment about 150,000 abortions are performed annually in the United Kingdom. The embryos and foetuses thus lost go almost entirely to waste. I cannot imagine the moral argument that would support the killing of 150,000 embryos annually to safeguard the 'health' of women, where 'health' is very broadly conceived and where their lives are seldom at risk, which would at the same time suggest that no comparable embryos should be studied, experimented upon or used as a source of transplant or graft material, where such use would very probably save lives and be of substantial benefit to the health of present and future individuals. I say 'comparable' embryos because all abortions carried out by doctors involve the killing of embryos or foetuses beyond the 14 days permitted by *Warnock*.

So any society which accepts that the health and well-being of its members legitimates abortion must also accept that the health and well-being of its members legitimates the beneficial use of embryos grown *in vitro*. Unless that is, some further consideration can be adduced which would show either that we should revise our views about *both* abortion *and* embryo experimentation, or which shows that there is something special about embryo experimentation which warrants its separation from the issue of abortion.

We will now look at examples of each type of argument before drawing some conclusions.

## POTENTIAL PERSONS

### *Two ways of protecting embryos*

The most powerful objections to embryo experimentation turn on the moral status of the embryo. They suggest that the embryo is protected in ways analogous to the moral protections usually afforded to normal adult human beings. Now of course the question arises as to why, in virtue of what, should the human embryo or the human foetus be protected as if it were a normal adult? There are two standard answers to this question.

One involves the suggestion that the human embryo is morally important in view of *what it is*, and the second argues that the human embryo is protected because of *what it might become*. Both of these suggestions run into a number of separate problems and interestingly they run ultimately into the same insuperable problem.

The suggestion that the human embryo is important for what it is takes a number of forms. One suggests that the embryo is important simply because it's *human*, that it is membership of the human species that carries with it moral protections of the sort that make its life sacrosanct in some sense. Another form of this argument attaches moral significance to a *natural kind* and suggests that since human beings are members of a natural kind that has moral importance, this importance extends to all members of that natural kind despite individual differences.

Many regard these suggestions as suspect, recognizing that there is something irredeemably arbitrary about a moral preference for one's own species or for something like a natural kind. Why this natural kind and not others? Such people are prepared to recognize that the human embryo and even the human foetus, judged in terms of what it is, may be less complex, intelligent, and interesting than many animals or other creatures to whom comparable protections are not extended. They recognize that the special thing that human embryos have going for them must be understood, not in terms of what they are, but in terms of what they will become. It is their *potential* to grow into paradigms of morally important individuals like you and me, that makes them important and makes mandatory their protection.

We should note that defenders of either of these types of position on the value or moral importance of human embryos, must also and for the same reasons object to abortion. For establishing the moral importance of the embryo or the foetus, either in terms of what it is, or in terms of what it will become, would confirm the moral importance and inviolability of those foetuses which might be the subjects of abortion quite as much as those embryos which might find themselves as experimental subjects.

### Objections

To take potentiality first, there are by now familiar and conclusive objections to the idea that we should regard an individual's potential to become something that is significantly different from its present state, as a reason for treating it as if it had already undergone the relevant changes when manifestly it has not. Acorns are not oak trees, all human beings are potentially dead, but no one regards this as a good reason for treating live humans as if they were already dead.

More disturbingly perhaps, it is not only the embryo or the foetus that is potentially a normal live adult human. The egg and the sperm taken together but as yet un-united have the same potential as the fertilized egg. Anyone who doubts this should ask themselves the question: what has the potential to become an embryo? Some things do, and whatever has the potential to become an embryo has the potential to become whatever it is that the embryo has the potential to become.[11]

Now some people are tenaciously myopic to this argument. They see a difference between the potential of *an individual* and the potential *to become an individual*. This distinction enables them to value the potential of the individual, but not the potential of that which will become the individual. Thus they can regard the fertilized human egg as a protected being without attaching any moral importance at all to the living human egg and the living human sperm which will become that embryo.

It is at this point that the two strands of argument we have so far separated unite in their susceptibility to a powerful objection. For both the defenders of a preference for members of the human species, or for the natural kind/human being, and those who rather value such beings for their potential to become normal adults, or to become self-conscious and rational individuals, or whatever other piece of potentiality is regarded as securing moral significance, both believe falsely that it is only the embryo, the fertilized egg, that qualifies. And they believe this because they believe falsely that it is only in the fertilized egg that there is, united in one place, in one individual, all that is necessary for continuous development to maturity.

Why there is this mystical reverence for unity of place is something that is never explained, and indeed it is inexplicable except as a misplaced reverence for Aristotle. However, we do not have to attack the unities, for there is a more radical difficulty at hand. Let's grant for the sake of argument that individuals are the stuff of which moral significance is made. Let's grant for the moment also that it is human individuals who uniquely matter. I think both the propositions that we have just granted are false, but no matter.

The possibility of parthenogenesis, both natural and artificial, sinks this line of argument utterly.

## Parthenogenesis

The eggs of most species including humans can be stimulated to grow without fertilization. This occurs naturally and randomly and may account for alleged examples of virgin birth, including that of Jesus; but only on the assumption that the son of the God of the Christians was in fact her daughter. For parthenogenesis only produces females. It is now possible to induce parthenogenetic growth simply, in the laboratory.[12] Only the most determined male chauvinist could suggest that adult human individuals resulting from parthenogenetic reproduction were not fully human and of moral importance comparable with that of any other human beings. This possibility shows that the human egg is an individual member of the human species if the embryo is, for they both share the same important features, namely that they both contain within the one individual all that is necessary for continuous growth to maturity under the right conditions.

Those who accept some ethic which involves either not killing or otherwise using human individuals without their consent, or who believe that we have an obligation to instantiate human potential, or at least that we have an obligation not to kill or otherwise use any individuals with the requisite potential, must all have the same reverence for the unfertilized egg that they have for the embryo.

## WARNOCK

We must at this point in our argument return briefly to the influential *Warnock Report*. Its recommendation was, it will be remembered, that a limit of 14 days beyond fertilization should be set on research on embryos. The reason given by *Warnock* was that the formation of the so-called 'primitive streak' occurs at about 15 days. The primitive streak is important because it confirms that the embryo is at this point an individual (rather than, say, twins). *Warnock* prefaces this conclusion with the reiteration, as an article of faith, that 'the objection to using human embryos in research is that each one is a potential human being'.[13] Now these two features whether taken separately or in combination provide no grounds at all for supporting the 14-day limit. For if the potentiality argument is sound, then human potential is present quite as much before 14 days as it is after that limit. And if, as I have suggested, the potentiality argument is unsound, the development of the primitive streak operates on nothing of moral importance. For it does not affect species or natural kind membership and it cannot be morally preferable to kill a known, rather than an unknown number of humans.

However, another consideration has very central importance for *Warnock*. It is the idea that moral sentiment – the strongly held feelings of ordinary people – are of great importance. This point is strongly made in the foreword to the report:

> [M]oral questions . . . are by definition, questions that involve not only calculation of consequences but also strong sentiments with regard to the nature of the proposed activities themselves.
>
> We were therefore bound to take very seriously the feelings expressed in the evidence . . . people generally want *some principles or other* to govern the development and use of the new techniques.[14]

Crudely the idea is that if people feel that something is wrong, that feeling must be respected and that respect must be reflected in law. But a first duty of any moral agent is surely to examine her feelings to see whether what she feels is actually right. We know of so many strongly held feelings – feelings that women are inferior or that it is unseemly for them to be involved in certain male occupations, for example – which should not be respected, however strongly held they are. So we must always examine our feelings to see whether they cohere with our principles. Now in the present case there is a radical inconsistency. For while *Warnock* believes (on very inadequate evidence it must be said) that people in this society feel strongly that clear and early limits should be set on embryo research, people in this society equally clearly feel strongly that abortion is permissible. Now, as we have seen, these two beliefs are clearly and simply inconsistent.

Of course an independent argument is required to reconcile these two views and that would involve a detailed examination of the moral status of the embryo and the foetus. I have not room for such an undertaking here[15] so I will attempt the following short cut.

## CONCLUSION

If the moral reasons which justify abortion are sound then we should permit embryo research and experimentation and the use of embryonic material on the same terms and set a limit to such research *at the same point* as the upper limit for abortion.

If, on the other hand, the sorts of arguments that are adduced for objecting to embryo research, or for setting a *Warnock*-style early limit, are sound, then two consequences follow. The first is that we must on the same grounds outlaw abortion and all but barrier methods of birth-control. We must not prevent implantation of the fertilized egg. The second is that we must protect the human egg, for it too is a human individual with the potential for successful development. Those who accept that fertilized *in vitro* embryos should always be implanted must accept that all eggs collected must be stimulated to grow either parthenogenetically or by fertilization and must then be implanted. Women who fail to attempt the fertilization of their own eggs are morally in the same boat as embryologists who fail to return embryos to the uterus.

I would guess that faced with these alternatives, public sentiment would be on the side of abortion and on the side of research on embryos up to the same point – about 28 weeks. I can see much to commend this as the right course to take in the light of present knowledge and beliefs. My personal view is that the limit should be substantially beyond 28 weeks. But the justification of such a view is another story entirely.[16]

## NOTES

1 *Report of the Committee of Inquiry into Human Fertilisation and Embryology (Warnock Report)* Cmnd 9314 (London: HMSO, 1984).

2 Department of Health and Social Security, *Legislation on Human Infertility Services and Embryo Research: A Consultation Paper*, Cm 46 (London: HMSO, 1986), and *Human Fertilisation and Embryology: A Framework for Legislation*, Cm 259 (London: HMSO, 1987). The announcement in July 1988 of a postponement of legislative action for at least 18–24 months means that the question will need to be reopened for a fourth time: see *Institute of Medical Ethics* Bulletin No. 40 (1988), p. 10.

3 R. Edwards and J. Purdy (eds), *Human Conception in Vitro* (London: Academic Press, 1981).

4 See my *The Value of Life: An Introduction to Medical Ethics* (London: Routledge & Kegan Paul, 1985), ch. 6, for further details.

5 Edwards and Purdy, *Human Conception*, p. 373.

6 Edwards and Purdy, *Human Conception*, p. 381.
7 ibid.
8 R. G. Edwards, Lecture at the Centre For Social Ethics & Policy, University of Manchester, 24 February 1987.
9 Harris, *Value of Life*.
10 The presumption of the Infant Life (Preservation) Act 1929 is that the infant is prima facie incapable of existing independently of its mother prior to 28 weeks; see *C* v. *S* [1987] 1 All E.R. 1230.
11 See Harris, *Value of Life*.
12 You just dip them in alcohol and they start to grow. Or so I am reliably informed.
13 *Warnock Report*, para. 11.22.
14 ibid., para. 8.17.
15 See Harris, *Value of Life*, ch. 1.
16 This story is told in Harris, *Value of Life*.

# 6

## 'WHAT SHALL WE TELL THE CHILDREN?' REFLECTIONS ON CHILDREN'S PERSPECTIVES AND THE REPRODUCTION REVOLUTION

*KATHERINE O'DONOVAN*

In discussion of the new technology of conception little attention has been given to the perspectives of the children thereby produced. There is, as yet, no language readily available for explaining to a child that egg, sperm, or embryo donation form part of its inheritance. And how is a child to respond? Available however, is the experience of adopted children, in whose case genetic and social parentage have been separated. It is this parental separation of genitor and child raiser that adoptees and the children of donation have in common.

As a result of *in vitro* fertilization the five stages of producing a child – female genitor, male genitor, female carrier, social mother, social father, can be implemented by five separate persons. In adoption the first three stages are separated from the last two. Where artificial insemination by a donor takes place the male genitor is separate from the social father, if any.[1] In egg donation the female genitor is neither carrier, nor caring mother. In embryo donation the genitors are separated from the other three functions. Surrogacy arrangements usually imply that caring mother is separated from female genitor and carrier. But carrier may be separated from female genitor/caring mother, as where the carrier is not the genitor, or does not intend to raise the child. The bond between sex and conception has been broken.

This essay examines debates surrounding the issue of information given to children on their genetic origins. It suggests that aspects of this discourse are based on the premise that the biological family is 'natural' and provides a model to which other families must conform. In the upholding of the biological family those children excluded therefrom are stigmatized in their 'artificial family'.[2] It is true that our knowledge of human and legal relationships are based on bonds between sex and conception. But adoption, and illegitimacy, have contributed to that knowledge, as stigmatized exceptions.

## THE BACKGROUND

The discourse on adoptions has traditionally been suffused with concepts of secrecy and anonymity. In recent years, however, the notion of identity has provided a challenge to these former concepts. By contrast, donation is considered to be a secret practice, protected by medical guarantees of anonymity. Examination of these three concepts reveals the contradictory nature of debates on adoption and donation, and an underlying uneasiness which is reflected in the legal response.

Law's role in this is not merely reflective of cultural values which are maintained in the face of unease. Law also constitutes social institutions, such as adoption, and this influences the way in which adoptees perceive themselves and are perceived.

*Anonymity* has been part of the legal institution of adoption since its inception in England and Wales in 1926.[3] It was believed that biological and adoptive parents' interests were best served by this policy. A special register was created to record and make traceable the connection between the entry in the birth register and the entry in the adoption register. This was maintained by the Registrar General. However, access to this special register was unobtainable except by special permission of a court. Approval for inspection was rarely granted. This meant that adopted persons, who did not know the names of genitors, could not obtain copies of their original birth certificates. Adoption practice has generally involved the giving of a new name to the child.[4]

Anonymity was reinforced by the Adoption Act of 1949 which

97

permitted adopters to conceal their identity from the biological parents during court proceedings. The theory of 'matching' the child's physical appearance to that of the adopters also enabled concealment. The adoption itself could be hidden, from the child and from the world. Social policy in adoption, until fairly recently, was to mimic so far as possible the arrival of a newborn child into a biological family. The notes of registration in the Adoption Act 1950 state: 'the substitution . . . of the original birth certificate is considered desirable where that certificate revealed the fact of illegitimacy or where it is desired to conceal the origin of the child'.[5]

Artificial insemination by a donor is almost as common a way of becoming a parent today as adoption. It is estimated that 2.5 per cent of live births in the United Kingdom are through AID, and that 250,000 people in the United States were conceived through this process.[6] Donors of sperm are guaranteed anonymity where the medical profession is involved. This policy is justified by the confidentiality of medical treatment, the doctor/patient relationship. It is also said to be necessary to protect donors, and to ensure that donation continues. Medical practice has been to advise AID parents to keep the matter secret. A leaflet from the Royal College of Gynaecologists (1979) advises that 'unless you decide to tell the child there is no reason for him (or her) ever to know that he (or she) was conceived by AID. Whether or not you do so is entirely up to you.'[7] This goes further than anonymity; for it introduces secrecy.

*Secrecy* is a darker concept than anonymity. It is possible for a child to know that its genetic and social parentage have been separated, even though the genitors remain anonymous. But where parentage is a secret, the child may not know anything.

The first indication that the policy of secrecy on adoption might not be entirely sound came with the Hurst Report in 1954. There it was stated: 'A number of witnesses in England thought that the adopted person has a right to this information [about origins] and expressed the view that it is not in the interests of adopted children to be permanently precluded from satisfying their natural curiosity.'[8] The committee recommended that the adoption application should include a pledge to tell the child of the adoption. This was not implemented in the subsequent Adoption Act 1958. The Home Office did produce an explanatory memorandum for all adopters. This stressed that children should be told of adoption but added: 'You may prefer not to tell him anything; but that would be unwise, because he would be likely to find out himself sooner or later and if you had not told him, the discovery might be a shock.'[9] The evidence from life histories of adopted persons is that discovery is more than a shock; it can undermine a lifetime's security.

The opinion was growing that not only was it good adoption practice to tell children of their status, but also that they should be given some information about their birth parents. The adoption law in Scotland, from its inception in 1930, had permitted adoptees, on reaching the age of 17, to apply for their original birth certificates direct from the Registrar General. John Triseliotis had done research on Scottish adoptees applying for birth records and was forceful in recommending to the Houghton Committee, set up in 1969, that England and Wales should follow Scottish practice. The reason was grounded on the concept of identity.[10]

The first Working Paper published by the Houghton Committee in 1970 still emphasized concealment:

> anonymity serves as a protection both for the child and the adoptive parents on the one hand and the natural parents on the other – for the adoptive home against interference from the natural parents or the fear of this, for the natural parents against any temptation to watch the child's progress or in any other way to feel the links still in existence.[11]

And although greater openness with the child about adoption was advocated, the committee still felt that this 'does not, however, necessarily entail a knowledge of the actual names of the natural parents and other identifying information'.[12]

Secrecy in family life is a strong subject in fiction and autobiographies. Philosophical reflections thereon suggest that family secrets, whilst forming part of the fabric and history of the group, may have a deleterious effect. Sissela Bok argues that deceit over an important matter, such as parentage, is a form of control and even assault. The secret excludes the child whom it concerns, evoking a sense of being an outsider.[13] There is both an attraction to, and a repulsion from, the secret. The telling may be experienced by the child as an aggressive attack on the centre of her life. Instead of clearing up the dark hints, the sense of exclusion, the feeling of not belonging, the revelation may create greater mysteries.

Underlying this are issues of interaction and power within the family unit.

Secrets and myths may . . . be started by an individual member of the family. Like everything else that happens in families, they do not remain the property of the individual, as the responses of other family members set in motion processes of interaction, which strengthen or weaken the effects of secrets and myths.[14]

The prevailing secrecy may set up doubts and insecurities. The awareness of a family secret may place the child of donation in a similar position to the child of adoption in the past. 'Silence and secrecy are a shelter for power';[15] feelings of powerlessness and guilt may follow.

The outcome of the Houghton Committee's 1972 report was the Children Act 1975. Section 26 provides that, on reaching the age of 18, adopted people have the right to receive a copy of their original birth certificate. Because of the promise of anonymity to parents, those adopted before 12 November 1975 receive mandatory counselling, as part of an official effort to ensure that genitors are not suddenly confronted by genes.[16]

The manner of discussion of access to birth certificates in Parliament reveals a number of assumptions surrounding the institution of adoption. On one hand were those who feared for the security of the biological mother confronted by the child placed for adoption. These feelings were expressed in terms of 'her guilty secret', her embarrassment and shame of her past, her rejection by family and neighbours.[17] This discourse reveals much about the status of women, notions of female chastity, and the stigma of bearing an illegitimate child. On the other hand there were those who spoke of 'a basic human right that every child should know his origins',[18] of being 'psychologically whole',[19] of the adopted child who 'wishes to know who and what he his'.[20]

The idea underlying section 26 has been summed up by Triseliotis in the words, 'no person should be cut off from his origins'.[21] But the notion of origins and its accompanying phrase 'identity' have not been subjected to critical scrutiny.

Rather they have been greeted with acclaim by writers on this area of social policy and law.

*Identity* in discussions of adoption policy serves as a concept concerned with psychology. Researchers have linked 'genealogical and personal information to the development of a positive sense of identity and of a whole self'. Triseliotis, who influenced the passing of section 26, writes of 'a psychological need', in 'the formation of a positive concept of self' for 'personal history material'. Such information is 'a fundamental right' in 'the quest for roots, origins and reunions', where adoptees are 'seeking to "complete" themselves.'[22] The question which is neither asked nor answered is whether the identity crisis suffered by adoptees is socially and discursively constructed.

Other writers have criticized this model of identity as pathological. Haimes and Timms argue that there is a distinction between ego identity and social identity.

The rhetoric of the pathological model uses concepts such as the 'identity crisis' to describe the effect of a bad adoptive experience on the individual's ego identity, that private 'internal' sense of self. We argue that adoption can be better understood in terms of the individual's *social* identity: adoption is, after all, a social arrangement rather than a natural process happening to the individual.[23]

The concept of social identity is explained as 'the presentation of self in everyday life'[24] and the appraisal and judgment of others. Adopted persons are aware of themselves as different but are, according to this view, attempting to account for themselves in their 'search for origins'.

A social identity open to questioning does not imply, as a damaged ego identity might, a degree of psychological disturbance, but rather that extra care is required by the social act or interaction, and often that extra work is needed to ensure the individual is taken as a serious, competent but non-threatening member of society.[25]

This idea of identity seems to be an 'image of ourselves projected to other people'.[26] But identity has other senses, such as that of oneself as a particular kind of person. The two models of identity, ego and social, erected by writers on adoption, are underpinned by visions of normality and difference. This is a vision of family structure in which there is a 'natural' family, which is assumed. Triseliotis, and Haimes and Timms are committed to a discourse which does not question the concept of identity as a response to socially produced situations. Yet, as Derek Morgan argues, 'appeals to the "natural order" of the family and claims of its necessary retention can be seen, from the perspective of social history, as an attempt to legitimate and reinforce a specific form of structure and specific relationships of authority and dependence'.[27] The 'search for identity' as the quest of adopted children for their genetic parents has been termed, does not exist in a vacuum. It is produced by legal and social structures which attach value to concepts of identity linked to genitors. The case histories of those whose searches have ended in finding a parent do not necessarily suggest that such quests should be encouraged.[28]

## THE EXPERIENCE OF ADOPTED CHILDREN

The literature on adoption and identity uses case-studies to bring out what are perceived as crucial issues. These are knowledge of genetic origins as important for psychological health and openness by genetic and social parents. Yet a recent popular account of nine case histories, revealingly entitled *Lost Children*,[29] shows that the quest and subsequent discoveries may be disastrous for the searcher. This account does not question the desire to trace genetic parents which is perceived as 'natural'; the adopted child is said to have 'some fate, some identity, some natural identity which drives him on to seek out his own origins'.[30] Adopted children are described as growing up with a desperate longing to discover more about themselves and their roots; even where the adoption has been successful and happy, many feel incomplete without some knowledge of their blood origins.[31]

It is an open question as to whether this description is accurate. But what is revealing is a language suffused with the notion that we are our genes; that blood matters. In this account secrecy is explained as having been necessary originally to overcome the stigma of illegitimacy, but now to be in the interest of the adopters: 'giving them the emotional security of knowing that the natural mother has gone for ever, and they are entirely free to simulate natural parenting as best they can'. However, a 'sense of alien, different, foreign, unknown blood and genes may not ever be totally obliterated from the relationship between new parents and child'.[32]

The concept of stigma is introduced by writers on adoption to account for perceived differences on the part of others between the adoptive family and the 'natural' family. Erving Goffman has argued that those who are perceived as different are stigmatized as a form of 'management of spoiled identity'.

> The attitude we normals have towards a person with a stigma and the actions we take in regard to him, are well known, since these responses are what benevolent social action is designed to soften and ameliorate . . . We construct a stigma theory, and ideology to . . . account for the danger he represents.[33]

Adoptive parents, it seems, are stigmatized because 'by admitting that their child is adopted, they are telling the world of the shame of their own infertility'.[34] Adoptive children are stigmatized as 'unknown blood, unknown genes' the 'cuckoo in their nest'.[35] The 'spoiled identity' of both arises, in part, from an inability on the part of normals to place the adoptive family.

In most literature on child care the concept of placement is used to convey a sense of a new family for a child whose initial placement with biological parents has broken down. But there is another sense of placement, to do with 'social identity – their ability to place themselves in their own and in the life-histories of others'. Section 26 is said to be important in this process 'not simply because it confers access to information but also because it allows for the public requesting of an account'.[36]

Uneasiness about adoption among normals and adoptees is reflected in stigma and marginal status. Adopted children are seen as having an 'achieved' role, as having to prove themselves and who they are; whereas the biological child has an ascribed role. One adoptee reflected: '[Y]ou know, I wasn't a blood relation – and blood counts in families – they never accepted me.'[37]

The hidden agenda of section 26 is that adopted children have an unrequited desire to know their genitors, and that this is a natural and understandable need which can be met by legislation. Although I have argued that writings on this need should be subjected to critical scrutiny, nevertheless we must take seriously the question whether other children brought up by a genetically unrelated parent also have this desire and require legislation to meet it.

Before we leap into extending section 26 of the Children Act 1975 to cover all children with 'unknown genes' perhaps we should investigate further the research data on adopted children. It has been said that all adopted children experience the need to contact their genitors. But does the empirical evidence support this assertion? Closer inspection reveals that there was an initial flood of applications on the coming into force of section 26 but that this has diminished to a trickle.[38] Furthermore, application for one's original birth certificate does not necessarily mean a desire to trace, or to contact genitors. Of the first 500 applicants to the General Register Office, only 46 gave locating a natural parent or relative as their prime reason, but 140 overall declared an intention to trace.[39]

This data does not suggest an overwhelming urge on the part of adoptees to seek out genitors. The literature is insufficiently critical of the idea of a 'search for identity'. There are two questions to be asked: first, to what extent is the perceived psychological need culturally produced? Second, might this need not be a displacement of other personal problems, or part of the adolescent crisis experienced by most persons?

It is true that in Polly Toynbee's popular account of the experience of adoptees the subjects wished to contact their genitors. Some were obsessed with this desire. However, this was a self-selecting group. Of the eight searchers, one found a mother who was a hopeless derelict, another was obsessed with a mother who refused to have anything to do with him, and a third discovered her mother to be Ruth Ellis, the last woman to be hanged in England.[40]

That these searchers experienced a desire to fill a gap in their lives cannot be denied. But the majority were not adopted as babies. Furthermore their quest appears to have arisen because they shared a popular view expressed by Toynbee that 'every human civilization has held family and blood kinship in high esteem'.[41] The literature on the search for origins continually emphasizes the blood tie. If this has any meaning then it ought to apply also to children of donation. Yet the unspoken text that the search for genitors is natural, that infertile adults are to be stigmatized, might be sufficient argument for secrecy on the part of social parents.

## BLOOD TIES MATTER

The notion of blood relationships suffuses the work on adoption and identity. But is it blood that is under discussion? Most subjects of case studies were interested in their mothers, rather than in their fathers. Does this mean that the nine months *in utero* create a perceived bond? If that is so, then children born through sperm, egg, or embryo donation may have identity problems. But children produced through surrogacy and womb-leasing arrangements may have similar experiences to adoptees. However, it seems that genes, inherited appearance, traits, intelligence, are emphasized by some subjects. As Oliver O'Donovan reflects: 'From now on there is no knowing what a parent is.'[42]

Modern social policy theory has been to de-emphasize the blood tie. Too many tragedies, such as that of Maria Colwell, have arisen from claims by parents based on biological relationships.[43] Feminist theorists have persistently attacked John Bowlby's depiction of mother love as based on genetic bonds.[44] Carers have been shown to form relationships with small children on a day-to-day basis and not on blood.[45] This resurrection of blood as of great significance in parent/child relationships seems a retrograde step.

In what sense might the blood tie matter? Elsewhere I have identified three aspects: materials, medical, and the cultural notion of identity.[46] In the case of adoption there can be no material interest, as the adoption order severs the legal tie with the biological parents, and therefore adoptees cannot look to them for inheritance or financial support. Donation, however, does not sever the legal tie between genitor and child.[47] So far as medical interest is concerned we do know that a genetic family history of certain diseases may be important knowledge to any person. When founding a family future parents will be greatly helped by knowledge of genetic diseases such as haemophilia or Huntington's chorea. No legislative effort has been made in ascertaining and recording such information for adoptees, although this is a feasible task. Nor has the medical profession shown any concern despite advances in scientific work or genetic diseases. The *Warnock Report* has proposed that this be done for children born through egg and sperm donation.[48] It is however the confused concept of identity that has been the focus of law makers, social workers and the published work on adoption.

## IMPLICATIONS FOR THE CHILDREN OF DONATION

What does this mean for the children of donation? Are they in an analogous position to the children of adoption, or can significant distinctions be drawn? At present it seems that donation is surrounded by the secrecy, anonymity, and stigma, so familiar from the adoption story. As secrecy has been an important aspect of the adoption experience it is likely to be so also of the donation experience. Why does secrecy surround donation? Medical ethics require confidentiality in the relationship between doctor and patient. In the case of donation the duty has been interpreted by the Royal College of Gynaecologists as owed both to the donor and to future parents.[49] Concern to protect the privacy of donors was the reason given by physicians in the United States for their failure to keep records of donations.[50]

There is also reason to suspect that donors would not participate in donation if anonymity were not guaranteed. A study of sixty-seven donors in Melbourne showed that half would not participate if their names were available to parents.[51] It seems however that fear of legal complications was one source of desire for anonymity and some donors held softer attitudes towards the children produced. Recent experience in Sweden, where anonymity is no longer promised to donors, supports the hypothesis that donations will be significantly reduced by the legislative creation of rights to know the donor's identity.[52]

Male infertility, the major reason for attempts at conception through artificial insemination by a donor, is a source of shame. Studies show that feelings of masculinity have been damaged by the discovery of infertility.[53] AID parents do not tell. Yet many of those interviewed by Snowden and Mitchell were tormented by the secrecy they had initially so eagerly sought.[54] The shame men feel because of infertility seems to be related to cultural attitudes, to meanings given to masculinity. A misfortune leads again to stigma.

Marginal status and a failure of placement are also said to be a common feature of adoption and donation. Although the children may suffer a marginal identity because of 'their ignorance about certain key people and events in their lives',[55] the parents are marginalized by their failure to conceive. Section 26 is said to be important to the children of adoption, not just in opening the way to secret information, but also by permitting the adoptee to request a public account of the adoption. The idea of an account or public explanation arises from the institution of adoption as legally constituted and sanctioned. Its intrusion makes the state accountable for the transfer of parental rights. Views are influenced by legal structures, and adoption is subjected to the full rigours of legal control. Private adoptions, and private contracts for transfer of parental rights are unenforceable, and illegal.[56] If the state takes control of donation, as it proposes to do,[57] then a similar accountability will be expected by the children of donation.

The experience of adoption is highly relevant in discussions of the new reproductive technology. What was seen in parliamentary discussions of section 26 as an issue of children's rights versus parents' rights, has become an issue of moral responsibility in terms of power and choice. It is true that power and choice are lacking for all children. The old taunt thrown by child at parent, 'I didn't ask to be born', is indicative of the powerlessness of all, not just the adopted. It is evident that adoptive children do not choose their adoptive parents, in most cases; but neither do they choose their birth parents.[58] Is there some sense in which the fusion of egg and sperm of biological parents is seen as outside their control, whereas the decision to adopt, sanctioned by law, is an exercise of power and choice? But choice is now exercised in the decision to become biological parents. It is odd that adoptive parents or parents by donation should be perceived as more powerful than biological parents. In adoption the process of application, interview, vetting, trial period and supervision before the adoption is granted emphasizes the powerlessness and marginal status of the infertile. State control of the new technology of conception is likely to increase the feelings of powerlessness of parents by donation, who are already subjected to the power of the medical profession.

Secrecy removes power and choice from the adopted. This is made clear in personal histories. It is highly likely to be true also of the children of donation. But secrecy arises from the stigmatizing of infertility and illegitimacy. It serves to preserve certain perceived standards of morality and normality. Perhaps it is these that must change.

It has been suggested that there is an uneasiness about adoption in society as a whole and that it is this which gives rise to stigma.[59] But the stigma attaches also to infertility. And recent debates suggest great unease in relation to new modes of conception. Therefore, a likely outcome is that the children will be stigmatized. Given this hypothesis, it is hardly surprising that social parents are reticent and secretive.

The general advice given by social workers to AID parents is to tell. Thus Haimes and Timms:

107

whether the children have a right to know their genetic origins, possibly at the expense of the adults involved, is a debate that was thoroughly rehearsed prior to the introduction of Section 26. It would seem that Section 26 is the answer. It is difficult to argue a special case for AID.[60]

We know very little about what AID children feel. There is pressure in the United States and elsewhere for information to be released. In Sweden this has led to legislation.[61] Given the prevailing secrecy and confidentiality of treatment, how many of the 250,000 people alive in the United States estimated to have been conceived after AID know of their status? The corresponding estimate for the United Kingdom is 50,000.[62] Writers have put forward the hypothesis that

> children and adults are likely to suspect something, not just through family interaction but also through basic genetic knowledge. Other temporal and social, as well as physical cues work to confirm their suspicion, but given the lack of publicity of AID until recently, they are far more likely to suspect adoption or even adultery, rather than the truth.[63]

The prevailing secrecy may set up doubts and insecurities. The awareness of a family secret may place the child of donation in a similar position to the child of adoption in the past. At first glance there seem to be distinctions to be drawn, but on closer inspection these seem less obvious. Is it likely that in future we shall regard telling the children of donation in the same light as we now regard telling the children of adoption? Or are the distinctions sufficiently great to put donation in a different light? In order to probe this, two aspects demand further thought. The first is the reasons why genetic parentage is of interest to children. The second is social attitudes to donation.

In its exclusive concentration on psychological needs the literature on 'the search for origins' overlooks the practical reasons why their genetic parentage is of interest to children. A major practical interest is medical and genetic history. It is not too far-fetched to suggest that a reason why more adopted women than men go in search of their origins is that women's particular closeness to family medical history raises these issues in an immediate way. There is also evidence to show that it is at the stage of the life cycle when considering founding a family of one's own that interest is highest. Thus Philip Whitehead, an adopted child, stated in the parliamentary debate on section 26 that the adopted child

> wishes to know who and what he is. This is true as he approaches marriage . . . It is at such moments that a person wishes to know all the relevant facts and data about his past.[64]

Furthermore, as Yoxen points out, the risks of genetic diseases, and of consanguineous marriage, do exist. Medical advances have enabled the identification of particular genes. Where these carry genetic disease parents should be informed. These are arguments for 'quality control' of donors,[65] but they are also directed at openness about genetic origins. This makes it all the more curious that the medical profession should encourage secrecy.

The *Warnock Report* recognized that medical information is of importance to the children of donation. It recommended that donation be controlled by the state through a licensing system, and that 'donor profiles' be used from which prospective parents could choose the genetic donor. The details of the donor's ethnic origins and genetic health would be contained in the profile. Legislation giving a right of access to the child to the information contained in the profile is proposed.[66] However, the Report emphasizes the anonymity of the donor and the confidentiality of the donor service.[67] The *Warnock* proposals would, to some extent, serve the need to know the medical history of ancestors, provided the child was aware of donation status. However, the recommendation that the words 'by donation' be entered on the birth certificate has not been supported in public debate.[68] So the opportunity not to tell the children will continue.

## ATTITUDES TO DONATION

The *Feversham Committee Report* of 1960 on artificial insemination by donor took the view that 'the role of donor is of such a kind that it is liable to appeal to the abnormal and the unbalanced'.[69] And the medical establishment's view is that anonymity of donors must be retained, for those who do not object to being identified are seen as psychologically suspect.[70] From the donor's point of view there are several good reasons for wanting guaranteed anonymity. These have arisen in part from legal structures which are slow to adapt to donation. Thus while the AID child was illegitimate at law, the genetic father had, in theory, the duties to the child of an illegitimate father, that is, of financial support. The child could have claimed against the donor's estate on his death.[71] Hence the recent change to remove all liabilities from the donor.[72]

Cultural attitudes raise other issues. There is no evidence that donors are stigmatized, but they do seem to share the general public unease about displaced children. The French example is of some interest here. The state controls a nationally co-ordinated network of AID centres. Donors are unpaid and are encouraged to see their donation as a gift to meet the needs of infertile couples. Only married donors are accepted and the gift is represented as being from the 'donor couple' to the 'recipient couple'. It is the cultural significance attached to the act which is of interest. The organizers intend to create 'a new social understanding'[73] of AID, as a social duty, a charity to others, something to be valued by those involved. Desirable though it may be to give a positive social meaning to donation, the French example also represents 'a pervasive system of moral control'[74] over AID.

No doubt cultural attitudes elsewhere could change. But would this cultural change lie in the direction of saying that egg and sperm donation are analogous to blood donation? The consequences of such a view might be that genetic parentage would not be considered important and the notion of a search for origins bizarre. Or would the cultural change lie in the direction of genetic parents identifying themselves without difficulty to their genetic offspring? The latter direction seems unlikely. Relationships are the result of social interaction, and not of blood. But if openness is a social goal then the cultural meaning of parenthood must change to give full recognition to those who care for children and are psychological parents. At the same time the stigmatizing of adoptive and other 'different' children must cease.

Feminists, particularly those involved in self-insemination, are attempting to alter the meaning of parenthood. However this view remains within a particular sub-culture and could not be said to be a majority attitude.[75]

## CONCLUSION

The trouble with the concept of need to know one's origins in the context of parentage is that it is an imprecise concept which is socially constructed. The imprecision of the concept has already been discussed and it has been suggested that it be broken down further into psychological, medical, and legal aspects. The assertion that the notion of need is socially constructed does not represent a denial that it may be experienced in a profound sense by adopted and other persons. But it does arise partially from the cultural significance attached to the blood tie. By this is meant that 'the psychological need to feel whole' through identification of genetic parents arises from the value placed on such blood relationship. This value is made up of self-interest, pride, love. But it also is reflected in and reflects the legal structures surrounding parent and child relationships.

In most cases genetic parentage and social parentage are united. Legal rights and duties of parents are designed to cover that situation. But where genetic and social parentage are separated, or where both genetic and social fathers are missing or unknown, law and social attitudes stigmatize those children conceived in a different pattern from the majority. Removing the stigma might ensure that some of the secrecy and tension surrounding these matters is dispelled.

## NOTES

1 See R. Snowden and G. D. Mitchell, *The Artificial Family* (London: Allen & Unwin, 1981, 1983 ed.).

2 This phrase is taken from Snowden and Mitchell, *Artificial Family*. The experience of illegitimate children, particularly in the past, might be drawn upon.

3 The Adoption of Children Act 1926. This followed the *First Report of the Child Adoption Committee* (The Tomlin Committee), Cmnd 2401 (London: HMSO, 1925).

4 Adoption of Children Act 1926, s. 11(7). It has always been possible for an adopted person to obtain the original birth certificate, provided the birth name is known. See J. Levin, 'Tracing the birth records of adopted persons', *Family Law*, vol. 7 (1977), p. 104.

5 Adoption Act 1950.

6 E. Yoxen, *Unnatural Selection? Coming to Terms with the New Genetics* (London: Heinemann, 1986), p. 21.

7 Snowden and Mitchell, *Artificial Family*, p. 84.

8 *Report of the Departmental Committee on the Adoption of Children* (the Hurst Report), Cmnd 9248 (London: HMSO, 1954), p. 53.

9 Appendix of Home Office Letter (HO58/59, March 1959). Cited by E. Haimes and N. Timms, *Adoption, Identity and Social Policy* (Aldershot: Gower, 1985), p. 15.

10 See J. Triseliotis, *In Search of Origins* (London: Routledge & Kegan Paul, 1973).

11 *Adoption of Children: Working Paper of the Departmental Committee on the Adoption of Children* (the *Houghton Report*) (London: HMSO, 1970), p. 231.

12 *Adoption of Children*, p. 234.

13 S. Bok, *Secrets* (New York: Vintage, 1984), ch. 3.

14 L. Pincus and C. Dare, *Secrets in the Family* (London: Faber & Faber, 1978), p. 16.

15 M. Foucault, *The History of Sexuality*, vol. 1 (Harmondsworth: Penguin Books, 1984), p. 101.

16 See H. Bevan and M. Parry, *Children Act 1975* (London: Butterworth, 1978), pp. 194–9.

17 *Official Report, House of Commons, Hansard*, vol. 893 (20 June 1975) on the Children Bill. See, for example, the views of Jill Knight, col. 1363.

18 ibid., L. Abse, col. 1862.

19 ibid., P. Whitehead, col. 1900.

20 ibid.

21 Triseliotis, *In Search*, p. 166.

22 J. Triseliotis, 'Obtaining birth certificates', in P. Bean (ed.), *Adoption: Essays in Social Policy, Law and Sociology* (London: Tavistock, 1984), pp. 38, 39, 41, 42.

23 Haimes and Timms, *Adoption*, p. 98.

24 The phrase is taken from E. Goffman, *The Presentation of Self in Everyday Life* (Harmondsworth: Penguin Books, 1971).

25 Haimes and Timms, *Adoption*, p. 77.

26 J. Glover, *What Sort of People Should There Be?* (Harmondsworth: Penguin Books, 1984), p. 69.

27 D. Morgan, 'Making motherhood male: surrogacy and the moral economy of women', *Journal of Law and Society*, vol. 12 (1985), p. 219, at p. 225.

28 P. Toynbee, *Lost Children* (London: Hutchinson, 1985).

29 ibid. See the criticism by S. F. Schaeffer, 'Kith, kin and cuckoo', *London Review of Books*, 5 December 1985, p. 16.

30 Toynbee, *Lost Children*, p. 10.

31 ibid., p. 11.

32 ibid., pp. 12–13.

33 E. Goffman, *Stigma: Notes on the Management of Spoiled Identity* (New York: Prentice-Hall, 1963), p. 45.

34 Toynbee, *Lost Children*, p. 22.

35 ibid., p. 24.

36 Haimes and Timms, *Adoption*, p. 73.

37 ibid., p. 67.

38 *Appendix to First Report to Parliament on the Children Act 1975.*

39 C. Day, 'Access to birth records', *Adoption and Fostering*, vol. 3, no. 4 (1979), p. 17.

40 Toynbee, *Lost Children*, ch. 5. This is the story of 'Georgina' whose father took her at the age of two and a half to visit friends, who became her *de facto* adoptive parents. When she was 8 her father died and soon thereafter she discovered that her mother had been hanged for murder. For a fictional account of an analogous situation see P. D. James, *Innocent Blood* (London: Faber & Faber 1980).

41 Toynbee, *Lost Children*, p. 180.

42 O. O'Donovan, *Begotten or Made?* (Oxford: Clarendon Press, 1984), p. 48.

43 *Report of the Committee of Inquiry into the Care and Supervision Provided in relation to Maria Colwell* (the *Field-Fisher Report*) (London: HMSO, 1974).

44 J. Bowlby, *Child Care and the Growth of Love* (Harmondsworth: Penguin Books, 1965); M. Rutter, *Maternal Deprivation Reassessed* (Harmondsworth: Penguin Books, 1981).

45 See, for example, J. Goldstein, A. Freud, and A. Solnit, *Beyond the Best Interests of the Child* (London: Burnett Books, 1973).

46 K. O'Donovan, 'A right to know one's genetic parentage?', *International Journal of Law and the Family*, vol. 2 (1988), pp. 27–45.

47 In the case of donation of sperm, s. 27 of the Family Law Reform Act 1987 severs the legal tie between donor and child.

48 *Report of the Committee of Inquiry into Human Fertilisation and Embryology (Warnock Report)*, Cmnd 9314 (London: HMSO, 1984).

49 Department of Health and Social Security, *Human Fertilisation and Embryology: A Framework for Legislation*, Cm 259 (London: HMSO, 1987), annex B.

50 Yoxen, *Unnatural Selection?*, p. 27, citing M. Curie-Cohen, L. Luttrell, and S. Shapiro, 'Current practice of artificial insemination by donor in the United States', *New England Journal of Medicine*, vol. 300 (15 March 1979), pp. 585–90.

51 Yoxen, *Unnatural Selection?*, p. 36, citing R. Rowland, 'Attitudes and opinions of donors on an artificial insemination by donor (AID) programme', *Clinical Reproduction and Fertility*, vol. 2 (1983), pp. 249–59.

52 *Guardian*, 28 February 1985. See DHSS, *Consultation Paper*, para. 29.

53 Yoxen, *Unnatural Selection?*, p. 35, citing E. Alder, 'Psychological aspects of HID', in A. Emery and I. Pullen (eds), *'Psychological Aspects of Genetic Counselling* (London: Academic Press, 1984), pp. 187–99.

54 Snowden and Mitchell, *Artificial Family*, ch. 5.

55 Haimes and Timms, *Adoption*, p. 50.

56 Adoption Act 1976, s.11; Children Act 1975, s. 85(2); Guardianship Act 1973, s. 1(2).

57 *Warnock Report*, recommendations. DHSS, *Human Fertilisation*, paras 14, 23, 24, 31, 32.

58 One of Toynbee's subjects was born as the result of rape.

59 Haimes and Timms, *Adoption*, p. 81.

60 ibid., p. 98. See also CSS Report, *Human Procreation* (London: Oxford University Press, 1984), paras 5.3–5.4.
61 *Guardian*, 28 February 1985. See DHSS, *Human Fertilisation*, para. 29.
62 Yoxen, *Unnatural Selection?*, p. 21.
63 Haimes and Timms, *Adoption*, p. 97.
64 *Official Report, House of Commons, Hansard*, vol. 893, col. 1901 (20 June 1975) on the Children Bill.
65 Yoxen, *Unnatural Selection?*, p. 29.
66 *Warnock Report*, para. 4.21.
67 ibid., para. 4.26. See also DHSS, *Human Fertilisation*, para. 29.
68 *Warnock Report*, paras 4.25, 6.8. DHSS, *Human Fertilisation*, para. 30.
69 *Report of the Departmental Committee on Human Artificial Insemination* (the Feversham Committee), Cmnd 1105 (London: HMSO, 1960).
70 Haimes and Timms, *Adoption*, p. 97.
71 Under the Inheritance (Provision for Family and Dependents) Act 1975.
72 Family Law Reform Act 1987, s. 27 *Warnock Report*, paras 4.22 and 6.8. DHSS, *Human Fertilisation*, para. 27. Children born as a result of egg or embryo donation are not covered by the Act; the White Paper recommends that 'where a husband and wife have agreed together that the wife should have treatment using donated gametes or embryos, any child born by her should be treated in law, both by way of its status and for purposes of the law of succession . . . as their child' (para. 89).
73 Yoxen, *Unnatural Selection?*, p. 29. Yoxen's discussion is based on G. David and J. Lansac, 'The organisation of the Center for the Study and the Preservation of Semen in France', in G. David and W. S. Price (eds), *Human Artificial Insemination and Semen Preservation* (New York: Plenum Press, 1980), pp. 15–25.
74 Yoxen, *Unnatural Selection?*, p. 30.
75 See F. Hornstein, 'Children by donor insemination: a new choice for lesbians'. and R. Duelli Klein, 'Doing it ourselves: self insemination', in R. Arditti, R. Duelli Klein, and S. Minden (eds), *Test-Tube Women* (London: Pandora Press, 1984), pp. 373–81 and 382–90.

# 7

# FATHERS IN LAW?
# THE CASE OF AID

## *JOHN DEWAR*

### INTRODUCTION

The practice of AID in the UK is shrouded in secrecy and silence. There are no official figures on the extent of AID provision;[1] no controls exist on the selection of sperm donors, of couples for treatment, on record keeping, or the maintenance of sperm banks, all of which are currently matters of good practice for the agency concerned. The couples themselves tend to keep their recourse to the treatment a secret even from the child, and they tend to conceal the true facts of conception from the register of births by entering the woman's partner as father.[2] Similarly, the anonymity of the donor is carefully maintained, and those professionals who practise AID regard themselves as obliged to maintain its use as confidential, to the extent of concealing the mode of conception from the mother's medical notes.[3]

This phenomenon is attributable to three features of AID which also serve to distinguish it from the other techniques for the alleviation of infertility discussed by the Warnock Committee.[4] First, unlike (for example) *in vitro* fertilization or surrogate motherhood, both of which may involve complex medical treatment, AID is remarkably 'low tech' – it requires no medical intervention and may be performed with the assistance only of a needleless syringe, a speculum and a willing donor.[5] One consequence of this is that the shroud of secrecy is easily maintained and any consequential birth may be presented as the 'real' thing (although there is an underlying issue here as to what real and artificial mean in this context – see below). Another is that not only is the practice of AID extremely diverse and therefore difficult to straitjacket within a uniform system of regulation, but also that any regime of prohibition or regulation would be extremely difficult to enforce. This fact has often been noted as an argument against either prohibiting or regulating the practice of AID by legal means:[6]

> attempts by the law to regulate and control every act of AI are unlikely to be effective. Legal regulation of the act of AI could not be policed or monitored and would be likely to be ignored, creating a risk of bringing the law into contempt.[7]

However, as we shall see, these difficulties did not prevent the *Warnock Report* from recommending a degree of legal regulation of certain aspects of AID practice; nor is this the only reason for the current absence of a legal framework.

The second distinctive feature of AID is that it is exclusively concerned with *male* infertility (except where it is employed as part of a surrogacy arrangement). In large part, the silence surrounding the practice of AID may have something to do with men's reluctance to face the consequences of their own infertility, possibly because our culture attaches much significance to the association between fertility and power. It cannot be that the fact of infertility itself is considered so embarrassing or so stigmatized as to demand secrecy – the alleviation of *female* infertility is a matter of widespread public interest and debate. Indeed, one might be forgiven for thinking that the *Warnock Report* was concerned only with surrogate motherhood and *in vitro* fertilization (both techniques focusing on the female body), so exclusively did public debate of the Committee's report focus on those aspects.[8] As the *Warnock Report* points out, 'a change in attitude to male infertility is .... required'.[9]

A third distinctive feature of AID is that if offers women a considerable degree of control over reproduction in that it has enabled lesbian and other single women to develop and communicate techniques of self-insemination.[10] In other words, the silence surrounding AID both preserves the shameful secret of the male while simultaneously enhancing women's ability to do without men in the reproductive process in all but the most basic biological sense: 'silence and secrecy are a shelter for power, anchoring its prohibitions; but they also loosen its holds and provide for relatively obscure areas of tolerance'.[11] However, it is precisely the opportunities offered to women through AID that have led to its being assigned a relatively low status in the hierarchy of reproductive technologies, and thus largely ignored.[12]

The various silences surrounding AID and the absence of any regulatory framework have not prevented lawyers from engaging in discussion of the legal aspects of AID.[13] These are usually perceived as raising such issues as the legal status of the child and parental rights with respect to it, the legal liabilities of the doctor or donor and whether or not AID amounts to adultery. It has quite rightly been pointed out that

> most of the legal literature reads like an answer to the following exercise: 'review all of the case law and statutes relating to AID and discuss all possible lawsuits that any participant or product of AID might have against anyone. If time permits, suggest a statutory scheme that might minimize these problems.'[14]

Although I am in this chapter concerned with the role of law in relation to AID, I do not propose to duplicate this mode of inquiry, which has been more than adequately performed elsewhere. Instead, I want to pursue two different lines of thought. First, how is the availability and practice of AID regulated, if at all, and how might it be regulated? To the extent that law is implicated in this, it is as part of a continuum or spectrum of different regulatory possibilities which also includes professional self-regulation and statutory licensing authorities. It will be argued that a common theme of these various forms of regulation has been a willingness to collude in the parties' desire for secrecy, and to promote a specific version of 'familialism' rooted in particular conceptions of good child rearing practice. The latter is well illustrated by the almost uniform condemnation of AID for single and lesbian women. For example: 'the encouragement of lesbian families can be seen as a threat to normal family life, to say nothing of . . . failing to provide a nurturing father-figure'.[15]

The second line of thought concerns the way in which paternity of AID children is to be determined. This is partly because the question of paternity is often asserted as being central to many discussions of AID: 'any consideration of the social effects of AID rests squarely on the issue of paternity'.[16] However, I wish to argue precisely the reverse – that a consideration of AID reveals a good deal of confusion surrounding the definition of paternity itself which extends beyond the particular case of AID. I shall treat this as a more directly legal question since it is primarily in the context of legal and related discourses on the paternity of AID children that the uncertainties inherent in the notion of paternity, inevitably a social construct, have been rendered most apparent.

A first step in understanding this confusion may be taken by asking the question: what is 'artificial' about artificial insemination? One answer might be that the artifice lies in the substitution of a mechanical procedure for 'natural' intercourse. However, it has been pointed out that

> 'artificial insemination' is only artificial because the male agent is not engaged in the act. But this account leaves out the female entirely, especially the fact that the natural process of conception occurs in the woman's body . . . 'Artificial Insemination' reflects a partriarchal male-centred mode of thinking.[17]

Further, it seems unlikely that the mechanical nature of the process is the cause of concern, since AIH (Artificial Insemination by Husband) is frequently stated to be unproblematic. The 'artifice' that causes concern is the substitution of donor sperm: 'the possible problems with AID . . . [come] down to the psychology, morality and legality of donation'.[18] It is in the apparent illogicalities of the legal response to the 'problem' of third-party donation and its consequences for paternity (outlined below) that we can see the nature of the artifice at issue in AID – for it lies not in the substitution of the real by an artificial father, but in the concealment of the truth that there is no 'real' fatherhood, only a supremely flexible notion whose shape is determined by the desired form of social reproduction: 'The very definition of the real becomes: *that of which it is possible to give an equivalent reproduction.*'[19] This suggests that the unproblematic status of AIH, which rests on the only recently fashionable privileging of biology as a means of ascribing paternity, ought to be reconsidered. It also suggests that the uncertainties in the notion of paternity revealed by a study of the case of AID are not confined to AID itself.

I shall pursue these themes by looking first at the evidence as to the existing practice of AID, then at the various views on AID as expressed in 'official' reports since the war; and finally at the way in which the issue of legal paternity has been resolved.

## THE PRACTICE OF AID

Although the techniques of artificial insemination have been known and practised for some years with respect to animals, it is only since the war that it has come to be widely applied to human reproduction. When the Feversham Committee reported in 1960, they estimated that there were less than twenty medical practitioners offering artificial insemination and that the number of AID births between 1948 and 1957 was 376.[20] Since then the practice of AID appears to have grown considerably – latest figures show that there are now about fifty clinics in the UK offering AID treatment (compared with three between 1960 and 1969) and that there are between 1,500 and 2,000 conceptions a year.[21]

There are many possible explanations for this increase in the use of AID. The first is an improvement in the techniques of sperm storage by freezing donated sperm and storing it until needed; another is the growing public awareness of the availability of the technique, together with a decline in the availability of children for adoption;[22] another is the wider availability of practitioners and agencies willing to offer insemination. For example, a committee of the British Medical Association recommended in 1973 that AID should be available within the National Health Service[23], and other private organizations, such as the British Pregnancy Advisory Service (BPAS), have introduced their own AID service. It is currently estimated that there are over thirty clinics offering AID treatment.

AID is most commonly used where a male partner is infertile, although it may also be used where there is a danger of the male transmitting an inheritable disease. The procedure itself is extremely simple – all that is needed is donated sperm and a syringe to inject the sperm as close to the cervix as possible at the right point in the woman's ovulatory cycle. The simplicity of this procedure, however, belies the potential complexity of its practice with respect to, for example, the selection of sperm donors, the selection and counselling of the recipients, procedures for record-keeping and of the maintenance of sperm banks. The simplicity of AID also means that it may be carried out without recourse to any medical practitioner or agency, a fact which has led to the creation of 'self-insemination' groups, such as the Feminist Self-Insemination Group and the Girl Babies Group.

Where AID is offered by an agency of some sort, the absence of any regulatory framework has meant that individual practice may vary widely. These differences stem from the nature of the agency itself. For example, while the BPAS describes its approach as 'multidisciplinary' in that it employs counsellors, nurses, doctors and technicians,[24] some medical practitioners claim to be able to perform all aspects of the procedure, from selection of donors and counselling of the recipients to performing the insemination itself.[25] Similarly, while it may be common practice for an NHS clinic to recruit medical students as sperm donors, private agencies that have no such formal link with a medical establishment may have to rely on informal contacts or advertizing. Again, criteria for acceptance for treatment may differ – there is evidence that while some doctors will only treat married couples whose relationship is 'stable and mature',[26] other agencies will offer treatment to single and lesbian women.[27] Fewer differences arise, however, in the matter of record-keeping and the maintenance of donor anonymity. While records of donated sperm are kept, only the barest genetic and physical information is stored, and the identity of the donor is never revealed to the recipients. A 'blind eye' is usually turned to the illegal practice of the parents registering the male partner as father in the register of births[28] – indeed some doctors suggest that the couple should have intercourse on the day of insemination so as to create the possibility of the child being the 'natural' child of the father.[29]

## OFFICIAL ATTITUDES TO AID

Official attitudes to AID, as evidenced by a series of official and semi-official reports since 1945, have changed markedly from outright rejection, through indifference, to qualified acceptance. Central to each of these differing attitudes have been differing conceptions of the role of legal regulation or prohibition of various aspects of the practice of AID. The consistent objective, however, has been and continues to be, the maintenance and promotion of a heterosexual two-parent family unit. The 'subversive' potential of AID, as evidenced by its use by lesbian and single women, is ignored or suppressed.

The early attitude to AID is exemplified by the 1948 report of a Commission appointed by the Archbishop of Canterbury to study the issue of AID.[30] The Commission regarded AID as fundamentally wrong, for a number of reasons. First, it was regarded as a breach of marriage in that it introduced a third party into the procreative process, and was thus analogous to adultery. The secrecy and deceit surrounding AID was also thought to have potentially harmful effects on the child, for example if the child accidentally discovered the nature of its conception. It was also thought to amount to a fraud on society in that it involved withholding information concerning 'questions of kinship, inheritance and actual identity'.[31]

> It would change the whole basis of society if a man could not safely regard his brother's child as of the proper common stock of his and his brother's parents, and could not feel assured that it was not the product of an anonymous 'donor'.[32]

AID was also thought to injure the 'essential nature and structure of the family, which is the community of *parents and children begotten by them*'.[33] For these reasons, the Commission recommended that the practice of AID should be made a criminal offence.

These views were substantially reiterated twelve years later in the report of the Feversham Committee on Human Artificial Insemination.[34] The Committee considered AID to present dangers for all the parties involved – the recipients, the donor, the child, and the medical practitioner – and also to pose a danger to society at large by weakening the institution of marriage (since it might lead to indifference concerning marriage vows)[35], by deceiving children, and by 'substituting an anonymous and mechanical procedure for an intimate personal relationship'.[36] Unlike the Archbishop's report, the Feversham Committee did not consider any legal prohibition or regulation of the practice to be either possible or desirable. Any criminal prohibition would be difficult to enforce, and would 'be considered to be an unjustifiable encroachment on the freedom of the individual in a sphere of behaviour where the law does not normally intrude'.[37] Any framework of regulation was also considered undesirable since 'any proposal to regulate AID by excluding certain cases as unsuitable implies that other cases are suitable for AID . . . we do not ourselves consider that AID is a desirable course in any circumstances'.[38] This was despite the fact that the Committee clearly regarded some instances of AID as clearly worse than others, for example the insemination of single women:

the importance and possible difficulties of AID are such that it should never be undertaken if there is not in the home a husband who is prepared to exercise the responsibilities of fatherhood from the beginning. It is manifestly unfair to the child to impose on him the additional handicap of having no one to look to as his father.[39]

Similarly, the Committee decided against recommending legislation that would legitimate the AID child of a married couple since this would also amount to an official recognition of the practice, and would be to introduce an entirely new dimension to the concept of legitimacy or legitimation in that it would render legitimate a child who was not the natural child of one of the married partners. Further, legitimacy for AID children would interfere with hereditary succession: 'succession through blood descent is an important element in family life and as such is at the basis of society'.[40] The Committee did, however, recommend that acceptance by a wife of artificial insemination with the seed of a donor without the husband's consent should be made a new ground of divorce or judicial separation.[41]

The recent increased acceptance of AID is evidenced by the 1973 report of a Committee set up by the British Medical Association (the Peel Committee).[42] The growth in the use of AID in the years since the Feversham Report led the Committee to believe that it was important to 'ensure that the practice of AID conforms to the highest ethical and medical standards' and that this could be ensured by making AID available within the National Health Service and hence subject to the ethical and professional standards of the medical profession.[43] The Peel Committee assumed, as the Feversham Committee had done, that AID would only be available to couples; unlike the Feversham Committee, the Peel Committee further recommended that the rules on legitimacy be changed so as to legitimate the AID child of a married couple where the husband consents to the treatment, and that a husband should be entitled to be entered as father in the register of births. The assumption of this report is that AID is an acceptable means of alleviating male infertility, but only within a marriage, and that a degree of official deception is justified in order to conceal the mode of conception. As we have seen, these assumptions also appear to underlie the current 'official' medical practice of AID.[44]

The acceptance of AID is thus conditional on its supporting rather than undermining the conventional notion of a two-parent heterosexual family unit. This emerges clearly from the most recent official consideration of AID, by the *Warnock Report*.[45] Warnock considered AID as one amongst a range of 'techniques for the alleviation of infertility'. As such, the Committee were in favour of AID, in line with their general conclusion that infertility is a condition meriting treatment. However, this general conclusion is limited by the Committee's view that 'as a general rule it is better for children to be born into a two-parent family, with both father and mother.[46] The Committee's conclusion with respect to AID was that it should be made available to infertile couples on a properly organized basis; that AID practitioners should be subject to the general licensing framework proposed for infertility practitioners, and that it should be an offence to provide an AID service without a license.[47] (The precise impact of this last recommendation is unclear – would it be a condition of, or one of the terms of, a license that the licensed practitioner only treat 'couples'? Would a self-help group offering advice about self-insemination fall foul of this new criminal offence?)

The remainder of the *Warnock* proposals for AID involve a mixture of legal reform and non-legal regulation. Into the former category fall the recommendations that the AID child of a married couple should be regarded as legitimate (provided that the husband consents), that the donor should be deemed to have no parental rights with respect to the child, that the husband should be permitted to register as the child's father (as to all of which, see further below) and that the child should have a right of access to non-identifying information concerning the donor on reaching the age of eighteen.[48] Other aspects of AID, such as the screening of donors, maintenance of donor anonymity, obtaining of written consents of the parties involved, limiting the number of children to be fathered by the sperm of one donor, and the payment of donors are to be left to the development of guidelines by the licensing body.

The *Warnock* proposals appear to represent a significantly more progressive approach to AID than, for example, the Archbishop's report of 1948. However, as has already been suggested, these two reports share in common the assumption that the two-parent heterosexual family is the basic unit of society, and the proposals for the regulation of AID are framed accordingly. The differences between the eventual proposals made may be explained by two factors. First, there is a recognition by the *Warnock Report* of the limits of effective legal control on a practice as simple as AID – far better to control through regulation than through attempted prohibition; in any case, *Warnock* was faced with AID as an established social practice, whereas this was not the case in 1948.

The second difference between the two reports lies in the differing emphases within the notion of the 'family' that both were seeking to conserve. The emphasis has changed from (in 1948) the family as an institution concerned with the regulation of sexual behaviour, the ordered devolution of inheritance and the establishment of identity through blood relationship, to (in 1984) the family as a forum for individual satisfaction and fulfilment, serving as the basic unit of child rearing where particular notions of good child-rearing practice predominate, essential to which is the requirement of a parent of each sex. The fact that this conventional two-parent family does not exist for all children suggests that what is being defended here is not an actual social practice, but what Barrett and Macintosh call an 'ideology of familialism';[49] and that central to that ideology is the preservation of a role for fathers in the upbringing of children. This familialism is a particularly strong weapon to be deployed in the context of AID, which, after all, threatens to subvert the role of fathers altogether in all but the most basic biological and genetic sense. But what do we mean by 'fatherhood'? In particular, how is paternity defined in law?

## FATHERS IN LAW?

The legal definition of parenthood is of practical importance in the sense that it identifies those individuals who are entitled to exercise 'parental rights' with respect to a child, those who are liable for the child's support, and those against whom the child may claim certain rights of inheritance.[50] In crude biological terms, motherhood is relatively easy to prove – the fact of having given birth is itself ample evidence of maternity. Difficulties may arise in cases of surrogate motherhood or where there has been an administrative mix-up in the hospital, but usually there will be no problem in determining the identity of the mother. Fatherhood, on the other hand, is much harder to demonstrate – there is no such obvious link between a father and a child.

There are three different legal ways of determining paternity, only one of which is directly concerned with the biological 'truth'. The underlying concern of all three is to ensure that, so far as possible, all children are regarded in law as possessing a father, in order to 'reproduce the nuclear family structure'.[51] The first method is marriage – by virtue of the 'presumption of legitimacy', a child is deemed in law to be the natural child of the mother's husband and hence legitimate. Although described as a presumption of legitimacy, it is also a presumption of *paternity* since it identifies a particular man as father. The strength of this presumption is now greatly diminished, and may be 'rebutted by evidence which shows that it is more probably than not that the person is illegitimate'.[52] Thus, an AID child born to a married couple is presumptively legitimate (and also, of course, presumptively the natural child of the father); and as long as the couple are prepared to conceal the manner of the child's conception, this presumption would remain undisturbed. Clearly, evidence that the child was an AID child would be sufficient to rebut the presumption, and the child would be rendered illegitimate.[53]

A second method of defining paternity is that of 'social fatherhood'. The best-known example of a legal formula giving expression to this concept is that of the 'child of the family', to be found in the legislation dealing with maintenance and custody on divorce, separation, or nullity.[54] For these purposes a child that is not the natural child of one of the parties to such proceedings will be deemed to be such if that party has 'treated' the child as his or her own.[55] However, this formula is employed in specific statutes for specific purposes and has no general application. Another example of reliance on 'social' parenting is in those cases involving custody disputes over surrogate children, where, in order to find in favour of the commissioning couple, the court will be forced to rely on some notion of social parenthood.[56]

The final method of determining paternity is to rely on biology. Improvements in techniques of blood testing have made it easier to determine the probability of a given male (or female) being the biological parent of a child. This has made possible a recent trend towards reliance on biological parenthood in the ascription of rights to fathers, exemplified in recent Law Commission proposals for the abolition of the status of illegitimacy. These involved according all biological fathers (married or unmarried) the same parental rights over children as married fathers currently hold.[57] This shift to biology in the determination of parentage was perceived as an attempt to retain a degree of legal power for fathers over children in the face of the decline of marriage as an effective institution for the ascription of paternal rights.[58]

AID poses a particularly difficult problem in this context, and reveals the extent to which the process of deciding on a definition of fatherhood for legal purposes may be almost entirely a matter of expediency. In the particular case of AID, as we shall see, the current proposals for the determination of the paternity of AID children are a compromise between, on the one hand, a policy of locating the child within a two-parent family unit, and on the other, of acknowledging the parties' wish for secrecy in the whole matter of the child's conception.

How, then, to determine the paternity of an AID child? To do so on a biological basis would be to treat the sperm donor as father for legal purposes – something which it is generally agreed should be avoided; but to do so on the basis of marriage (so that the husband of an AID mother would be deemed to be father) would be to run contrary to the avowed policy of removing all legal differentiation of treatment as between marital and non-marital children, as evidenced by the Law Commission proposals on illegitimacy.[59] This would also mean that where the AID mother is unmarried, the sperm donor would continue to be father for legal purposes. Yet, to attribute paternity on the basis of social parenthood would be to ask the couple involved to make public precisely that which they hope to keep secret, namely that the father is not the natural father of the child.

In the final result, the Warnock Committee resolved to follow the Law Commission's recommendation that an AID child born to a married couple, where the husband has consented to the treatment, should be deemed in law to be the legitimate child of the couple, and that the father should be entitled to be registered as father in the register of births.[60] In other words, the marital link is the preferred method of attributing paternity. This would amount in effect to what the Feversham Committee had earlier set its face against – namely, the extension of the present meaning of legitimacy, in a way that makes the child's status turn on the father's consent. Both the Law Commission and the Warnock Committee recognized the inconsistency of privileging marriage in this way, since both elsewhere deny the significance of marriage to their proposals as a whole,[61] but both described this as 'inescapable' in the particular case of AID.[62] However, this is only the case given a willingness to collude in maintaining the secrecy surrounding AID, since attributing paternity on the basis of marriage avoids inquiring into the biological facts altogether. This is possibly borne out of a recognition that it would be difficult to do otherwise;[63] but also, at the same time, there is the given objective of locating as many AID children as possible within a two-parent legal family framework – far better to do this at the expense of consistency (by relying on marriage) than not at all. The consequences of this inconsistency are most peculiar, however – for AID children born to unmarried mothers, or to married mothers whose husband has not consented to AID, the sperm donor continues to be the father; or, as the Warnock Committee would have it, the child has no legal father at all, since they recommend that the sperm donor should be deemed to have no parental rights.[64] As Carol Smart has put it, 'the Warnock Report attempts to create a new form of illegitimacy, but one in which the child has fewer rights than illegitimate children born without the help of . . . [AID]'.[65]

This overt reliance on the ties of the marital family to supply the legal link between father and child is thus not only peculiarly inconsistent with prevailing social policy (as evidenced by both the reports in question themselves) but also leads to consequences that can only be described as bizarre, although many women may not find them unwelcome. This retreat into marriage both as the medium of paternal rights over children, and as a convenient shroud for male infertility, illustrates the extent to which AID both casts confusion on, and threatens to undermine, the notion of fatherhood.

## CONCLUSION

The current mood of acceptance of AID is conditional on the assumption that it supports rather than undermines the conventional two-parent family by remedying the perceived 'life crisis' of infertility. Implicit in this assumption is a particular view of good child-rearing practice as including a role for fathers. For this reason, the opportunity AID offers single women to escape this conventional structure of child rearing is almost uniformly condemned; but the simplicity of the practice ensures that it will continue to offer such women the possibility of 'acts of rebellion', even on the widest interpretation of the *Warnock* proposals for regulation of infertility techniques.

But what is the role of fatherhood that is so carefully protected? It cannot be the biological role, since all AID children have a biological father. Thus it must be the social role of fatherhood. But, as we have seen in relation to the determination of paternity for legal purposes, social fatherhood is abandoned in favour of marriage, which is not synonymous – there may be many 'social' fathers who are not married, and many husbands may not be social fathers. The confusion appears to be compounded by the fact that men are reluctant publicly to admit to their infertility, and appear to be supported in this by both AID practitioners and official policy-makers.

The case of AID offers an illustration of the constructed and flexible notion of paternity, and of the form of social reproduction sought to be achieved through it.

## NOTES

1 The first official guidance on any aspect of AID practice is contained in *Acquired Immune Deficiency Syndrome (AIDS) and Artificial Insemination – Guidance for Doctors and AI Clinics* (London: DHSS, July 1986).

2 R. Snowden and G. D. Mitchell, *The Artificial Family* (London: Allen & Unwin, 1981); R. Snowden, G. D. Mitchell, and E. M. Snowden, *Artificial Reproduction: A Social Investigation* (London: Allen & Unwin, 1981, 1983 ed.), ch. 6.

3 M. Brudenell, A. McLaren, R. Short, and M. Symonds, *Artificial Insemination*, Proceedings of the Fourth Study Group of the Royal College of Obstetricians and Gynaecologists (London: RCOG, 1976), p. 45.

4 *Report of the Committee of Inquiry into Human Fertilisation and Embryology (Warnock Report)*, Cmnd 9314 (London: HMSO, 1984), chs. 3–9.

5 Francie Hornstein, 'Children by donor insemination: a new choice for lesbians', in Rita Arditti, Renate Duelli Klein, and Shelley Minden (eds), *Test-Tube Women* (London: Pandora Press, 1984), pp. 373–81.

6 *Report of the Departmental Committee on Human Artificial Insemination* (the Feversham Committee), Cmnd 1105 (London: HMSO, 1960), ch. IX; Mary Warnock, *A Question of Life* (Oxford: Basil Blackwell, 1984), p. xii.

7 New South Wales Law Reform Commission, 1, *Artificial Conception, Human Artificial Insemination* (Melbourne, 1986), p. vii.

8 As an example of this, see Simon Lee, *Law and Morals: Warnock, Gillick and Beyond* (London: Oxford University Press, 1986), ch. 8, where the

discussion of the *Warnock Report* is concerned exclusively with surrogacy and embryo experimentation.

9 *Warnock Report*, para. 4. 28.
10 Renate Duelli Klein, 'Doing it ourselves: self insemination', in Arditti, Klein, and Minden (eds), *Test-Tube Women*, pp. 382–90; Jalna Hanmer, 'Sex predetermination, artificial insemination and the maintenance of a male-dominated culture', in Helen Roberts (ed.), *Women, Health and Reproduction* (London: Routledge & Kegan Paul, 1981), pp. 163–90.
11 Michel Foucault, *The History of Sexuality*, vol. 1 (Harmondsworth: Penguin Books, 1984), p. 101.
12 See H. B. Holmes, B. Hoskyns, and M. Gross, *The Custom-made Child? Women-centred Perspectives* (New Jersey: Humana Press, 1981), pp. 70–1.
13 Marylin Mayo, 'Legitimacy for the A.I.D. child', *Family Law*, vol. 6 (1976), pp. 19–24; Diana Parker, 'Legal aspects of artificial insemination and embryo transfer', *Family Law* vol. 12 (1982), pp. 103–7; D. J. Cusine, 'Artificial insemination', in S. McLean (ed.), *Legal Issues in Medicine* (London: Gower 1981), pp. 163–75; O. Stone, 'English law in relation to A.I.. and embryo transfer', in *C.I.B.A. Foundation Symposium: Law and Ethics of A.I.D.* (Amsterdam: Associated Scientific, 1977), pp. 68–76.
14 George Annas, 'Fathers anonymous: beyond the best interests of the sperm donor', *Family Law Quarterly*, vol. 14 (1980), pp. 1–13.
15 Council for Science and Society, *Human Procreation: Ethical Aspects of the New Techniques* (London: Oxford University Press, 1984), p. 61; see also 'Lesbian couples: should help extend to A.I.D.?', *Journal of Medical Ethics*, Vol. 4 (1978), pp. 91–5.
16 Snowden and Mitchell, *The Artificial Family*, p. 23.
17 Holmes, Hoskyns and Gross, *The Custom-Made Child?*, p. 255.
18 E. Yoxen, *Unnatural Selection? Coming To Terms With The New Genetics* (London: Heinemann, 1986), p. vii.
19 J. Baudrillard, *Simulations* (New York: Semiotext(e), 1983), p. 146.
20 *Report of the Departmental Committee on Human Artificial Insemination* (Feversham Committee), para. 21.
21 RCOG Fertility Sub-Committee, *Donor Insemination Survey*, (London: RCOG, 1984–5).
22 J. R. Newton, 'Current status of A.I. in clinical practice', in M. Brudenell *et al.*, *Artificial Insemination*, pp. 25–41.
23 'Report of Panel on Human Artificial Insemination' (the Peel Committee), *British Medical Journal Supplement* (7 April 1973) pp. 3–5.
24 *Evidence and Opinion from British Pregnancy Advisory Service to the Government Inquiry into Human Fertilisation and Embryology*, p. 2.
25 M. Brudenell *et al.*, *Artificial Insemination*, pp. 51–2.
26 ibid., p. 82; similarly, the RCOG *Handbook on Artificial Insemination* (1979) describes it as being available to 'happily married couples'.
27 *Evidence and Opinion from British Pregnancy Advisory Service*, pp. 4–5.
28 In contravention of s. 4 Perjury Act 1911.
29 M. Brudenell *et al.*, *Artificial Insemination*, p. 45.

30 *Artificial Human Insemination*, The Report of a Commission Appointed by His Grace the Archbishop of Canterbury (London: SPCK, 1948).
31 ibid., p. 53.
32 ibid., p. 42.
33 ibid., p. 51.
34 *Report of the Departmental Committee on Human Artificial Insemination* (Feversham Committee).
35 ibid., para. 214.
36 ibid., para. 218.
37 ibid., para. 237.
38 ibid., para. 261.
39 ibid., para. 113.
40 ibid., para. 163.
41 ibid., para. 117.
42 'Report of Panel on Human Artificial Insemination', *British Medical Journal, Supplement*, 7 April 1973, pp. 3–5.
43 ibid., paras 13, 25.
44 See text accompanying notes 17–21.
45 n. 4 above.
46 *Warnock Report* para. 2.11.3.
47 ibid., para. 4.16.
48 ibid., paras 4.17, 4.21, 4.22, 4.24–5. For a critical view of the Warnock proposals regarding access to information regarding the donor, see J. priest, 'The Report fo the Warnock Committee on Human Fertilization and Embryology', *Modern Law Review*, vol. 48 (1985), pp. 73–85, and Katherine O'Donovan (ch. 6).
49 M. Barrett and M. Macintosh, *The Anti-Social Family* (London: Verso, 1985).
50 For a full discussion of the law see B. Hoggett, *Parents and Children*, 3rd edn (London: Sweet & Maxwell, 1987).
51 C. Smart, ' "There is of course a distinction dictated by nature": law and the problem of paternity', in Michelle Stanworth (ed.), *Reproductive Technologies: Gender, Motherhood and Medicine* (Oxford: Polity Press, 1987) p. 98, at p. 114.
52 Section 26, Family Law Reform Act 1969.
53 For a discussion of the consequences of the status of illegitimacy, see Hoggett, *Parents and Children*, ch. 6.
54 Matrimonial Causes Act 1973, ss. 23–5, 27, 41–4; Domestic Proceedings and Magistrates Courts Act 1978, ss. 1–5, 8–14.
55 Section 52(1) Matrimonial Causes Act 1973.
56 J. Montgomery, 'Constructing a family – after a surrogate birth', *Modern Law Review*, vol. 49 (1986), pp. 635–40.
57 Law Commission, *Illegitimacy*, Working Paper no. 74, (London: HMSO, 1979); the proposals have now been withdrawn – see Law Commission, *Illegitimacy*, Report no. 118 (London: HMSO, 1982).
58 Rights of Women Family Law Subgroup, 'Campaigning around family law: politics and practice' in J. Brophy and C. Smart (eds), *Women in Law* (London: Routledge & Kegan Paul, 1984) p. 188.

59 Law Commission, *Illegitimacy*, Report no. 118 (1982).
60 ibid., Part XII; *Warnock Report*, paras 4.24–5; see now s. 27 Family Law Reform Act 1987. Similar legislation has already been enacted elsewhere – see s. 5(a), Uniform Parentage Act (US); see also New South Wales Law Reform Commission, 1 *Artificial Conception, Human Artificial Insemination* (Melbourne, 1986), ch. 2, for an overview of existing legislation.
61 e.g. *Warnock Report*, para 2.6.
62 Law Commission, *Illegitimacy*, Report no. 118, para. 12.10; *Warnock Report*, para. 4.24.
63 Law Commission, *Illegitimacy*, Report no. 118, paras 12.19–20.
64 *Warnock Report* para. 6.8; DHSS, *Human Fertilisation and Embryology: A Framework for Legislation*, Cm 259 (London: HMSO, 1987), para. 88.
65 Smart, 'Distinction dictated by nature', p. 116.

# 8

## A LESSER SACRIFICE?
## STERILIZATION AND
## MENTALLY HANDICAPPED
## WOMEN

### ROBERT LEE and DEREK MORGAN

Reproduction has come to occupy a central position in the theatre
of the personal. It has moved upstage, from being seen as a minor
bit part of personhood, to being cast as one of the essential characteristics of its successful production and realization. This has been
accompanied by an increasingly public presence and debate about
its determinants and its control. The ground rules of fertility have
been opened up for scrutiny and assessment, and the courts have
been drawn more critically into a debate about the respective merits
and claims of the producers and players in this contemporary
morality play. Two recent scenes can be used to illustrate the
confusing nature of the dynamics involved.

Victoria Gillick's endeavour to pre-empt the provision of contraceptive advice and treatment to her daughters by medical practitioners sought two declarations from the courts:

(i) that the Department of Health and Social Security (DHSS)
Service Notice (HN(80)46) carried no legal authority since it gave
advice which was unlawful in both contravening parental rights
and duties and encouraging doctors to aid and abet unlawful
sexual intercourse, and

(ii) that no doctor or other professional within the Family Planning Services would be permitted to give contraceptive advice or
treatment to any child of Mrs Gillick below the age of sixteen
without Mrs Gillick's consent.[1]

The DHSS notice had advised that a doctor consulted at a family planning clinic by a young woman under 16 would not be acting unlawfully in the prescription of contraceptives to her, as long as this was done in good faith and to protect her against the harmful effects of sexual intercourse. Note the inherent contradiction here. If the offences of causing or encouraging unlawful sexual intercourse with a girl under 16, contrary to the Sexual Offences Act 1956, section 28(1), or of being an accessory to such intercourse under section 6(1), were satisfied by providing contraceptive services to a girl under 16 as suggested in (i), then this would be true irrespective of the consent of the parent, as required by (ii). This hints at the subsidiary significance of the criminality of the doctor. It was a tactic in a more fundamental battle – for parental control over the social and sexual relationships of the Gillick daughters. However, the battleground was consent to medical treatment, so that any victory by Gillick was likely to have far reaching implications in the continuing struggle for patient autonomy within medicine.

Two outcomes of the case deserve immediate comment. First, it established a type of parental control over the consent of minors seeking medical services; it simply did not take the form desired by Mrs Gillick. Parental rights were recognized, but only to the extent that they were forced to yield to the child's autonomous decision-making. The point at which that matured was not to be arbitrarily fixed at 16 years of age, but emerged as the child reached a sufficient understanding and intelligence to assess the medical procedures proposed.

The second important feature of *Gillick* is that determining the capacity to consent to medical treatments was established as being a matter of clinical judgment. The logical extension of this principle is that medical opinion regarding capacity in different settings becomes the dominant source of information and opinion used by the courts to support their analyses.[2] What judges do with that is another matter; judicial perceptions of the best interests of the child, the guiding legal formula in cases such as *Gillick*, varied throughout the three courts which heard the arguments. The view of Lord Templeman, however, dissenting in the final appeal, was clear; 'there are many things which a girl under sixteen needs to practise but sex is not one of them.'[3]

133

## A SIMILAR CASE?

Some eighteen months later the House of Lords was asked to consider again the provision of contraceptive treatment for those felt to be incapable of exercising rational choice. Here, the logical extension of the second limb of *Gillick* is displayed.[4] Sterilization had been proposed for a mentally handicapped 17-year-old, Jeanette. The Court did not refer to their earlier decision in *Gillick*, although that case had also concerned the extent to which individual autonomy could be overridden in relation to procreative liberties.[5] There was no mention here of aiding and abetting rape of Jeanette, despite claims that she did not fully understand the nature of sexual intercourse.

Lords Brandon and Templeman who had been in dissent in *Gillick* formed part of the majority in *Re B*. It was not (in their analysis) in the best interests of Gillick's daughters to be given contraceptive advice, but it was in Jeanette's best interests that she be sterilized. Whereas in *Gillick* it had been felt appropriate for parents to exercise consent on behalf of a minor lacking the necessary capacity, in *Re B* Lord Templeman suggested that leave of a High Court judge should henceforth be necessary to authorize sterilization of a female minor.[6]

Different procedures are thus proposed for sterilization and other contraceptive treatments. The effect of this (and perhaps the intention) is to treat mentally handicapped young women in a manner quite distinct from other young women. In practice, sterilization has been sought for women thought to be at risk of pregnancy. This is reinforced by the supposed recognition of the advantages of sterilization over other forms of contraceptive measure in the case of certain categories of mentally handicapped young women.[7] It may be that one consequence of this approach will be a separate legal process for women whose understanding of contraceptive treatment is impaired by a lack of maturity, compared with those impaired by disability. Parents remain free to decide for the former but not the latter.

## SAPPING THE STRENGTH OF THE STATE?

The broad assumption revealed in *Re B* is that the interests of mentally handicapped young women are best protected by the courts exercising wardship jurisdiction. This is a conclusion else-where refuted; for example, the Canadian Supreme Court in a parallel case declined to accept that it could ever use its *parens patriae* jurisdiction to authorize non-therapeutic sterilization.[8] Indeed, the notion that the courts ought now to act *only* to protect and safeguard the reproductive autonomy of the mentally handicapped will be familiar to American observers.[9]

When the American Supreme Court in the notorious case of *Buck* v. *Bell* came to review the proposed sterilization of a mentally handicapped woman, herself the daughter of a mentally handi-capped woman, Justice Oliver Wendell Holmes displayed clearly the fear of the drain which the handicapped could place on the national economy:

> the public welfare may call upon citizens for their lives. It would be strange if it could not call upon those who already sap the strength of the state for these lesser sacrifices, often not felt to be such by those concerned, in order to prevent our being swamped with incompetence. It is better for all the world, if instead of waiting to execute degenerate offspring for crime, or to let them starve for their imbecility, society can prevent those who are manifestly unfit from continuing their kind. The principle that sustains compulsory vaccination is broad enough to cover cutting the Fallopian tubes . . . Three generations of imbeciles are enough.[10]

A contemporary note in the *Kentucky Law Journal* endorsed this view forcefully:

> From time immemorial the criminal and the defective have been the cancer of society. Strong, intelligent, useful families are becoming smaller and smaller; while irresponsible, diseased, defective families are becoming larger. The result can only be race degeneration.[11]

The long-term care of the elderly and disabled does indeed absorb state resources.[12] When the House of Lords in *Re B* stated that there was no issue of eugenics involved, compared with the sentiments which Carrie Bell's case generated it is possible happily to concur with this assessment. But there is a need to be careful and watchful. We are too close in history to the eugenic sterilization programmes of the 1930s, when thirty American states adopted sterilization

ROBERT LEE AND DEREK MORGAN

legislation and over 16,000 people had been sterilized by January 1933. Germany passed similar legislation in the same year, and within four years had sterilized 225,000 people; a figure which grew eventually to 350,000.[13]

Against such recent histories of the use of sterilization for overtly eugenic purposes, the stance of courts at least in the United States as bulwarks against proposed sterilizations is so dominant that it is seriously argued that the difficulty in obtaining sterilization for the mentally handicapped infringes their freedom to choose an appropriate contraceptive regime.[14] In Britain an entirely contrary danger is apparent. It may prove difficult to envisage the judiciary as protectors of mentally handicapped women when the leading case permits a widely criticized sterilization operation. Reports of the use of sterilization as a precondition for abortion operations on women regarded by their doctors as feckless and in need of protection from themselves[15] alone give sufficient pause for thought about the relationship between sterilization, procreation and the courts' protection of human rights. The judges in *Re B* anticipated such criticism by decrying it as based on 'erroneous or, at best, incomplete appreciation of the facts and on mistaken assumptions as to the grounds on which the decision proceeded'.[16] Lord Bridge's contention that 'it is difficult to understand how anybody examining the facts humanely, compassionately and objectively could reach any other conclusion'[17] invites three responses. We might identify them as the 'human rights' ground, the 'slippery slope' argument and the 'alternative facts' analysis.

### A right to reproduce?

The first challenge to the House of Lords' assessment argues for the recognition of a basic human right – the right to reproduce or the right to safeguard reproductive capabilities. In view of the irreversible nature of the procedure, any sterilization performed in the absence of the consent of the woman herself and for non-therapeutic reasons involves a deprivation of that right. Such a conclusion has been reached not only in Canada,[18] but, on one interpretation,[19] was apparent in the earlier English case of *In Re D (A Minor)(Wardship: Sterilisation)*.[20] In *Re B*, the House of Lords sought to confine the unequivocal judgment of Mrs Justice Heilbron

136

in *Re D* to its facts.[21] Clearly, the two cases disclose a very different perception of the notion of a basic human right.

The House of Lords suggested that Jeanette would be deprived of no basic rights which she was capable of valuing since, lacking maternal instincts, pregnancy would mean little to her. Contrary views appeared to Lord Hailsham 'wholly to part company with reality'.[22] Yet it is difficult to see what is 'human' on this analysis of a basic human right, since the right does not seem to attach by virtue of a person's humanity, but is capable of being pushed aside for certain classes of person. Nor is this right 'basic'. It is contingent upon the person having the capacity to value that right. But to confer rights only on those thought to be able to enjoy them opens the way for rights to become exclusive property of the rich and powerful.[23] Moreover, as Sheila McLean points out, 'by dismissing the impact of the removal of capacities from certain people on the grounds that they may not in any event recognize their worth [is to minimize] the status of reproduction as a human right'.[24] It is only a short step from here to a more dangerous argument in relation to the mentally handicapped – that their liberties generally are dependent upon usages that others consider reasonable or valuable.[25] This is a familiar complaint against any mediation in contemporary reproductive ethics; it characterizes the slippery slope or thin end of the wedge argument.

### *Which slopes are slippery?*[26]

All the judges who heard argument in *Re B* were led to the conclusion that it was a case of last resort.[27] But where are the margins to be drawn? The second ground on which to challenge the judicial handling of *Re B* proposes that Jeanette's case gives a glimpse of the crest of a gradient from which there is a descent to more questionable uses of sterilization.

The slippery slope argument is always a difficult and contested one to run. It is an essentially *practical* argument, which must demonstrate the undesirable outcome, rather than rely on speculation or hypothetical fears. Bernard Williams distinguishes two approaches; the 'horrible result' and the 'arbitrary result' arguments. The horrible result argument points at clearly objectionable practices to which the slope leads. The arbitrary outcome suggests that once on the slope any subsequent distinction between one case and another will disclose unsupportable discrimination;[28] the slipperiness of the slope is disclosed by the fact that once on the slope any exit point is arbitrary. This argument is applicable to *Re B*.

Margaret Shone has suggested that to refuse the non-therapeutic sterilization of a mentally handicapped woman is 'to fragment the person'.[29] On the contrary, to view the person as a whole, rather than in atomized bits, mandates a wider view of what is at issue than simply reproductive organs. In his rumbustious speech in *Re B*, Lord Hailsham specifically disavows reliance on the distinction between therapeutic and non-therapeutic procedures, so carefully drawn by Justice La Forest in *Re Eve*.[30] But how does the use of a vague predicate such as the welfare principle affect the arbitrary result objection?

Hailsham's approach attempts to rely on what Williams has called 'the resource of restricted judgment'.[31] In separating arguments which distinguish between cases two important conditions must be satisfied. First, specific cases can be disposed of as if they display almost unique features only if the judgment is made under relatively informal procedures, or reflects a high degree of consensus; if it is not made under pressure, and clearly displays only features of the predicate in question, or clearly does not. Secondly, the judgment must not be called to concern itself with hypothetical cases that have not actually arisen or will be likely to arise. In other words, the resource of restricted judgment is not available where decisions are called for in formal, public circumstances. Such cases demand a declaration of the principles being employed, so that the practices advocated can be publicly understood and criticized and so that people can have determinate expectations of how they will be affected by them.

Notwithstanding the attempt to restrict its judgment by demanding that requests for all future sterilization operations on young people should be channelled through the wardship jurisdiction of the Court, the House of Lords fails in its appeal to the restricted judgment resource for four reasons. There is not a wide degree of consensus on how to proceed in sterilization cases; the wardship jurisdiction is a formal exercise of judicial logic, often with publicly declared outcomes; the notion of 'welfare' is such a malleable concept, that it has in fact no agreed core,[32] and finally, identification of the principles involved in judicial proceedings of this nature is a *sine qua non* of entrusting courts with the responsibility to make them. The argument, then, is that the authorization contemplated in Jeanette's case is the thin end of a routine procedure in which the scalpel replaces security, the operative course replaces the contraceptive career.[33]

On the conclusion of *Re B*, a host of similar applications for sterilization were pending. Jeanette was not an isolated individual, but part of a much larger circle of mentally handicapped women for whom sterilization was to become routine.[34] It is difficult to discover precisely how many operations take place. Certainly the number of sterilizations on young women under 18 had grown from thirty-six in 1973–4 to ninety on women aged under 19 by the mid-1980s.[35] Stories appeared in the press of an 11-year-old whose hysterectomy had overcome the problem of her grandfather having to cope with her periods, and of a woman in her late teens who was sterilized when she developed a relationship with a mentally handicapped boy.[36]

Note that there is no appearance on the agenda of any equivalent medical procedure for men as a solution to the elimination of the risk of pregnancy. The reason why it is thought permissible to destroy the reproductive capacities of women but not of men is difficult to answer. The fact that it needs to be addressed, raises the issue of whether the power to make those choices and decisions can ever properly be delegated to an overwhelmingly male judiciary, or even determined by a Parliament composed almost exclusively of men.

### *Wholly parting company with reality . . .*

The third method of contesting the assertion of Lord Bridge that only one conclusion was possible on the facts is to challenge the nature of those facts. Facts are selectively chosen to support legal analysis and judgment; in *Re B* few facts are given in the reports of the case. The crucial basis for the decision seems to be as follows: Jeanette was beginning to show signs of sexual awareness; she and her carers would not be able to cope with contraceptive procedures (a consultant obstetrician and gynaecologist put the chances of successfully devising a regimen of the progesterone pill at 30–40 per cent with attendant risks of side effects); she would not fully comprehend the pregnancy and would be unable to undergo a normal delivery; she would have no inclination or capacity to care for the child. These 'facts' are actually a series of assessments as to Jeanette's capabilities and prospects. They involve speculation as to Jeanette's future capacity, and judgments as to the desirability and nature of her environment, the sexual attractions she might form and the consequences flowing from them.

Even where we are offered more detail, a curious pattern emerges. It is of a girl who can manage 'the necessary hygienic mechanics of menstruation', but could not cope with contraception; who can understand the link between pregnancy and babies, but 'is unaware of sexual intercourse and its relationship to pregnancy'.[37] No information is offered about Jeanette's sex education and why it has failed to overcome her ignorance of one of the outcomes of sexual intercourse.[38] Nothing explains why her carers are able successfully to manage the regime of medication necessary to control her epilepsy, but would be unable to supervise the use of an oral contraceptive because 'it would not be possible in the light of her swings of mood and considerable physical strength to ensure the administration of the necessary daily dose'.[39]

Lord Oliver, whose speech details more of her medical and developmental history than those of his fellow judges, lets pass almost without comment the fact that Jeanette's present medication includes danazol, a drug prescribed to alleviate the pre-menstrual tension which she suffers. Danazol is described in the ABPI *Data Sheet Compendium* as causing 'some degree of fluid retention'. Hence, 'patients with conditions which may be influenced by this factor, such as . . . epilepsy . . . require careful observation'.[40] It may also result in weight increase. This factor was contra-indicated in the use of an earlier medication, Microgynon 30, which Oliver states was given to Jeanette to assist in controlling her outbursts of violence. It had had, he recognized, the additional benefit for her of being a combined oral contraceptive.[41] This passage is especially puzzling. Microgynon 30 is not a psychotropic drug. Its stated uses are solely as an oral contraceptive and the recognized gynaecological indications for such oestrogen-progestogen uses.[42] Lord Oliver does not disclose the nature of the 'significant increase in weight' attendant on its earlier use, which was discontinued because of Jeanette's obesity.

Her irregular menstruation is given by Lord Hailsham as an additional reason why the agreed risks of pregnancy should be specially guarded against. Detecting the pregnancy would be compromised by this irregularity and her overweight, meant that '[it] would be difficult to detect or diagnose in time to terminate it easily'.[43] The reasons why visual detection of the pregnancy is here assumed to be the only efficacious method of alerting Jeanette's carers to abuse are again opaque. Sterilization, on the contrary, removes that very visual form of protection of handicapped women, the growing foetus, thus rendering them potentially open to more abuse.

The certainty of the sterilization operation, compared with Jeanette's developmental prognosis, is striking. All the judges seem prepared to accept that from her present position she will never be able to develop, either on her own or in the company of a sympathetic and supportive partner or community, into a woman who might just be able to form the affective links with children which would enable her meaningfully to exercise her procreative capacities. And yet, the evidence surveyed by the House of Lords indicates that she has already developed from the age of 4, when she was first received into care, from being a 'wild animal' to someone who will in a short time be going to an adult training centre at which it 'will not be possible to provide the degree of supervision that she presently experiences'.[44] To arrest Jeanette's metamorphosis at the age of 17 and to treat her as though she will never become 27, 37 or 40, abandons twenty-five years of potential reproductive capacity, affinitive development and emotional maturing to expert evidence which is necessarily speculative in nature, imprecise and heavily opinionated.[45] It is used to justify a procedure which is certain in its consequences, definite and irreversible.[46]

None the less, the House of Lords expended considerable effort to promote the exactitude of the evidence and marshalled carefully the postulates as to Jeanette's abilities to cope with reproduction, which were then passed off as fact. These approaches were particularly necessary following criticism of the earlier judgment in the Court of Appeal. There Jeanette had been described as suffering 'a moderate degree of mental handicap'.[47] The word moderate was used in a technical sense to describe shortly the extent of the handicap, but it was widely (and wrongly) interpreted as meaning that the handicap was slight.[48] The House of Lords took care to emphasize the expert assessments relating to Jeanette and to argue that other issues were irrelevant. Lord Hailsham stated that:

the first and paramount consideration is the well being, welfare and interests of the human being concerned . . . In this case I believe it to be the only consideration involved. In particular there is no issue of public policy other than the application of the above principle which can conceivably be taken into account, least of all eugenics.[49]

In denying the relevance of wider policies, Lord Hailsham and his fellow judges who rejected sterilization for 'social purposes'[50] confined themselves to considering Jeanette's medical interests. This is to interpret the words 'first and paramount' to mean 'sole'. Yet, as two sets of commentators have pointed out,[51] it is far from clear whether the 'interests' to be considered are indeed solely medical, or whether wider social interests need properly to be assessed.

One burden of our later argument will be to question whether sterilization was in Jeanette's wider interests, and to moot that it may well have run counter to them. In addition, we shall argue that *Re B* suggests that there is reason to be troubled about judicial handling of ethical issues.

## RISKS AND BENEFITS

Risk-taking is part of everyday life. Therefore in any process which attempts to assist a handicapped person's development there may be serious drawbacks in policies which tend towards overprotection. Clearly there is a need to achieve a balance between protection and exposure to danger. Sterilization may curtail the need for an intrusive form of supervision. This is an important issue which ought not to be overlooked. Sexual pleasures and freedoms are not the exclusive possessions of unhandicapped people. Great care should be taken not to trample these values in our attempts to serve the best interests of the handicapped. However these were not factors which motivated the courts in *Re B*. This is hardly surprising; no firm evidence suggested that Jeanette was sexually active.[52]

This must be weighed in the balance when considering risk under the courts' protective model. The fears of undetected pregnancy, abortion, or traumatic childbirth must all be subject to some real likelihood of Jeanette's becoming pregnant. Moreover, had Jeanette been sexually active, pregnancy is not the only risk that she would face; the hazards of AIDS and other sexually transmitted diseases are ignored. One fear of the risk of pregnancy was said to be the difficulties attached to birth following caesarian section, but the difficulties of surgical sterilization procedures apparently deserved no consideration.[53] Similarly there was little mention of the dilemma that whilst sterilization might increase Jeanette's freedom, it could only do so at the cost of increasing her vulnerability to sexual exploitation.

A *Times* editorial in the aftermath of the House of Lords decision argued that there were competing rights at issue in the case but that the greatest of these was the right not to be sexually exploited. The conclusion was that the Court had acted wisely in upholding this right by authorizing sterilization. How this protects Jeanette from sexual abuse is not explained. An earlier *Times* editorial, following the Court of Appeal decision, had argued that this was a new problem, since in the past men and women were segregated in institutions.[54] A similar point is made by Lord Hailsham in *Re B*.[55]

We have grown to accept such unsubstantiated opinion from the Press, but are entitled to expect more from the judiciary in deciding such fundamental issues. No more than 15 per cent of mentally handicapped people have ever lived in institutions. Yet women within that sector have had a consistently higher rate of pregnancy than have the 85 per cent cared for in the community.[56] Not all institutional carers were or are above sexual exploitation.[57] Even if it were otherwise, it is curious to contrast the horror with which judges such as Lord Templeman in *Gillick* view the prospect of sexually active young women under 16 with what seems to be a resigned acceptance of the possibility of sexual abuse of mentally handicapped women, as in *Re B*.

## THE PROBLEM OF MENTAL AGE

If the Law Lords appear to have been woefully uninformed as to the reality of life for mentally handicapped women, they are also less than convincing in showing an understanding of their capacities. One of the most persistent criticisms of the decision in the professional press concerned the emphasis ascribed to the criteria of mental age, and the use to which this was put.[58] Having stated that Jeanette had a mental age of 5 or 6, the judgments in *Re B* seem to treat Jeanette as if she were simply a child of that age. Jeanette, like all other handicapped people, would be expected to demonstrate different functional abilities across a whole range of skills. Intelligence testing offers little information as to many of these abilities, and in so far as it leads to labels such as 'mental age of 5', it misdescribes the mentally handicapped person in a discriminatory fashion. Jeanette may not read at all, unlike many 6-year-olds, but she may consistently out-perform most children of that age in terms of socialization or self-help. In addition, the criterion of 'mental age' was treated as static. Yet, as Woolrych has observed:

> the use of the discredited concept of 'mental age' is disturbing, since current experiences indicate learning potential is dependent on the quality and variety of services available in developing an understanding of issues such as the connection between sex and having babies.[59]

Nor will the concept of mental age shed much light upon Jeanette's biological and emotional state as a 17-year-old woman. While it may be difficult to grapple with the concept of a physically mature woman manifesting child-like intelligence in some respects, we must be careful that we do not discount and become repulsed by the notion that this person manifests adult sexual desires. This is a problem facing many parents of mentally handicapped young women.[60]

Can we expect judges to be aware of the controversy which surrounds the notion of mental age? It is used, in part, to justify an irreversible surgical procedure. This procedure eliminates reproductive capacities, infringing what some would claim to be a basic human right. If the courts are to be used to channel issues of controversial ethical dilemmas, and if they are to legitimate their authority to resolve them, then informed judgment is a starting-point for that practice.

## CONVENIENCE AND COST CUTTING

The issues relating to both community care and parental wishes lead to another widely voiced criticism: that such sterilizations are a matter of convenience for those who care for women such as Jeanette rather than in her interests.[61] The Court took a good deal of trouble to deny this, but the convenience factor appears almost inevitably to have been taken into account. When the Court admitted the carers claim that they could not easily administer oral contraception, their convenience was being preferred. This is true whatever Jeanette's interest in the matter, for the two are not mutually exclusive. Such interests are continually balanced against other options within the present social services regime. Indeed, what made sterilization appear so desirable was the lack of effective alternative strategies within the budgetary constraints of the community care programme.

What emerges on this analysis is a grim picture of life for young handicapped women. For example, an apparently cogent reason for sterilization was that Jeanette was about to attend an Adult Training Centre. Is the assumption that Centre trainees have the opportunity to disappear to explore sexual intercourse?[62] Why are Centres so underfunded and understaffed that they cannot adequately protect women vulnerable to sexual abuse? There is an implicit judicial echo of Lord Templeman's remarks in *Gillick*: there are many things which the mentally handicapped should be trained in, but sex is not one of them.

The Court does not say that it is *impossible* to serve Jeanette's best interests in a community care programme. With the best of intentions, these have sought a limited integration of mentally handicapped people with the wider community. It has, however, been used by the government as a manoeuvre to obtain community care on the cheap. Resources saved through the closure of institutional facilities for the mentally handicapped are being appropriated by hard-pressed health authorities to supplement other heads of their budget.[63] These policies go unchallenged in the court. Instead it declares that, as no policy issues arise, it is the critics of sterilization who fail to recognize and advocate Jeanette's best interests.

There is a grave danger that, as with all medical technology, it will lead to the adoption of widespread change in traditional healthcare practices for no better or more rational reason than that they are now possible. If the anaesthetic, scalpel or laser proved hideously expensive, then no doubt governments would be reluctant to sanction their use. Courts would then be forced to consider different methods to secure and support Jeanette's best interests. If we could envisage a society in which sterilization was not such a straightforward economic option, or not a technical possibility, it would still be necessary properly to provide for Jeanette. This would require a Jeanette who was better cared for, better educated about her own sexuality, and better trained in retaining and exercising control over her own life each day. It would also require a society of adult men who were similarly educated about the responsibilities which their sexuality imposed on them, and the limitations which that demands. This responsibility is no different whether it is borne by those who are institutionalized with Jeanette, whether suffering from mental handicap or as carers, or whether they are those with whom she will come into contact at work, in her education, or in her home. Would her interests really be any worse served?

## A COMPARISON WITH CANADA

A further challenge to the House of Lords' determination of Jeanette's best interests is approached by comparing her case with the outcome of a parallel case in the Supreme Court of Canada. The fact that the Canadian courts reached a differing conclusion does not render them any more suitable to decide sterilization issues. Rather, it allows us to suggest that, even using the same base elements, any legal alchemist can produce a very different understanding of the social and sexual chemistry involved.

In *Re Eve*, Justice MacDonald in the Supreme Court of Prince Edward Island laid down definite and elaborate criteria whereby the 'best interests' could be determined. These operated from a presumption that sterilization was unlikely to be an appropriate solution and required those seeking the operation to satisfy the courts in line with the criteria. In the Supreme Court of Canada not even this approach proved acceptable. In the words of Justice La Forest;

> The grave intrusion on a person's rights and the certain physical damage that ensues from non-therapeutic sterilisation when compared to the highly questionable advantages that can result from it, have persuaded me that it can never safely be determined that such a procedure is for the benefit of that person. Accordingly the procedure can never be authorised for non-therapeutic purposes under the parens patriae jurisdiction.[64]

Reference to the Court's jurisdiction is significant. The Supreme Court spent some considerable time reviewing the ambit of their *parens patriae* powers. In the House of Lords, this review was described as 'helpful', but no account seems to have been taken of it. Yet it could have facilitated a more leisurely and detailed consideration of the issue. There was frequent mention in *Re B* of the speed at which the case had to be processed. This arose largely out of the necessity, as the House of Lords perceived it, to decide the case before the courts' statutory wardship jurisdiction ceased upon Jeanette reaching the age of 18.[65] In Canada, it had been argued and accepted that powers in wardship emanated from feudal sovereign duties to protect any individual in the jurisdiction incapable of exercising legal rights on their own behalf. This included, but was not confined to, minors.

On this view, the wardship proceedings in Jeanette's case were but a statutory form of a wider common law precursor. This raises complex issues relating to the scope of the statutory powers of the Court of Protection and residuary prerogative powers.[66] These were swept aside without detailed analysis on the basis that the issue needed to be decided quickly. Yet Jeanette was not sexually active and had the House of Lords given themselves more time by invoking the *parens patriae* jurisdiction we might have achieved a more thoughtful result. The mischief of the House of Lords approach is underlined by the fact that proceedings in *Re B* had been initiated ten months before the final decision was rendered, and there appears at no time to have been directions to expedite the trial of the case. In *Re Eve*, the Supreme Court of Canada took an overlong time to produce its judgment – almost a year and a half – but avoided in the process basic misunderstandings, such as the relevance of mental age and the meaning of moderate handicap, and produced in the result a significantly more thorough and considered judgment.

Within a few weeks of *Re B*, one of a number of cases in the queue behind it came to court. *Re T; T v. T*[67] involved the application by the mother of a 19-year-old mentally handicapped woman for a declaration which would protect doctors should they perform a sterilization upon her daughter. Whilst not following *Re Eve* – Justice Wood decided that the inherent *parens patriae* jurisdiction was now entirely covered by statute – he none the less concluded that the sterilization could be carried out in the absence of the woman's consent. In his view, there were exceptional circumstances where a doctor was free to take such steps as good medical practice dictated. This would include circumstances where a court, faced with a patient suffering such mental abnormality as never to be able to give consent, could find no one able to give consent on the patient's behalf, or could find no other legal provision which appeared to cover the question of consent. This is a clear illustration of the extent to which *Gillick* has legitimated clinical judgment as the appropriate yardstick against which to measure proposed treatment of the mentally handicapped.

## HOSTAGES TO FORTUNE: HANDICAP, COMMUNITY, CARE

One final point arises out of the *Re Eve* case. It helps to illustrate very different judicial perspectives. The remarks of Justice La Forest contrast sharply with those of Lord Bridge, although they have similar rhetorical qualities:

> it is difficult to imagine a case in which non-therapeutic sterilisation could possibly be of benefit to the person on behalf of whom the court purports to act, let alone one in which the procedure is necessary in his or her best interest.[68]

This view stems from an implicit worry in *Re Eve* that there was a large degree of convenience for the child's carers in the solution proposed. This is apparent in statements such as 'there are human rights considerations that should make a court extremely hesitant about solving a social problem like this by this means'. [69] Indeed there is genuine doubt as to whether courts can solve such social problems:

> Judges are generally ill-informed about many of the factors relevant to a wise decision in this difficult area. They generally know little of mental illness, of techniques of contraception or their efficacy. And however well presented a case may be, it can only partially inform.[70]

In spite of all the protestations that Jeanette's sterilization was not merely for convenience, in a broad sense this is clearly untrue. The necessity for the sterilization in the eyes of the Court arose out of their perception that she was at greater risk of pregnancy in the community. The policy to remove Jeanette and women like her from institutional care is that of the government. Whatever the motives, this policy has been seen to have the strategic advantage of generating savings in permitting the closure of large institutions. Health Authorities have come to absorb half of the £1 billion total spent on services provided in relation to mental handicap, yet they provide care for only 25 per cent of the estimated 160,000 people concerned.[71] The location of the mentally handicapped in the community was always likely to prove especially costly, and it is beyond argument that the whole process has been massively under-resourced. Jeanette's vulnerability is a consequence of this; she is but one victim, one hostage to fortunes which are redirected away from mental health care.

How should we expect judges to mediate these conflicts? They have no immediate means by which to effect a cure even if they had been prepared to recognize the symptoms. The cure which they proposed, however, seems to be a striking example of iatrogenic disease. But the courts are having to face more and more dilemmas in which they will find it impossible to provide answers which will command wide acceptability or appeal to a broad consensus. This is an inevitable consequence of attempts to constrain spending on health care as newer and more appropriate regimes of therapy become available. The fact of handicap means that choosing appropriate regimes can never be a simple issue of rationing resources for health care. Most controversy about rationing surrounds curative medicine.[72] Yet it is the longer-term care of the elderly and the handicapped that has the most profound capacity to sap the economic strength of the state.[73] Jeanette is not only a victim, she also provides an unusual example of this.

To question in this way the development of state intervention in reproductive liberties and choices, and to debate the nature of its interest, appears far removed from Mrs Gillick's crusade. However, the two cases we have highlighted have more in common than the fact that they concern young women alleged to lack the capacity to be fully autonomous in relation to sexual and reproductive choice. Both cases perpetrate a peculiarly rosy view of mechanisms which might encroach on such freedoms. Thus, in *Gillick*, families are presented as warm, open and supportive institutions, not the context in which sexual or psychological abuse could take place. The same approach can be identified towards mental hospitals in *Re B*. Can we detect a hint of Victorian values here?

These cases fit into, and may be a part of, a modern paradox which seems at the heart of Thatcherism, and which, as we argued earlier,[74] concerns the familization of political life and the politicization of family life. Thus, at the same time as the job of rolling back the state continues, more and more attempts are made to devolve responsibility onto the family. The move away from welfarism, evident in relation to proposals for the social fund,[75] will mean for young people a loss of independence as they are thrown back into the family home. This assumes, of course, that all families are well placed to receive them, and that the arms of the family exist and are strong enough to do the catching, without in the process suffocating their developing autonomy. Within this programme, it becomes vital to uphold the stereotype of the family unit. This suggests a parallel with health care policies for the handicapped.

As community care policy becomes little more than the residualization of support for the handicapped, far more responsibility will devolve onto the family. What happens when it appears that 'the family' is not there to receive handicapped people? – Jeanette's father had left the home many years before and 'plays no part in the story'.[76] This judicial aside reminds us of the caring roles into which men and women are frequently cast. It reflects the limited range of characters with which women are frequently confronted; as carers they too are hostages to fortunes sought out and spent elsewhere. It also illuminates a stark fact which escapes the dimmed footlights of the judicial pantomime. When it appears that carers such as Jeanette's mother can no longer cope, the imperative will be to support the flagging and damaged family unit so as to camouflage those who might sap the ideological strength of the state and plunder its purse. Reach for the scalpel.

## NOTES

1 *Gillick* v. *West Norfolk and Wisbech Area Health Authority* [1985] 3 W.L.R. 830.
2 We owe this point to Phil Fennell. Carol Harlow has argued that the Gillick case did not serve the public interest and ought never to have reached court; 'Gillick: a comedy of errors?', *Modern Law Review*, vol. 49 (1986), p. 768. Les Moran has identified the hierarchies of power competing for recognition in the case; see 'A reading in sexual politics and law', *Liverpool Law Review*, vol. 8 (1986), p. 83.
3 *Gillick*, at p. 869.
4 *Re B (A Minor) (Wardship: Sterilisation)* [1987] 2 All E.R. 211.
5 cf. Andrew Bainham, 'Handicapped girls and judicial parents', *Law Quarterly Review*, vol. 103 (1987), p. 334.
6 *Re B*, p. 214.
7 See the extensive references in Elizabeth Scott, 'Sterilisation of mentally

retarded persons: reproductive rights and family privacy', *Duke Law Journal* [1986], p. 806, nn. 120–5.

8  *Re Eve* (1987) 31 D.L.R. (4d.) 1.

9  *In Re Guardianship of Hayes* 93 Wash. (2d) 239, P. (2d) 635 (1980) represents an early example of the adoption by the United States courts of this new protective role. A host of cases and statutes have followed in its wake, see Scott, 'Sterilisation of mentally retarded persons', and Elaine Krasik, 'The role of the family in medical decision making for mentally incompetent adult patients', *University of Pittsburg Law Review*, vol. 48 (1987), p. 539.

10  274 US 200 (1927). For a fascinating account of the background to this leading case, see Paul Lombardo, 'Three generations, no imbeciles, new light on *Buck* v. *Bell*', *New York University Law Review*, vol. 60 (1985), p. 30. Neither Carrie Bell (the young woman whose sterilization was authorized in *Buck* v. *Bell*) nor her mother, nor her daughter were in fact 'feebleminded'. The daughter died at the age of eight, but had by that time a school record well above average. What seems more significant is that both Carrie Bell and her daughter were 'born out of wedlock'.

11  'A sterilisation statute for Kentucky?', *Kentucky Law Journal*, vol. 23 (1934), p. 168. And see W. Burgdorf and T. Burgdorf, 'The wicked witch is almost dead: *Buck* v. *Bell* and the sterilisation of handicapped persons', *Temple Law Quarterly*, vol. 50 (1977), p. 995.

12  For a comparison of the cost of support in different settings, see Audit Commission Occasional Paper no. 4, *Community Care: Developing Services for People with a Mental Handicap* (London: HMSO, 1987), para. 27 Table 1; and Audit Commission, *Making a Reality of Community Care*, (London: HMSO, 1986), p. 30, Table 12 and pp. 29–48, *passim*.

13  J. Van Der Merwe and J. P. Roux, 'Sterilisation of mentally retarded persons', *Obstetrical and Gynaecological Survey*, vol. 42, no. 8 (1987), p. 48.

14  Scott, 'Sterilisation of mentally retarded persons'; Margaret Shone, 'Mental health – sterilisation of mentally retarded persons', *Canadian Bar Review*, vol. 66 (1987), p. 635, at p. 635. For a recent review of sterilization use in Canada, see also *Sterilization Decisions: Minors and Mentally Incompetent Adults*, Report for Discussion no. 6 (Edmonton: Institute of Law Research and Reform, March 1988).

15  Sometimes known as 'the abortion package'; see Elizabeth Kingdom, 'The sexual politics of sterilisation', *Journal of Law and Society*, vol. 12 (1985), p. 19, at pp. 26–7.

16  *Re B*, *per* Lord Bridge at p. 213.

17  ibid., at p. 214.

18  *Re Eve*.

19  cf. Sheila McLean, 'The right to reproduce', in Tom Campbell, David Goldberg, Sheila McLean, and Tom Mullen (eds), *Human Rights: From Rhetoric to Reality* (Oxford: Basil Blackwell, 1986), p. 99, at p. 112.

20  [1976] 1 All E.R. 326.

21  *Re D*, at p. 332: 'The type of operation proposed is one which involves a deprivation of a basic human right of a woman to reproduce, and

therefore it would, if performed on a woman for non-therapeutic reasons and without her consent, be a violation of such a right.'

22  *Re B*, at p. 213.

23  See Tom Campbell *et al.* (eds), *Human Rights*, pp. 2–14.

24  McLean, 'The right to reproduce', p. 108, discussing *Buck* v. *Bell*.

25  Tom Campbell, 'The rights of the mentally ill', in Tom Campbell *et al.* (eds), *Human Rights*.

26  The shape of the argument in this section and its terminology is modelled on Bernard Williams, 'Which slopes are slippery?' in Michael Lockwood (ed.), *Moral Dilemmas in Modern Medicine* (London: Oxford University Press, 1985), pp. 126–37. As Williams adroitly concludes (p. 137), 'there is no slippery slope more perilous than that extended by a concept which is falsely supposed not to be slippery'. We are grateful to Celia Wells for her comments on this section.

27  See particularly the judgment of Dillon L. J. in the Court of Appeal [1987] 2 All E.R. 209, at p. 210.

28  Williams, 'Which slopes are slippery?', p. 127.

29  Shone, 'Mental health', p. 639. Similarly, Shone appears to overlook the important caveat entered by Dickens that the transition from regarding sterilization of retarded adults upon their guardians' consent as an act done *to* them into consideration of it as an act done *for* them must be treated with caution; 'the population of competent adults making autonomous choices for the procedure is not comparable to the retarded population whose guardians may seek their sterilisation. Competent adults are often of relatively advanced age for reproduction and have usually completed their desired child-bearing, whereas the retarded are often lower in age and parity.'

30  *Re Eve*, p. 32. Below we argue that Jeanette's sterilization was manifestly non-therapeutic; see also Elizabeth Kingdom, 'The right to reproduce', *Archiv für Rechts und Sozialphilosophie*, vol. 32 (1986), p. 55.

31  Williams, 'Which slopes are slippery?', pp. 130–1.

32  The 'welfare criterion' which motivated the Law Lords approach to the case is analysed by Peter de Cruz in 'Sterilisation, wardship and human rights', *Family Law*, vol. 18 (1988), p. 6, at pp. 9–11.

33  For the notion of a contraceptive career, see Hilary Thomas, 'The medical construction of a contraceptive career', in Hilary Homans (ed.), *The Sexual Politics of Reproduction* (Aldershot: Gower, 1985), pp. 45–63.

34  Mencap reported twenty approaches from parents or hospitals in a two-year period; *Times*, 19 March 1987.

35  Clare Dyer, 'Sterilization of mentally handicapped woman', *British Medical Journal*, vol. 294 (23 March 1987), p. 825.

36  *Times*, 19 March 1987; *Times*, 20 March 1987.

37  *Re B*, p. 216.

38  The suspicion, of course, is that she has had none. Compare the experiences of the mentally handicapped members of the Lothian Rights Group in 'Sterilisation debate: why weren't mentally handicapped people consulted', *Social Work Today*, 11 May 1987, p. 5, and the opinion

of Morgan Williams, 'Sexual and personal relationships of the disabled', cited in *Social Work Today*, 23 March 1987, p. 3.

39  *Re B, per* Lord Hailsham, at p. 212.

40  ABPI, *Data Sheet Compendium*, Winthrop Laboratories, Danol.

41  *Re B, per* Lord Oliver, at p. 216.

42  ABPI, *Data Sheet Compendium*, Schering Chemicals Limited, Microgynon 30.

43  *Re B, per* Lord Hailsham, at p. 212.

44  ibid., *per* Lord Oliver, pp. 215–16.

45  Audit Commission, *Community Care*, para. 5, 'Ideas about the abilities of handicapped people and their place in society'; and see para. 45.

46  This point is eloquently made in an excellent contemporary comment on the Court of Appeal decision, *Social Services Insight*, 20 March 1987, p. 2.

47  *Re B, per* Lord Hailsham, at p. 209.

48  e.g. 'The sterile debate', *Spectator*, 21 March 1987, p. 5.

49  *Re B, per* Lord Hailsham, at p. 212.

50  ibid., *per* Lord Oliver, at p. 219; *per* Lord Bridge, at p. 213.

51  Simon Lee and Ian Kennedy, 'This rush to judgment', *Times*, 1 April 1987; Andrew Grubb and David Pearl, 'Sterilisation and the courts', *Cambridge Law Journal*, vol. 46 (1987), p. 439.

52  'She was beginning to show recognisable signs of sexual awareness and sexual drive exemplified by provocative approaches to male members of staff and other residents and by touching herself in the genital area;, *per* Lord Oliver, at p. 216; 'she has . . . been found in a compromising situation in a bathroom', *per* Lord Hailsham, at p. 212.

53  In the unlikely event of carrying a pregnancy to term, Lord Hailsham offers this warning as an additional reason indicating sterilization: Jeanette 'would probably have to be delivered by Caesarian section, but . . . she would be quite likely to pick at the operational wound and tear it open'. As Peter de Cruz pertinently asks, 'Suppose . . . that she had appendicitis?' ('Sterilisation, wardship and and human rights', at p. 11.)

54  *Times*, 1 May 1987 and *Times*, 18 March 1987 respectively.

55  He assumes (at p. 212) that incarceration would provide sufficent protection against pregnancy, though he then disapproves of this solution. Repeated examples of either abuse of patient-carer relationships are found in various literatures; for an analysis of the sociological roles implicated here see Erving Goffman, *Asylums: Essays on the Social Situation of Mental Patients and Other Inmates* (Harmondsworth: Penguin Books, 1961), esp. pp. 187–266, 'Hospital underlife'.

56  Chris Heginbotham 'A storm has raged', *Social Services Insight*, 27 March 1987, p. 6. That such information was overlooked strengthens the case for *amici curiae* in such cases. 'Community care' is, of course, often used here as a euphemism for parental care, or, if institutionalized, for private care.

57  As reported in *Day-to-Day*, BBC Television, 19 March 1987. And see *Social Services Insight*, 27 March 1987, p. 2.

58 *Social Work Today*, 11 May 1987, p. 3.
59 Quoted in *Social Work Today*, 11 May 1987, p. 3.
60 David Sines, Chair of the Royal College of Nursing Community Mental Handicap Nursing Forum, quoted in *Nursing Times*, 25 March 1987, p. 7.
61 Are we to assume (as was done throughout *Re B*) that we should always seek to prevent this; see David Carson, 'The case for castration M'lud?', *Health Service Journal*, 26 March 1987, p. 354.
62 There was a sharp reaction from the Adult Training Centres at the implicit slur on the quality of their supervision: see, for example, *Community Care*, 23 April 1987, p. 8.
63 There is an irony here. The move away from institutional care is aimed at establishing the individuality and personhood of the handicapped and establishing their value within society. Yet we seek to protect Jeanette from the consequences of her sexuality which her community status attempted to promote. On deinstitutionalization see Andrew Scull, *Decarceration: Community Treatment and the Deviant – A Radical View* (Englewood Cliffs, N.J.: Prentice-Hall, 1977 edn), *passim*; and also Audit Commission, *Making a Reality of Community Care*.
64 *Re Eve*, at p. 32.
65 Lee and Kennedy, 'This rush to judgment'.
66 Grubb and Pearl, 'Sterilisation and the courts', pp. 461–2.
67 *Re T*; *T* v. *T* [1988] 1 All E.R. 613.
68 *Re Eve* at p. 32.
69 ibid., at p. 31.
70 ibid., at p. 32.
71 Audit Commission, *Community Care*, para. 16 and exhibit 1.
72 Robert Lee, 'Legal control of health care allocation', *Archiv für Rechts und Sozialphilosphie*, vol. 32, (1986), p. 93.
73 Recalling Justice Holmes in *Buck* v. *Bell*.
74 See Chapter 1 of this volume.
75 For a recent analysis of the development of policies of community care and the social fund, see, for example, Clare Ungerson, *Policy is Personal: Sex, Gender and Informal Care* (London: Tavistock, 1987).
76 *Re B*, *per* Dillon L. J., at p. 209.

# 9

# ABORTION: A RIGHTS ISSUE?

## *LINDA CLARKE*

It is now twenty years since David Steel's Private Member's Bill became the Abortion Act 1967. That Act provided that in certain circumstances doctors had a defence to the crimes set out in s. 58 of the Offences Against the Person Act 1861, and s. 1(1) of the Infant Life (Preservation) Act 1929. Safe, legal abortions became generally available to women for the first time and many women have made use of the facility: 54,819 women had abortions in 1969, rising to 171,873 in 1985.[1] After twenty years, abortion continues to arouse passionate feelings and disagreements between those who believe that the foetus should be accorded the status of a human being (and thus its destruction be prohibited by law) and those who believe that the individual woman should have the choice to terminate her pregnancy if she chooses, and that she should be able to do so freely and legally up to term.

Both these positions are logically defensible if one accepts certain premises as to the personhood or non-personhood of the foetus. The middle ground, that abortion should be permitted at certain stages of pregnancy, and in certain circumstances, is a much more problematic area and has been the main focus of political debate.

Steel's Private Member's Bill was the seventh such bill to be introduced in Parliament; and almost as soon as it became law movements began to reform it, with the first bill introduced by Norman St John Stevas MP after only fifteen months. This continued concern over abortion law has been attributed to the activities of pressure groups, most notably the Society for the Protection of the Unborn Child (SPUC), LIFE and the National Abortion Campaign (NAC).[2] Following the passage of the 1967 Act the

155

anti-abortion lobby, consisting of SPUC and LIFE, became increasingly active at a time when the Abortion Law Reform Association (ALRA) was losing membership and influence. Throughout the first half of the 1970s the anti-abortion lobby dictated the tenor of the abortion debate and kept up constant pressure for restrictive reform. This led to the government establishing a committee to investigate the working of the 1967 Act, but the report of the Lane Committee in 1974 disappointed the anti-abortion lobby, with its findings which broadly supported the Act, recommending in general only administrative reforms. The anti-abortion lobby kept up the pressure nevertheless and some MPs began to express concern over the rise in the number of legal abortions performed (from 54,860 a year in 1969 to peak at around 167,000 in 1973), leading to allegations that the Act provided 'abortion on demand'. Other features of the debate were concern over London becoming 'the abortion capital of the world' and stories of 'abuses' in private abortion clinics. Periodically abortion horror stories appeared in the popular press; most notable amongst these were a series of articles in the *News of the World* by Susan Kentish and Michael Litchfield containing sensationalist and sometimes horrific allegations about abortion clinics. These articles formed the basis of a book, *Babies for Burning*, which influenced several MPs despite the fact that many of the allegations were later proven to be false.[3]

The course of James White's Private Member's Bill in 1975 (which ultimately fell) was important in that the success of the anti-abortion lobby in mobilizing support and influencing MPs made it apparent that pro-choice groups must begin to act together to defend the 1967 Act. The National Abortion Campaign was formed, initially as a co-ordinating body, but it quickly developed into a broad-based, non-hierarchical movement which drew strength and support from the women's movement. The lessons learned by the pro-choice lobby during the debates on the White Bill and the Benyon Bill of 1978/9 (both of which ultimately fell) were invaluable bulwarks against John Corrie's Private Member's Bill in 1979. This bill appeared to have a real chance of succeeding in the new Conservative-dominated Parliament and it is a tribute to the skill of the pro-choice lobbyists that the bill ultimately fell.[4] This surprise defeat appeared to take the wind out of the anti-abortionists' sails for the next six years: although there were further attempts to amend the 1967 Act it was notable that even known anti-abortion MPs coming high in the Private Members' Ballot failed to use the opportunity to introduce amending legislation (including John Corrie himself in 1982). However, there will be further attempts to introduce amending legislation which will narrow the grounds for abortion, and there are indications that such legislation may be successful. The twenty years between 1967 and 1987 may become the high-water mark for legal abortion in England and Wales.

Although abortion remains a highly contentious and hotly debated issue, the focus in the 1980s has shifted towards other areas of the politics of reproduction, and in particular to technical advance in the treatment of infertility. Since the birth of the first test-tube baby in July 1978 the debate on control of human reproduction has focused on the various developments aimed at helping the childless, both medical, such as *in vitro* fertilization, and social/non-medical, such as surrogacy. This has some hidden implications for abortion law reform. The concern and sympathy shown to those who are involuntarily childless often carries with it an implied (rarely explicit) criticism of those who advocate easy access to abortion. At the same time, the liberalization of abortion law in 1967 is frequently given as one reason for the shortage of children (which usually means white, healthy babies) for adoption. But it is the issue of embryo experimentation which is likely to have most impact on the abortion debate. The new technological developments designed to help the childless have led to the creation/existence of embryos (or pre-embryos) outside the womb and the question has arisen as to whether or not it is permissible to use human embryos for research.[5] The *Warnock Report* included a recommendation that embryo experimentation should be allowed up to the fourteenth day of development; to keep an embryo alive for experimental purposes after that should be a criminal offence.[6] There are obvious implications of restricting embryo research for the law on abortion. As *Warnock* noted in a footnote,

> it seems to us totally illogical to propose stringent legislative controls on the use of very early human embryos for research, while there is a less formal mechanism governing the research use of whole live embryos and foetuses of more advanced gestation. Although we understand that these mechanisms have worked well, we consider that there is a case for bringing any research that makes use of whole live aborted embryos and foetuses —

whether obtained from in vitro fertilisation, uterine lavage, or termination of pregnancy - within the sort of legislative framework proposed in this report.

*Warnock* refers to research on aborted foetuses under guidelines drawn up by the Peel Committee[7] but highlights the potential inconsistency in protecting embryos from experimentation after 14 days but allowing foetuses to be killed up to 28 weeks and then experimented on.

Following the *Warnock Report*, Enoch Powell introduced a Private Member's Bill, the Unborn Child (Protection) Bill, which proposed to make it an offence to create, keep or use a human embryo for any purpose other than enabling a child to be born by a particular woman, thus effectively barring all embryo research. The bill fell.[8] The government has not yet introduced legislation in this area, although the Conservative manifesto for the 1987 General Election proposed a Bill with alternative clauses, one allowing experimentation up to 14 days, the other offering a complete ban. Given that Powell's bill was passed by a majority of 286 on a free vote, embryo experimentation may well be banned with all the consequent implications for abortion. It is significant that anti-abortion groups such as LIFE and SPUC are leading the campaign for banning embryo research and pro-choice groups must be alert to the dangers.

Such technological advances also raise the spectre – as yet very much in the future – of the 'artificial womb', which could sustain the foetus *ex utero* from a relatively early age. This could raise questions as to the permissibility of abortions from this early age, given the general opposition to aborting 'viable' foetuses. Those who believe in a woman's right to choose would have to face the issue of what rights a pregnant woman would have in relation to the foetus: can she demand that the foetus be allowed to die? Conversely, should the foetus have the right to live, even though life can only be sustained with the help of complex and expensive technology? What rights, if any, would any resulting 'child' have in relation to its mother?[9] What duties, if any, would medical staff performing the abortion have towards the foetus? Any technological advances in this area will raise difficult questions with important implications for abortion.

Recent legal developments concerning the mother's behaviour during pregnancy could also have implications for the legality of abortion. In California, a mother was prosecuted but acquitted for contributing towards her baby son's death because she took amphetamines during her pregnancy: the baby was born brain-damaged, with traces of amphetamines in his blood, and later died. In Britain, the House of Lords has ruled that in deciding whether to make a care order under the Children and Young Persons Act 1969 a juvenile court was entitled to consider treatment of the child before it was born.[10] Here a mother who took heroin during her pregnancy had her baby taken into care by the local authority, who relied on the mother's behaviour during the pregnancy as evidence that the child's development was being avoidably impaired or neglected. The House of Lords upheld the care order, although Lord Goff stated that had the mother irrevocably given up the taking of drugs before the child was born, then the case would be different. The possible implications of this kind of legal control of behaviour during pregnancy were spelt out in an editorial in *The Independent*:

> Neither woman would have had difficulty in finding someone and some reason, lawfully to terminate her pregnancy. Had they decided not to carry their respective babies – perhaps because of their drug dependence – few outside 'moral majoritarians' would have blamed them. . . . Instead, Mrs Stewart faces grave charges. As for Mrs X, she is . . . deemed unworthy of raising her child because of pre-natal damage caused by her drug dependency. But perfectly lawful activities are also known to endanger the foetus. Smoking, for example. Or drinking heavily. Some sports can do harm. So can sexual intercourse, practised too often and too energetically, too early or too late in a pregnancy. We are approaching a situation in which society effectively tolerates abortion on demand – the destruction of a foetus on grounds of convenience – yet insists upon policing the mother's social life during pregnancy.[11]

Similarly, Mrs Nuala Scarisbrook of LIFE has said that prosecuting drug-addict mothers could lead to an increase in abortions among patients who feared action after their baby was born.[12] Like legal controls over embryo experimentation, any greater control over the treatment of the foetus *in utero* will lead people to ask; why is foetal destruction still permissible?

LINDA CLARKE

## THE LEGAL POSITION

Despite the familiarity of the abortion debate, the law is often misquoted and misunderstood. The primary offence is contained in section 58 of the Offences Against the Person Act 1861. This provides that

> whosoever, with intent to procure the miscarriage of any woman, whether she be or not be with child, shall unlawfully administer to her or cause to be taken by her any poison or other noxious thing or shall unlawfully use any instrument or other means whatsoever . . .

commits the crime of abortion. In addition, the Infant Life (Preservation) Act 1929, s. 1(1) creates the offence of child destruction where 'any person who, with intent to destroy the life of a child capable of being born alive, by any wilful act causes a child to die before it has an existence independent of its mother'. There is a statutory presumption that where a woman has been pregnant for 28 weeks or more, the foetus is capable of being born alive. However, if the act was done 'for the purpose only of saving the life of the mother', then no offence is committed. In the famous test case of *R* v. *Bourne*[13] in 1938 McNaghten J. held that the 'unlawful' provision in section 58 of the 1861 Act imported the same proviso at common law, so that abortion could be carried out at any time during the pregnancy for the purpose of preserving the mother's life. Further, he held that 'preserving the life of the mother' included where a doctor was 'of the opinion, on reasonable grounds and with adequate knowledge, that the probable consequence of the continuation of the pregnancy will be to make the woman a mental or physical wreck'.[14]

The Abortion Act 1967 provides that no offence is committed under the law relating to abortion when pregnancy is terminated by a registered medical practitioner if two such practitioners are of the opinion that continuance of the pregnancy would involve risk to the life of the pregnant woman, or injury to her physical or mental health, or to the physical or mental health of any existing children she may have. The risk must be greater than if the pregnancy were terminated.[15] In reaching this decision, doctors are entitled to consider the woman's actual or reasonably forseeable environment. In addition, no offence is committed if there is a substantial risk that the child would be seriously handicapped. So far, there has only been one case alleging that the provisions of the Abortion Act 1967 were not complied with,[16] but there are two areas where current medical practices may involve the commission of criminal offences.

First, questions have arisen as to the legality of post-coital contraception in the form of the 'morning after' pill, and the practice of fitting an intra-uterine device (IUD) within a few days of sexual intercourse. It has been argued that these techniques are in fact very early abortions and that unless the terms of the 1967 Act are complied with, an offence under section 58 of the Offences Against the Person Act 1861 is committed. The issue has yet to be tested in the courts, but in May 1983 the Attorney General stated that the use of the 'morning after' pill did not amount to a criminal offence, as it worked by preventing implantation and that ordinary nineteenth-century usage of the word 'miscarriage' did not cover a failure to implant, whether spontaneous or otherwise. Similarly, the legality of endometrial aspiration, or the 'mini-abortion', which has been described as 'the safest and least disturbing form of abortion',[17] is uncertain; the procedure involves an evacuation of the uterine contents within days of a missed period. The difficulty is that this occurs *before* pregnancy is diagnosed, and the Abortion Act 1967 only legalizes abortion 'where a pregnancy is terminated'. So it could be argued that even where the provisions of the 1967 Act are purportedly complied with, the abortion is still illegal. (The same reasoning would make post-coital contraception an offence, despite purported compliance with the 1967 Act). The Lane Committee recommended in 1974 that the 1967 Act be amended to cover the situation where it is intended to terminate a pregnancy if such exists. This has not happened, although in March 1979 the government's Law Officers stated that the words 'termination of pregnancy' in the 1967 Act included steps taken to terminate a pregnancy which two practitioners believed in good faith to exist.[18] The legal problems involved in endometrial aspiration can, however, be largely avoided by making use of more sophisticated tests which can diagnose pregnancy within ten to fourteen days of conception. However, given the uncertainty of the timing of implantation and lack of knowledge as to exactly how post-coital contraception works, it may be that doctors prescribing the morning-after pill or fitting IUDs should comply with the provisions of the Abortion Act 1967.

Second, the Abortion Act 1967, s. 5(1) states that nothing in the Act shall affect the provisions of the Infant Life (Preservation) Act 1929. This raises the question of the legality of late abortions; if the foetus is 'capable of being born alive' then the offence of child destruction is committed, regardless of whether or not the abortion takes place before 28 weeks. As the technology available for keeping premature babies alive improves, babies can survive earlier and earlier. The House of Lords Select Committee on the Infant Life (Preservation) Bill found 'some evidence of the occasional possibility of earlier survival than at 24 weeks gestation . . . [and] a substantial survival rate among normal babies born after the completion of the 24th week of pregnancy, amounting probably to over 50 per cent after 26 completed weeks of pregnancy'.[19] Foetal viability is an ever-shifting standard. The effect of the 1929 Act would appear to be to make many late abortions illegal despite purported compliance with the Abortion Act 1967.

However, prosecutions under the 1929 Act are very rare; there have been only five since 1957, of which the last two in 1981 and 1987 were cases where the mother was assaulted in the latter stages of pregnancy.[20] The Director of Public Prosecutions, in his written evidence to the House of Lords Select Committee on the Infant Life (Preservation) Bill, gave a summary of four cases referred to him by the Chairman of LIFE in 1979 and 1980 where it was alleged that despite a termination under the Abortion Act 1967 a child was born and lived for a short time afterwards. Such cases, according to the DPP, usually invoke allegations of manslaughter or gross negligence and

> are always difficult to prove and in the rare cases where sufficient evidence may exist it is unlikely that the public interest will require proceedings. The difficulty in such cases is that the mother will have wanted the termination . . . we have always been mindful of the distress which would be caused to her by proceedings.[21]

Criminal proceedings would therefore seem unlikely whilst such a policy exists. However, in *C* v. *S*[22] an Oxford student sought an injunction to prevent his former girlfriend having an abortion, on the grounds that such an abortion would constitute an offence under section 1(1) of the 1929 Act. The woman was between 18 and 21 weeks pregnant. Mr C produced affidavit evidence that a foetus of

18 weeks gestation would be live born, as defined by the World Health Organization, and was therefore 'capable of being born alive' even though it would be unable to sustain an independent existence. It was argued that 'being born alive' is a much more restrictive concept than viability, but that the words of the 1929 Act were unambiguous and could not be extended to cover the concept of viability. The Court of Appeal rejected this interpretation, ruling that as a foetus of between 18 and 21 weeks gestation 'would be incapable ever of breathing either naturally or with the aid of a ventilator', then it was not 'a child capable of being born alive' within the meaning of the 1929 Act, even though it could be said to demonstrate real and discernible signs of life. So adequate lung development, occurring at around 24 weeks, would appear to be crucial. The Court of Appeal's judgment therefore opens up the possibility of an injunction being granted to prevent the termination of a 24-week pregnancy, as such a termination could constitute a criminal offence.[23]

## A RIGHTS ISSUE?

It is common to hear abortion discussed in terms of rights – of the mother, the foetus and also of the father; the law, however, recognizes none of these. The Abortion Act 1967 gives a 'right' only to doctors; to form an opinion as to whether or not abortion is justified. A woman has no 'right' to an abortion even if her circumstances are such that she falls within the terms of the Act. Similarly, where two doctors form the relevant opinion, she has no right *not* to have an abortion (although in practice any such abortion would amount to an assault).[24]

Nor does English law give the father of the foetus any rights. In *Paton* v. *BPAS*[25] a man failed to get an injunction to stop his wife having an abortion. Sir George Baker stated that the 1967 Act gives the father no right to be consulted in respect of the termination of a pregnancy: as long as two doctors acted in good faith that was the end of the matter. The European Commission similarly rejected the father's claim,[26] holding that the right to respect for family life did not extend to him a right to be consulted about the proposed abortion, as this principally raised a question of a woman's right to respect for her family life. In so far as termination of pregnancy on health grounds was an interference with the prospective father's right to respect for his family life, the Commission found this justified as being necessary for the protection of the rights of another person. In *Paton*, the father was attempting to prevent a lawful abortion: *C* v. *S* raised the question of whether a prospective father could stop an unlawful abortion. Even if one assumes that the abortion of a foetus of 24 weeks gestation would amount to the offence of child destruction under the 1929 Act, the right of individuals to restrain breaches of the criminal law are fairly limited.[27] Sir George Baker in *Paton* v. *BPAS* would have recognized such a right only if the complainant 'would suffer personally and more than the general public'.[28] In *C* v. *S* the matter of whether a father would have *locus standi* was left open, the case having been decided on the grounds that the proposed abortion would not in fact constitute a criminal offence. However, it is certainly arguable that a prospective father would have the necessary *locus standi* to prevent criminal abortion. Similarly the European Commission's decision is couched in limited terms; only where the pregnancy is terminated 'in order to avert the risk of injury to [the mother's] physical or mental health' is the interference with the father's rights justified. Another application by a prospective father from Norway currently before the Commission may give further indication of the extent of the father's rights. The crux of the matter is how injury to physical or mental health is interpreted. Under the Abortion Act 1967 the risk must be greater than if the pregnancy were terminated, and around 70–80 per cent of all terminations are carried out on these grounds. Kenyon[29] states that the vast majority of legal abortions carried out are for the sake of the mental health of the mother, but that

> there are no guidelines as to the *degree* of danger to health that should be involved nor to what is actually meant by 'mental health' in this context. This allows for the widest possible interpretation, from the view of hardliners who say there are no psychiatric indications at all (taking risks to mental health to refer to psychosis, maintaining there is no particular danger of deterioration during or after pregnancy) to the opposite extreme, that of abortion virtually on demand, when minor worries, unhappiness at not being able to cope, are taken to mean injury to mental health.[30]

So it all depends on which doctor the woman consults, as Mr Paton realized: in his application to the European Commission on Human

Rights he claimed a right that the mother be examined by different doctors appointed by the father, or by a designated court or tribunal. Given the existence of private abortion clinics and the charitable referral agencies, the Abortion Act 1967 does in practice provide abortion on demand for those who can pay,[31] but it seems unlikely that the courts will begin inquiring into the 'good faith' of the doctors' opinion: Sir George Baker said in *Paton* that 'it would be quite impossible for the courts . . . to supervise the operation of the 1967 Act. The great social responsibility is firmly placed by the law on the shoulders of the medical profession.' It remains to be seen to what extent the European Commission on Human Rights (and also the Court) is prepared to examine the reasons for the abortion, and determine what constitutes 'injury to mental health'.

Nor does the foetus have any legal rights: in order to have any 'rights' the foetus must first be born and be a child.[32] So in *Paton* and *C* v. *S* the father was unable to seek an injunction on behalf of the foetus. More interestingly, it seems that the foetus has no right to be aborted; the so called 'wrongful life' claims by children subsequently born handicapped have so far been rejected as contrary to public policy as a 'violation of the sanctity of human life'.[33] Again, the European Commission on Human Rights, in *Paton* v. *United Kingdom* did not decide whether the 'Right to Life' in Article 2 covered the foetus at all, but assumed that if it did, then an abortion at the 'initial' stage of pregnancy is covered by an implied limitation protecting the life and health of the woman at that stage. Exactly what is the 'initial' stage is uncertain. *Paton* concerned an abortion at ten weeks, so presumably this would cover first trimester abortions.

## A WOMAN'S RIGHT TO CHOOSE?

So in English law mothers, fathers and foetuses have no rights with respect to abortion, but doctors have rights (to form opinions in good faith) and medical staff have rights (to object on grounds of conscience to participating in the majority of abortions).[34] Insufficient consideration has been given as to why it is a matter of clinical judgment whether or not a woman may have an abortion. The vast majority of abortions are carried out on the grounds that the continuance of the pregnancy would involve risk of injury to the physical or mental health of the pregnant woman greater than if the pregnancy were terminated; there is no legal guidance as to the degree of risk necessary, and a great deal is therefore left to the 'clinical judgment' of the doctors. In practice, doctors can impose on to women their own views of when abortion is permissible.

Abortion itself is a medical procedure but the decision whether a woman should have an abortion or not is not necessarily a medical one, and it has yet to be established why doctors are particularly well qualified to make such decisions. However, if one wishes to remove the decision from doctors it becomes necessary for the law to establish when abortion should be available, and who should decide, as otherwise the medical profession will effectively continue to regulate the availability of abortion, either as individuals or through a professional code of practice.

There are strong arguments for making safe, legal abortion generally available, leaving the decision to the individual woman. Biologically it is the woman who must accommodate the growing foetus in her own body for nine months, with all the discomfort and restrictions which this brings with it. Then she must go through a painful labour resulting in the birth of a child for which she remains responsible for many years to come. For all the rhetoric about 'the best interests of the child' our society provides little in the way of practical support for mothers once their children are born. It is on the woman that the greatest part of the heavy burden of child rearing falls. Ultimately it must be the woman who decides whether or not to bear a child, because only the woman has to live with the consequence of her decisions.[35] The law should therefore make abortion available to women on demand.

To argue that ultimately women must have the right to choose for themselves is not necessarily to ignore the moral framework of the abortion debate; one can be pro-choice but not necessarily pro-abortion. Indeed, once the legal right to choose is conceded, the discussion of abortion may concentrate on providing a suitable moral framework within which women should exercise that choice.[36] It is also a mistake to see abortion as an isolated issue; rather it is part of a much wider issue of reproductive freedom, and child-rearing, areas where many women have little real control or choice. In order to have real choice about abortion, society must provide the necessary support to enable women to choose to *have* a child, in terms of financial aid, housing provision, child care provision and support within the home.

## TWENTY YEARS ON: TIME FOR A CHANGE

It is not realistic to expect in the near future a change in the law which gives women the general right to choose to have an abortion. The last twenty years have been spent defending the 1967 Act from attacks by anti-abortionists, rather than fighting for improvements. David Alton's Private Member's Bill, seeking to reduce the statutory presumption in the 1929 Act from 28 weeks to 18 weeks, was merely the latest in a line of attempts to reverse that initiative.

Some change in abortion law appears likely within the next few years. The main reason is that there is a growing consensus that it is wrong to attach legal significance to a period of 28 weeks gestation when this is no longer of biological significance. Rather it is currently felt by many that 24 weeks represents viability and that this should be reflected in the law. There are good reasons why this reduction should (and will) be opposed by many; there are always women who for a variety of reasons present late for abortions, and these are often tragic cases.[37] However, abortions after 24 weeks are very rare, with only thirty-one carried out in 1985; in 1985 the DHSS acted to prevent late abortions being carried out in the private sector by refusing to license clinics unless they agreed not to carry out post-24-week abortions. As post-24-week abortions represent a tiny fraction of abortions, there are pragmatic reasons for conceding a new 24-week standard for viability and concentrating instead on the real problems with the 1967 Act. If the law is to restrict abortions to pre-24 weeks, then it is essential that women insist that the choice pre-'viability' is theirs, and not that of the medical profession, and that free, legal abortions are available promptly. It is inequitable that women who can afford a private abortion in reality have a right to choose, but women dependent on the NHS do not. There are regional variations in the availability of NHS abortions,[38] and a study carried out by the Royal College of Obstetricians and Gynaecologists in 1984 revealed serious delays in NHS procedures, with one in five women referred before the twelfth week of pregnancy not having an abortion until between 20 and 23 weeks.[39] It may be advisable to concentrate on these deficiencies rather than defending the very late abortion. The danger, however, is that any reduction in the time limit for abortion has a knock-on effect, as doctors currently err on the side of caution because of difficulties in accurate measurement of the length of

167

pregnancy, and a reduction to 24 weeks in practice effects some several hundred women who seek abortions after 22 weeks. Nevertheless it may be more effective to campaign for improved access to abortion in the earlier stages of pregnancy than to fight to retain a standard of 28 weeks which no longer reflects viability.

'A woman's right to choose' is an old slogan, but one which highlights three important issues. First, for the reasons outlined above it is essential that *women* must have the legal right to decide whether or not to have an abortion. It is for this reason that proposals for the 'medicalization' of abortion should be carefully examined; whilst it is essential that abortion be decriminalized it is not sufficient that it be seen simply as another medical procedure within the area of the individual doctor's 'clinical judgment'. Second, abortion should be a *'right'* with a corresponding duty on the state to provide safe, free abortions.

Once women have the *legal* right to abortion, it will be possible to focus attention on the morality of abortion. The foetus (and the father) can have no *legal* rights *vis-à-vis* the mother, but many have strong moral rights which vary from case to case. There is a pressing need for a morality of abortion, which confronts the notion of competing rights of mother and foetus (and perhaps father) and gives women guidance and support in making the choice.[40]

Lastly, there must be a real *choice*. Many women feel they cannot possibly decide to bear the child they have conceived because of their economic and social circumstances. For very many women, deciding to have a child condemns them to a life on the breadline, living in sub-standard housing, existing on inadequate social security payments and unable to see any prospect of improving their situation through finding employment. State nursery provision, more council house building and adequate financial support for children would probably prevent more abortions than any reduction in the time limit, yet no Private Member's Bill advocates these measures.

Pro-choice campaigners have spent the last twenty years defending the 1967 Act from attack. Perhaps now is the time to make concessions on the time limit, rather than fighting to retain a standard which no longer has any biological significance, and in practice affects only a tiny minority of women. However, such a concession should only be made in return for giving women, not doctors, the power to decide over abortion pre-'viability'. Concern over late abortions should be channelled into ways of preventing these through sex education, counselling, improved contraception and automatic access to early abortion.

In twenty years from now it is to be hoped that 'A woman's right to choose' will be more than just another slogan.

## NOTES

1 Currently the last full year for which statistics are available; *Select Committee on the Infant Life (Preservation) Bill* [HL], 1986–7, Memorandum by the DHSS, Annex C (HI, 153).

2 See J. Lovenduski, 'Parliament, pressure groups, networks and the women's movement; the politics of abortion law reform in Britain (1967–83)', in J. Lovanduski and J. Outshourn (eds), *The New Politics of Abortion* (London: Sage Publications, 1986).

3 See, for example, *Sunday Times*, 30 March 1975, 'Abortion horror tales revealed as fantasies'.

4 There is a remarkable parallel with the fate of the Alton Bill in the 1987/8 session. For a fascinating account of the Corrie Bill, see D. Marsh and J. Chambers, *Abortion Politics* (London: Junction Books, 1981).

5 The aims of such research include further improvements in the treatment of infertility, aiding the understanding, detection and prevention of genetic defects, improved understanding of miscarriage, and developing more effective forms of contraception.

6 Fourteen days was chosen as the time of the development of the so-called 'primitive streak' which marks the 'beginning of the individual development of the foetus'. It is also the last stage at which twins can develop. For a persuasive critique of the logic behind this time-limit, see John Harris, *The Value of Life* (London: Routledge & Kegan Paul, 1985), pp. 134–5, and his essay (Chapter 5) in this volume.

7 *The Use of Fetuses and Fetal Material for Research* (the *Peel Report*) (London: HMSO, 1972).

8 There have been three other similar bills: two introduced by Ken Hargreaves, and a third by Alastair Burt.

9 Cf. The rights of adopted children in relation to their biological mother.

10 *D (a minor)* v. *Berkshire C.C.* [1987] 1 All E.R. 20.

11 *Independent*, 9 October 1986.

12 *Observer*, 5 October 1986.

13 [1939] 1 K.B. 687, [1938] 3 All E.R. 615.

14 ibid.

15 This provides the basis for the so-called 'statistical grounds', in that statistics show that the risks of early abortion are always smaller than the risks of continued pregnancy and childbirth.

16 *R.* v. *Smith (John)* [1974] 1 All E.R. 376.

17 Angela Phillips and Jill Robinson, *Our Bodies Ourselves* (Harmondsworth: Penguin Books, 1978), p. 306.

18 The Director of Public Prosecutions in a letter to Renée Short, MP, 13 March 1979, quoted in V. Tunkel, 'Abortion: how early, how late and how legal', *British Medical Journal*, 28 July 1979, p. 253.

19 *Select Committee on the Infant Life (Preservation) Bill (HL)*, 1986–7, (HL 15), p. 7.

20 See Memorandum by the Director of Public Prosecutions to the *Select Committee on the Infant Life (Preservation) Bill* for the case of *Poulton* (DPP Defence 7076/80), p. 170. For the case of *Virgo*, see *Times*, 26 September 1987.

21 *Select Committee on the Infant Life (Preservation) Bill*, p. 170.

22 [1978] 1 All E.R. 1230.

23 Although Mrs Justice Heilbron's judgment at first glance highlights some of the difficulties in establishing that such an abortion would be a crime: 'If a doctor were to be charged . . . any such offence would have to be proved to the standard of certainty, the burden of proof, a heavy one, would be on the prosecution to produce evidence to establish all the elements of their case, including proof of the accused's requisite mens rea.' Also, see below as to the problems of *locus standi*.

24 This lack of a woman's right is highlighted by recent cases concerning abortions carried out on mentally handicapped women. In *Re T, T* v. *T* [1987] 1 All E.R. 613, Wood J. granted a declaration that the termination of the pregnancy of a 19-year-old severely handicapped woman would not be an unlawful act despite the absence of the woman's consent; see Chapter 8 by Lee and Morgan in this volume.

25 [1979] Q.B. 276, [1978] 2 All E.R. 987.

26 Application No. 8416/79.

27 See *Gouriet* v. *Union of Post Office Workers* [1977] 3 All E.R. 70.

28 *Paton* v. *B.P.A.S.* [1978] 2 All E.R. 376.

29 Edwin Kenyon, *The Dilemma of Abortion* (London: Faber & Faber, 1986), p. 120.

30 ibid., p. 121.

31 Cf. the position in the United States where *Roe* v. *Wade* 401 U.S. 113 (1973), legitimizing first trimester abortions as part of the right to privacy, was effectively undermined by *Harris* v. *McRae* 448 U.S. 297 (1980), which provides that state funding need not be made available for abortions.

32 See, *inter alia, Paton* at p. 990; *Re F* (in utereo) [1988] 2 All E.R. 193. Law Commission, *Report on Injuries to Unborn Children*, Report no. 60, Cmnd 5704 (London: HMSO, 1974); and the Congenital Disabilities (Civil Liability) Act 1976.

33 See *McKay* v. *Essex AHA* [1982] 1 W.L.R. 890, and Chapter 10 by Lee in this volume.

34 See Abortion Act 1967, s. 4.

35 This raises the question of whether women should lose the right to choose if men were to take an equal share in child rearing.

36 For a feminist discussion of the morality of abortion, see R. Petchesky,

*Abortion and Women's Choice* (Boston: North Eastern University Press, 1985), ch. 9.

37 See, for example, W. Savage, 'Requests for late terminations of pregnancy – Tower Hamlets 1983', *British Medical Journal*, vol. 290 (23 February 1985), p. 621.

38 See F. R. G. Fowkes, J. C. Catford, and R. F. L. Logan, 'Abortion and the NHS – the first decade', *British Medical Journal* (27 February 1979), p. 217.

39 *Late Abortions in England and Wales: Report of a National Confidential Study* (London: Royal College of Obstetricians and Gynaecologists, 1984).

40 See Petchesky, *Abortion and Woman's Choice*, pp. 341–50, for the argument that women are also most likely to make the most morally informed choice of abortion, and indeed have an implicit moral code.

# 10

# TO BE OR NOT TO BE:
# IS THAT THE QUESTION?
# THE CLAIM OF
# WRONGFUL LIFE

*ROBERT LEE*

This is not a paper in favour of the claim of wrongful life. It would be difficult to adopt such a stance without asserting the merit of such a claim for compensation in advance of, for example, that of a congenitally disabled infant, thereby adding to the piecemeal process by which our tort law system handles victims of misfortune. Rather it is an attempt to put the wrongful life claim under a microscope so that we may learn more of the nature of the tort law system of which it is a part. The aim is to explain and expose the tort law system as one which depends for its maintenance upon the rejection of certain claims in order to preserve for itself authority to determine the outcome of many others which better serve its vested interest.

## WRONGFUL LIFE

As the study of human genetics develops apace, it becomes increasingly possible to predict the probability of children handicapped by genetic disorders.[1] Timely advice to potential parents will allow the avoidance of conception, and even thereafter techniques such as amniocentesis and ultrasonography can locate foetal abnormality with a high degree of accuracy. The issue of whether tort law is the most appropriate mechanism to regulate such new biomedical skills is an issue which is debated later in this paper and elsewhere in this book. For now it is sufficient to make two points. First, neither the 'high tech' nature of the science nor its recent development lessens the claims of the parents to have the medical procedures applied to their benefit, or that of the foetus once conceived. Also, as with most technology, the mistakes in its application are often straightforward and obvious examples of human error.

Thus in this sphere it may consist of the failure to screen for genetic problems,[2] to test satisfactorily for genetic conditions, or to offer sufficient and appropriate advice on hereditary disorders. Similarly there may be a failure to offer amniocentesis to a pregnant rubella-contact, or a mother whose child is susceptible to Down's syndrome.[3] Alternatively, if offered, such procedures could be negligently performed, or their results not communicated or delayed beyond the point at which abortion is permitted. Finally, failed sterilizations or abortions could result in the birth of an unwanted child.

At this point it is useful to clarify the legal terminology particularly in relation to the labels of wrongful birth and wrongful life. Teff has been critical of these terms.[4] It is argued later that they are a misnomer. Certainly their emotive appeal is essentially unattractive, but in view of their widespread usage they are adopted here. Wrongful life describes an action brought on behalf of a handicapped child. It asserts that had the parents known of the child's likely disability either prior to conception or sufficiently early in the pregnancy, then they would have ensured that the child would not have been born. It is commonly said that the child is claiming that (s)he would have been better unborn. The cause of the injury lies therefore in (e.g.) the negligent failure to advise the parents, since, but for this, the child would not have been born. The child cannot allege that the defendant caused the defects, but asserts that as a result of the negligence (s)he now undergoes pain, suffering, and financial hardship attributable to the handicap.

In many such cases, the parents will also sue in their own right - a wrongful birth claim − for damages in respect of an unwanted child. That child may or may not be handicapped.[5] Damages may include both financial and emotional injury. Note the commonality of these two species of claim. Both arise out of similar (or the same) negligent acts, and both allege that but for that negligence the child would not have been conceived or would have been aborted.

## THE LACK OF LEGAL RECOGNITION

In view of the similar basis of the two claims, it seems surprising that the courts have been prepared to sanction recovery in wrongful birth claims while rejecting out of hand those based on wrongful life.[6] In *McKay* v. *Essex AHA*[7] the only UK authority on wrongful life, the plaintiff was born deaf and partially blind following her mother's contact with rubella during pregnancy. Following the mother's approach to the defendants, they failed to inform her of the risk of foetal abnormality. Had the mother been so informed she would have terminated the pregnancy in line with s.1(1)(b) of the Abortion Act 1967.

All three judges in the Court of Appeal described the claim as a 'one-off' case. They were alluding to the Congenital Disabilities (Civil Liability) Act 1976 which came into force shortly after the plaintiff's birth and which in the view of the Court excluded wrongful life claims. The Law Commission[8] had drafted the bill in order to allow recovery for a 'child born with disabilities which would not otherwise have been present'.[9] It is possible to argue that this falls short of precluding wrongful life claims since a wrongful life case embodies the argument that had a pregnancy been terminated no disability would have been present. However, the court expressed the opinion (*obiter*) that all future cases would be barred by the Act. Hence in the view of Ackner L.J. the case raised 'no point of general public importance'.[10]

None the less, forced to consider the issue at common law, all three judges had little hesitation in reaching 'the firm conclusion that our law cannot recognize a claim for wrongful life'.[11] The reasons put forward were fourfold: (i) there was no duty owed by the doctor to the child to perform an abortion; (ii) there was no damage; (iii) even if there was damage it was impossible for the courts to assess; (iv) it would be contrary to public policy to allow recovery.[12]

### Absence of duty

Since it is freely admitted that the duty concept is a useful policy device for extending or limiting liability, grounds (i) and (iv) above have much in common. The former represents one mechanism by which the values inherent in the latter may be effected. If the courts are to deny the existence of a duty in wrongful life cases it ought to be because there is no relationship falling within the neighbour principle as between doctor and plaintiff. One question which could arise in wrongful life is whether a duty could be owed to a child as yet unborn or (especially in genetic screening cases) not yet conceived. It might be argued that this would fall outside the neighbour principle which applies to 'persons who are so closely and directly affected by my act that I ought to have them in contemplation as being so affected when I am directing my mind to the acts or omissions which are called in question'. Such arguments formed no part of the judgment in *McKay*, perhaps because the Court was reluctant to wander into the legal quagmire of the status of the foetus. To argue the foreseeability point might mean that any negligent act (such as the production of a defective product) occurring prior to the conception of the eventual plaintiff would fail to give rise to liability. The 1976 Act permits recovery for preconception injury[13] and nowhere is this more obviously necessary than in those situations in which the parents may seek (e.g.) contraceptive advice. These points did not trouble the Court in *McKay*, and they presumably accepted the prima-facie application of the duty principle,

What did prove more troublesome was the nature of that duty: 'the only duty which either defendant can owe to the unborn child is a duty to abort or kill her or deprive her of that opportunity'.[14] Having thus circumscribed the concept, Stephenson L.J. then refused to impose a duty 'to take away life',[15] whilst Ackner L.J. stated that 'such a proposition runs wholly contrary to the concept of the sanctity of human life'.[16] The parameters of that concept and its underpinning values are explored later, but it is sufficient to note two points at this stage. The first is that the formal tort law requirements for the imposition of a duty of care are met in *McKay*, and the refusal to follow legal principle is based upon 'policy' grounds. Second, the policy objections are not pursued in relation to wrongful birth. Yet in such cases the failure of the doctor successfully to perform an abortion, or to inform parents of a foetal abnormality so as to allow abortion, has been accepted as a breach of duty giving rise to the foreseeable damage of the child's birth.[17] Why does the same analysis of duty (to 'abort or kill')[18] not apply in such cases? As Weir has written:

To assert that one cannot owe a duty to a foetus to kill it is plausible enough, but the plausibility fades a bit when one has to admit that a duty to kill the foetus may well be owed to the mother: if a duty is owed to one of the affected parties, why not to the other?[19]

## No damage

Weir does not make clear why he believes it is plausible to argue that one cannot owe a duty to kill the foetus. However, he would prefer to argue that the *McKay* claim might be most easily rejected on the basis of no damage rather than no duty, since:

> The child would not have been *better* if the defendants had done their duty: she would not have been at all. To damage is to make worse, not to make simpliciter. The child was deformed *ab initio*, just like Mr Anns's house. And just as Merton Borough Council did not damage Mr Anns's house (although they did damage him financially), so the defendants did not damage the child here (though they damaged the mother, both financially and emotionally).[20]

However, the excessive legalism which leads to the analogy of the house and the child does not produce good logic. The child here is presented as no more than a piece of property owned by the mother, but she is in reality a living person towards whom a duty may possibly arise (on Weir's analysis), and the issue is whether that child is damaged in her own right. Weir is forced to conclude not, because he begins with the statement that the child would not have been *better* if the defendants had fulfilled their duty. Yet this is precisely the issue at stake. The child alleges that non-existence would have been preferable to her life, and that she lives and suffers because of the defendants' negligence. To damage is not always to make worse in the law of tort, for it can consist of not making things better when there was a duty to do so.

In fact, in *McKay* these issues are bypassed in favour of arguments about the cause of damage; for example:

> But to make those who have not injured the child pay for that difference (the difference between the value of life as a healthy child and the value of life as an injured child) is to treat them as

if they injured the child when all they have done is not to take steps to prevent its being born injured by another cause.[21]

Ackner L.J. goes on to ask what injuries the doctor has caused, and he answers the question by saying 'none in any accepted sense'.[22] But the fact that the doctor did not cause the rubella damage does not mean that he did not cause the plaintiff to suffer under the rubella damage. But for the obvious negligence of the defendants, the plaintiff would not be suffering handicap and pain. The notion that non-existence might be preferable to such suffering will now be explored, but note that the 'no damage' argument is a policy-based assertion of the desirability in all circumstances of life over death.

### The impossibility of assessment

A related but separate reason for rejection is the impossibility of evaluating the loss suffered. All three judges rely upon this ground. Indeed for Griffiths L.J. 'the most compelling reason for rejecting this claim is the intolerable and insoluble problem it would create in the assessment of damages'.[23] It is difficult to envisage that if there is negligent breach of duty leading to foreseeable harm, otherwise deserving of compensation, the courts should deny the claim outright because it cannot devise a method of quantifying the damage. No one need pretend that this calculation is accurate any more than in a host of other situations covered by tort law. Thus in *Lim Poh Choo* v. *Camden AHA*[24] the House of Lords managed to award damages to 'a wreck of a human being'[25] existing in 'a living death'.[26] What is it that makes this state capable of evaluation whilst it is impossible to measure 'non-existence of which the court can know nothing'?[27]

There have been many similar exercises performed by the courts over time, including awards for the loss of expectation of life. Again, however, wrongful birth cases provide an immediate point of comparison. Here the judges have been prepared to assess 'the value of a child's aid, comfort and society'[28] in order to offset this against the cost of upbringing the unwanted child. This does not involve the same excursion into metaphysics as a comparison between life and non-existence, but nor is it more easily ascertainable.

The Law Commission in rejecting the possibility of an action for wrongful life considered the damages problem and concluded:

> Nor would it be easy to assess . . . the damages on any logical basis for it would be difficult to establish a norm with which the plaintiff in his disabled state could be compared. He never had a chance of being born other than disabled. We have given this problem the most careful consideration and have not, we think, been unduly influenced by these considerations of logic. Law is an artefact and, if social justice requires that there should be a remedy given for a wrong then logic should not stand in the way. A measure of damage should be artificially constructed.[29]

This is not dissimilar to the views expressed by Stephenson L. J. in *McKay* when he states that 'if public policy favoured the introduction of this novel cause of action, I would not let the strict application of logic or the absence of precedent defeat it'.[30] However, it seems impossible to reconcile this view with that expressed earlier by the same judge: 'if difficulty in assessing damages is a bad reason for refusing the task, impossibility of assessing them is a good one'.[31] If the former statement is accepted, then behind the claims of the inability of the tort system to provide compensation lies, once again, the judicial perception that the public interest is not best served by a policy of compensating the handicapped child.

Indeed, for the court which is willing to offer compensation for the negligence of the medical practitioner in wrongful life cases, there is a relatively straightforward and obvious formula to which many writers have pointed.[32] Despite judicial implications to the contrary, it was not a necessary part of the claim in *McKay* that the child should recover a sum equivalent to the whole of the rubella damage. The plaintiff child could not compare her life with that of a healthy unhandicapped child since, from the time that she contracted rubella, there was no possibility that she could have such an existence. She could claim for damages in respect of the degree to which her handicap was worsened by the negligent failure to arrest the onset of rubella. Little is said of this in *McKay*, since the case concerned the preliminary point of whether a claim for wrongful life should be allowed to stand. At this stage full details of the child's injury were unknown to the court. But, in denying the claim for wrongful life, they were happy to assume that damages could be assessed on the basis that at some point, but for the negligence of the defendants, rubella damage could have been arrested by an injection of globulins to combat the disease, leaving the child injured none the less, but by some speculatively lesser degree.

The wrongful life assessment is a no more difficult case than this. Rather than seek comparison with an existence without handicap, the child seeks a comparison between the defective life which she now possesses and the possibility that through a termination of the pregnancy she might never have existed. The objection in *McKay* is: 'how can a court begin to evaluate non-existence. "The undiscovered country from whose bourn no traveller returns." '[33] Here the courts clutch at the wrong straw. Even if they cannot evaluate non-existence, they claim to be able to place values upon life. The child in *McKay* will benefit from some of those facets of life that make it valuable. However in her case there are some benefits she will have to forgo, so that as in many personal injury cases the courts would agree that her life is reduced in value. Against these benefits she claims that she suffers positive hardships − burdens which are a part of her life which follow from the fact of her existence. Her damage flowing from the negligence would seem to be the extent to which those burdens outweigh the benefits. If they do not − and it is likely to be only in cases of severe handicap that they will − then (and only then) the courts can respond with the finding of no damage. This calculation does not seem especially unusual in a tort action, and certainly seems a sufficiently ascertainable notion of damage to allow recovery.

The above grounds form the basis of the rejection of the wrongful life claim in *McKay*, but there are a number of other obstacles placed in the way of recovery which deserve consideration because they throw more light upon the judicial usage of tort law devices as a vehicle upon which to smuggle unspoken value judgments.

### Lack of precedent

Wrongful life is described as 'a novel cause of action for or against which there is no authority in any reported case in the courts of the United Kingdom or the Commonwealth'.[34] In fact this is mistaken as it overlooks at least one Commonwealth authority,[35] but the assertion is sufficient to allow unbridled judicial hostility to the claim in the name of 'public policy' since 'allusion to policy considerations [is] exemplified by cases which [moot] a novel claim'.[36] The absence of direct authority (despite all the necessary components of a tort action) allows 'policy' to form a bulwark against what is presented as a novel and unwelcome departure from existing law.

Notwithstanding their readiness to cite the novelty of the action as a justification for the rejection of the claim, the court is prepared none the less to adopt such precedent as is available from the USA (which cases are 'of no more than persuasive authority but contain valuable material')[37] in support of their stance. These decisions, it is claimed, would lead to the rejection of the case. All three judges rely upon the decisions, although only one, Stephenson L.J., attempts any analysis of them. He rejects the approach of the 'only' decision in favour of wrongful life, *Curlender* v. *Bio-Science Laboratories*,[38] by saying that he has not found in the *Curlender* judgment 'any answer to the reasoned objections to this cause of action'.[39] Simply that – no further analysis of *Curlender* is offered but the objections are presented as 'reasoned' and by implication the decision in *Curlender* is unreasoned and unreasonable. Stephenson L.J. adds that 'California may now be coming into line with the rest: see *Turpin* v. *Sortini* (1981) 174 Cal. 128'.[40] Ironically, within three months this decision had been overturned on appeal and now stands in support of *Curlender*. The Washington Supreme Court soon followed in allowing wrongful life actions.[41]

Moreover the only decision from the USA to be subjected to anything approaching detailed analysis in *McKay* was the 1967 New Jersey case of *Gleitman* v. *Cosgrove*.[42] However, this case was heard some years before *Roe* v. *Wade*,[43] the landmark decision on abortion, in which the Supreme Court ruled (in effect) that a woman has the right to an abortion during the first trimester of pregnancy and ought not to be impermissibly denied (e.g. by state legislation) a meaningful opportunity to make her decision. In advance of *Roe* v. *Wade* it was difficult to recognize a wrongful life action depending as it does on the ability to terminate a pregnancy when this may not have been an available option. In the words of Capron: 'it is difficult to separate the abortion issue from the court's conclusion in *Gleitman*'.[44] *Gleitman* had been subject to a good deal of criticism on this and other grounds,[45] but the only academic opinion cited was an even earlier article by Tedeschi[46] which takes a firm line against the wrongful life action but is based upon that genus of case which is now referred to as dissatisfied life.[47] The New Jersey Supreme Court had, apparently unbeknown to the Court of Appeal, overruled *Gleitman* in the 1979 case of *Berman* v. *Allan*[48] – a case which Stephenson L.J. cites in *McKay*. Ironically, by 1984 New Jersey had shifted even further to allow the child to recover special damages for wrongful life.[49]

### Floodgates

The argument that to allow a claim would 'open the floodgates'[50] seems to be adopted by the courts, with little consistency, to express one of two supposed fears: either (i) that the courts will be over-whelmed in the future with claims of a similar species, or (ii) that the imposition of liability in a particular case may lead to indeterminate amounts of money awarded against an indeterminate class of defendants. This policy of rejecting otherwise valid claims is to be expected in test cases. Yet cases like *McKay* hardly hold out the prospect of thousands of actions waiting in the wings. Moreover, on the analysis offered above, the tort law system is likely only to allow compensation where the burden of the handicap outweighs the benefit of life and for the amount by which the burden outstrips the benefit. The likelihood in the legal lottery is of limited damages in rare cases.

Yet both Stephenson and Ackner L.JJ. raise the floodgates spectre lest 'a child born with a very minor disability, such as a squint, would be entitled to sue the doctor for not advising an abortion.'[51] The argument here would seem to be that if the doctor failed to detect (e.g.) foetal infection with rubella, and the child is born, but merely with a slight disability, then the child would be able to sue notwithstanding the fact that greater handicap did not befall her. Such reasoning is fundamentally flawed, since the consequences do not follow from the imposition of a duty of care. The duty exists and is breached, but damage does not result since the damage lies in being born, and no child with a squint (unhappy though the condition may be) is likely to wish to assert that non-existence would be preferable.

## Actions against the mother

If the doctor owes a duty to the foetus to prevent its birth, then in the view of the Court of Appeal the child would have a cause of action against its mother for the unreasonable refusal of an abortion.[52] This would raise complicated religious and philosophical issues, disrupt family life and cause much bitterness. So it might, if it was likely to happen, but there are a number of reasons why it could not. What is conjured up here as a ghastly spectre is, in reality, an elaborate illusion. It arises out of the formulation of the duty as one of preventing birth. If the duty is seen as one owed by the doctor to the mother, to provide the information which will form the basis of a decision on behalf of the child, then the equation falls down. It is impossible to envisage an action against the mother if the outcome of that informed choice is a live child. The mother's choice is the child's choice, for who else would we have exercise it?

Even accepting the *McKay* concept of duty – to prevent birth – why does it follow that there can be an action against the mother? Whatever the reasons for the mother's wishing to bear a handicapped child, it seems improbable in the extreme that her failure to prevent birth will result from negligence. It is unnecessarily confusing to equate her position with that of the doctor even for the purposes of formal legal analysis. It is the doctor's negligence which will deny to the mother the right to make a conscious decision to give birth to a child in the knowledge of the probability of that child's disability. Assertions of the possibility of the action against the mother implicitly refute the woman's autonomy in birth choices. Even if there was a technical possibility of such actions, the judiciary could thwart them and reassert the woman's choice – by a policy restriction upon such actions. Whereas elsewhere the judiciary claim the role of trainers and handlers of a law obedient to their policy, when it suits them they are happy to recast themselves as dealing with a law which they struggle to control lest it slips the harness and runs amok.[53]

Two final points illustrate the scaremongering nature of the concept of an action against the mother. One is the simple and obvious point that the action would need to be brought by the parent as 'next friend'. Even if the mother chose to sue herself, the damages would take the form of the money which a parent would expend upon upkeep of the child ordinarily, without a court award.

The second is that the mother is given immunity from liability in respect of antenatal injury by virtue of s.1 of the 1976 Act. The court can hardly claim ignorance of this statute since its existence rendered the action in *McKay* as not one of 'general public importance'.[54]

## Action by the mother

In contrast it was also said that the mother might sue – rather than be sued – by bringing an action in negligence for wrongful birth, thus undermining the necessity for its wrongful life counterpart. Yet such an action would have been no less novel in English law. The only case prior to 1982[55] had been brought in contract and that had failed to make any award in respect of the child's upbringing by restricting damages to reliance losses under the contract. In Canada, the wrongful birth case of *Cataford* v. *Moreau*[56] had rejected the claim for the cost of upbringing the eleventh child of a native Indian family 'in very humble circumstances' following a failed sterilization performed upon the mother. The court were reluctant to allow the family to 'cash in on their healthy child'. The additional burden of his arrival was outweighed by 'moral and financial advantages'. The husband was awarded damages for 'the loss of consortium of his wife'.

Against this background, Mrs McKay can hardly be blamed for taking a less than rosy view of her prospects of success in a wrongful birth action before a male-dominated judiciary whose thinking is typified by cases in which loss of sexual favours to the man is seemingly ranked a greater loss than that stemming from the unwanted consequences of those favours – an eleventh child in the family unit. Indeed the post-*McKay* English cases threatened to follow the Canadian path.[57] The following passage from *Udale* v. *Bloomsbury AHA*, which refused to countenance the cost of the child's upkeep as a separate head of damage, is illustrative of a similar view:

> A plaintiff such as Mrs Udale would get little or no damages because her love and care for her child and her joy, ultimately, at his birth would be set off against, and might cancel out, the inconvenience and financial disadvantages which naturally accompany parenthood. By contrast, a plaintiff who nurtures

bitterness in her heart and refuses to let her maternal instincts take over would be entitled to large damages. In short virtue would go unrewarded; unnatural rejection of womanhood and motherhood would be generously compensated.[58]

In subsequent cases, the notion of setting-off damages or barring recovery has been gradually overcome. However, the battle has been one in which arguments have concentrated largely upon technical legal concepts such as *novus actus interveniens*, mitigation of damage, reliance losses, etc., without any call for a fundamental reappraisal of the suitability of those concepts as a tool for analysis. Thus, even if the eventual answer is no, there is no hesitation in posing the question of whether a woman ought not to undergo an abortion in these cases in order reasonably to mitigate her loss.[59]

Moreover, it is by no means clear that the battle is won simply because some costs of upkeep are awarded. In 1984 in *Emeh* v. *Kensington AHA*,[60] Mrs Emeh was awarded a sum of £507 per annum in respect of her child's maintenance. At the time, she was separated from her husband. In 1986 in *Thake* v. *Morris*,[61] the Court of Appeal approved an assessment based upon costs of a baby's upkeep to first birthday of £717. As was said at first instance:

> They have made their calculation on the basis of the supplementary benefit scales. This is right. Samantha has been born into a humble household and the defendants should not be expected to do more than provide her with necessities.[62]

This was Mrs Thake's sixth child by her railway guard husband. All lived in a three-bedroomed council house in which three of the boys shared one bedroom and the two girls shared with another brother. Mrs Thake had worked, when possible, as a cleaner, and provided for the children by shopping at jumble sales. In such contexts the tort law framework of compensation is exposed as a mechanism for the legitimation and maintenance of existing forms of economic domination – especially domination of women.

### Defensive medicine

Not surprisingly the tort law system has its defenders amongst those whose economic interests it serves. However, in the face of overwhelming evidence as to its inefficiency as a mechanism for compensation, it has become fashionable to propound its deterrent qualities. Within the context of biomedical technology we might anticipate an argument that tort law can provide the vehicle for standard-setting within this developing field. However, as with medical negligence claims generally, the reality is a judicial reluctance to invoke principles of deterrence when faced with 'the professional man'.[63] Rather we are offered the figment of defensive medicine, and in *McKay* we see a particularly extreme account of this in the argument that an action for wrongful life might actually lower professional standards. Two judges make reference to reports of the Law Commission and to the Royal Commission on Civil Liability and embrace the reasoning of the latter[64] (quoting the Mothers' Union):

> if [wrongful life] actions were allowed, a doctor would be obliged to urge a woman to have an abortion if there was the slightest chance that her child would be born defective.

and the former,[65] who point to

> the danger that doctors would be under subconscious pressures to advise abortions in doubtful cases through the fear of an action for damages.

Accepting that we have a law which labels cases as doubtful or (presumably) meritorious, this seems a particularly sinister form of the defensive medicine argument, since it asserts that doctors will respond to wrongful life actions by acting unlawfully. There is no other way to describe actions such as *'urging'* abortion or advising it outside the scope of the 1967 Act. Not to allow compensation to A, on the basis that it might cause B to engage in unlawful activity at the expense of C, is a form of moral blackmail which the judiciary would decry in many other contexts. If uttered by any other critic, this type of allegation concerning the likely behaviour of doctors would be met by resentful indignation on the part of the medical establishment. Moreover, since the same negligent conduct may give rise to a wrongful birth action which the courts will now countenance, it seems illogical to deny wrongful life actions on the basis that only in these cases will defensive medicine be practised.

## POLICY ISSUES

It was stated by Stephenson L.J. that 'it would be . . . against public policy for the courts to entertain [wrongful life] claims'.[66] We are not told which precise policy is at issue, but he makes specific reference to 'the sanctity of life'.[67] Ackner L.J. is more direct. The wrongful life action 'runs wholly contrary to the concept of the sanctity of human life'.[68] Teff has pointed to an intriguing paradox here. To assert the primacy of life 'logically entails the measurability *in principle* of non-existence, simply by virtue of the assertion that it is necessarily worth less than life in any form'.[69] Thus the policy issue at stake here sits uneasily alongside other legal analysis both in this case and elsewhere.

### Selective non-treatment

The courts have had to face the proposition that it may be in the child's best interests to die. Indeed they have accepted such a proposition in the context of selective non-treatment. Thus in *Re B*[70] although the Court of Appeal used its wardship jurisdiction to allow a local authority to authorize and direct life-saving treatment for a Down's syndrome child, it was accepted that the criteria for deciding whether to preserve life was the 'best interests of the child'.[71] This entails the implication that there will be cases where the court would feel that it was not in the best interests of the child to insist upon life-saving treatment. This may be, as Templeman L.J. stated, in the case 'where the child's life is so bound to be full of pain and suffering'.[72] *Re B* was cited in *McKay* but the above statement was said to be a concession for the sake of argument.[73] The basis upon which we must place this construction upon Lord Templeman's words is not explained. Instead we are further told that the opinions in *Re B* are *obiter*. They result from 'an urgent application' which was made 'in the vacation and the two judgments were *ex tempore*'.[74]

Stephenson L.J. in *McKay* is not quite so sceptical about the quality of judicial reasoning during holiday periods. He disposes of the possibility of selective non-treatment raised by Templeman L.J. by saying that 'I would not answer the question until it is necessary to do so'.[75] Yet he does answer the question, albeit unwittingly, and in a particularly stark manner – by reference to the public policy criteria of the sanctity of life. For if it is against public policy to entertain claims that babies may be better off dead, then the public policy is that babies are always better off alive. We cannot administer DF118 so that a severely handicapped baby dies free of pain. We cannot offer 'Nursing Care Only', and passively allow a handicapped child to die which would have lived with food and nursing and the like.[76] We cannot allow children with fatal but remediable defects to die. We must positively strive on all occasions to keep them alive, for that is always in their best interests. This is unpalatable. Unless the judges themselves would be prepared to opt to live their lives in states of severe physical and mental handicap then they have no right to enforce that existence upon other children, at least (and we need take the argument no further than this) where, but for the absence of positive surgical intervention, the child would die quickly and naturally. Moreover, since public policy is said to reflect public sentiment,[77] it is not improper to take account of the common, perhaps intuitive, feeling that it would be preferable not to exist in certain states of disability.

### The value of life

Moreover, it is beyond argument that we do not as a society place a value upon life that even approaches 'sanctity'. Indeed we could depict the tort law system as mediating in the aftermath of life-taking or disabling activities which it not only permits but probably bolsters. Central to the concept of a requisite standard of care is the notion that certain activities entail risks which may be outweighed by the benefit which is seen to result from them. Thus the loss of production during a night shift is too great a price to pay for the elimination of a potentially disabling injury to a worker.[78] It is true, and it may even be vital to the continuation of the process, that we leave such values unspoken. But that is not to say that they are not part of our law. It is no less plausible to assert that, rather than treating life as sacrosanct, the courts are inexorably involved in a system which cheapens life by exposing some lives to threat for comparatively trivial rewards for other people.[79]

Within the framework of the legal regulation of health care, the issue of life choices is no longer a matter of academic dispute but a pressing reality. Health authorities are recruiting health economists to assist with the prioritizing of competing claims for health care resources. Demand for such resources is escalating and will continue to do so, but there is a limit to which society is prepared to foot the bill – hence rationing. This implies choices made amongst competing applicants for welfare services. As yet, law imposes few requirements with a view to ensuring a fair and accountable process by which choices can be made.[80] Economists have been more ready to provide a solution – latterly in the form of QUALY (Quality Adjusted Life Year).[81] This formula involves the ranking of certain states of health as less desirable than others. In the final analysis it permits those with the best chance of a prolonged post-operative life of good quality to live; and others to die.

It may be that such processes will escape legal challenge in the future, and that lawyers may be happy to concede this ground to economists. But neither seems likely. More probably judges will be called upon to arbitrate, in which case statements that life is beyond value or the espousal of the 'sanctity of life' will not assist greatly. By excluding themselves from the battlefield now, the judiciary may find it difficult to re-enter the war which will surely wage in the future. On performance thus far this may be no bad thing.

## UNDERPINNING VALUES

Thus far this paper has sought to assert that the overt policy claim of the sanctity of life is an emotive appeal of dubious philosophical pedigree, inconsistent with other legal standpoints. If this is so then it is necessary to seek to locate underpinning and unspoken values pertaining to the judicial interpretation of the wrongful life problem. It is suggested that these form part of a wider political debate concerning control of health care provision, and that they may be summarized in a series of polemical statements which would assert the judiciary to prefer:

- medical paternalism in advance of patient autonomy;
- male dominance over the reproductive choices of women;
- a legal forum for the resolution of issues of medical ethics.

It is obvious that the final preference is capable of advancing the earlier two. We see in the case of wrongful life that the very categorization of problems assists in the determination of outcomes. Thus there is a battle for compensation in the absence of a contract – a tort problem. The adoption of the concept 'tort' may now be imposed upon shaping the lines of argument. A protestation by the woman that she has been wronged by the denial of her choice in the birth of a handicapped child is relevant only in so far as it advances the claim for compensation, and in this case, where the action is brought by the child, it is largely irrelevant. Thus the process of legal classification confers the attribute of significance on certain facts alone. We see a narrowing of this focus as the particular elements of the tort are then considered. It is this which allows the Court of Appeal in *McKay* to isolate the duty as that of terminating another's existence. In so framing the duty the court implicitly denies an alternative analysis: that the duty is to inform as to likely handicap, and since the mother is the only person who ought to be permitted to decide on behalf of the foetus, then in order to be meaningful, the information must be imparted to the mother. Failure to fulfil this duty may give rise to actionable damage on the part of the child. The latter interpretation respects autonomy in so far as this is possible, and leaves choices concerning pregnancy and childbirth vested in the woman. The interpretation of duty actually adopted denies choice by placing the continuing control over informed decisions in the hands of the (predominantly male) medical profession under the supervision of their legal counterparts.

This supervisory jurisdiction is maintained and supported by the process of classification. In order to satisfy the demands of the legal concepts of damage and causation, the plaintiff finds it necessary to assert the preferability of non-existence over life. This is a legal fiction[82] which conceals a far more basic assertion – that handicapped children need financial support. Perhaps the reason for the fiction is its intrinsic lack of appeal. It is far easier to deny an assertion of the attraction of non-existence than the more basic claim for the support of society. Since society will choose to refuse that support, it is possible to countenance its rejection when it is presented in a sufficiently distasteful manner. Equally it is more convenient to convince ourselves that it is some failure to meet essential legal criteria which leaves Mary McKay uncompensated, rather than society's refusal adequately to provide for the handicapped.

Thus in this area, and in many others, where medical advance demands the resolution of ethical issues, disputes will be resolved in the courts. It does not matter that the legal framework may be particularly ill-suited to the task. Rather that is its advantage, for ethics are not easy. How much better if harsh choices can be obscured in the seemingly technical neutrality of statutory interpretation and the application of precedent. It might be thought that if we could face squarely the issue of whether handicapped children deserve financial support, irrespective of cause, life would be much simpler. But sadly, it is easier to obscure the issue by debating the intriguing question of whether that simpler life is preferable to non-existence.

## NOTES

1 American studies have shown that some 6–9 per cent of paediatric admissions have unambiguous genetic disorder. See Maxine A. Sonnenburg, 'A preference for non-existence: wrongful life and a proposed tort of genetic malpractice', *Southern California Law Review*, vol. 55 (1982), p. 477, pp. 482–3 and the works cited therein. It is claimed that up to 40 per cent of childhood deaths are in part attributable to genetic factors. See also W. Reilly 'Genetic counselling: a legal perspective', in Y. Hsia, K. Hirscharn, and R. Silverberg (eds), *Counselling in Genetics* (New York: Liss, 1979), p. 311.

2 Difficulties may arise where the plaintiff is a heterozygous carrier (i.e. not bearing a handicap but bearing the genes by which that handicap may be passed on) as opposed to a homozygous carrier.

3 The likelihood of this disease for a woman aged between 35 and 40 is 1 in 280, but over 40 the risk increases to 1 in 50; see F. Chapman, 'What are your odds in the prenatal gamble?' *Legal Aspects of Medical Practice*, vol. 31 (March 1979), p. 32.

4 H. Teff, 'The action for wrongful life in England and the United States', *International and Comparative Law Quarterly*, vol. 34 (1985), p. 423; and see also J. S. Kashi, 'The case of the unwanted blessing: "wrongful life" ', *University of Miami Law Review*, vol. 31 (1977), p. 1409.

5 It is increasingly common in the USA, however, to confine the term 'wrongful life' only to those cases concerned with negligent failure to inform of handicap so as to disallow contraception or termination, and to label those cases concerning the birth of a healthy child (usually due to failed sterilization, abortion or contraception) 'wrongful pregnancy'. Indeed there is an earlier category of 'dissatisfied life' cases, an early form of wrongful life (see, for example, *Zepeda* v. *Zepeda* 4 Ill. App. (2d) 240, 190 N.E. (2d) 849 (1963) in which the claim is brought by a healthy though illegitimate child claiming injury on the grounds of illegitimate status, and wrongful death is used to apply to cases in which life was terminated when it should not have been; see generally T. K. Foutz, 'Wrongful life: the right not to be born', *Tulane Law Review*, vol. 54 (1980), p. 480, at pp. 483–6.

6 This is true also for the USA where recovery for wrongful life is recognized in only certain jurisdictions; see *Curlender* v. *Bio-Science Laboratories*

106 Cal. App. (3d) 811, 165 Cal. Rptr 477 (1980); *Siemieniec* v. *Lutheran General Hospital* 134 Ill. App. (3d) 823, 480 N.E. (2d) 1227 (1985); *Procanik* v. *Cillo* 97 N.J. 339; 478 A. (2d) 755 (1984); *Azzolino* v. *Dingfelder* 71 N. C. App. 289; 322 S.E. (2d) 567 (1984); *Harbeson* v. *Parke-Davis Inc.* 98 Wash (2d) 460, 656 P. (2d) 483 (1983); *Turpin* v. *Sortini* 31 Cal. (3d) 220, 643 P. (2d) 954, 182 Cal. Rptr 337 (1982). The more recent trend is towards recognition of the claim.

7 [1982] Q.B. 1166. Hereafter page number references only are given in the *McKay* judgment.

8 Law Commission, *Report on Injuries to Unborn Children*, Report no. 60, Cmnd 5709 (London: HMSO, 1974), paras 85–91. Section 1 of the Act is the same as clause 1 of the draft bill annexed to the Report.

9 See now s. 1(2)(*b*) of the 1976 Act.

10 At p. 1187.

11 *Per* Griffiths L.J. at p. 1190.

12 Grounds (i) – (iv) are supported by Stephenson and Ackner L. JJ. with Griffiths L.J. relying primarily on ground (iii) but also supporting ground (i).

13 See s. 1(1) and (2) of the Act. These issues may be significant in cases where the transfusion of the mother's blood with an incorrect blood group may cause injury to a child later conceived; see, for example, *Renslow* v. *Mennanite Hospital* 67 Ill (2d) 348, 367 N.E. (2d) 1250 (1977).

14 *Per* Stephenson L.J. at p. 1178.

15 At p. 1179.

16 At p. 1188.

17 For those wrongful birth cases see *Scuriaga* v. *Powell* [1979] 123 S.J. 406; *Udale* v. *Bloomsbury AHA* [1983] 2 All E.R. 522; *Emeh* v. *Kensington & Chelsea AHA* [1985] 1 Q.B. 1012; *Thake* v. *Maurice* [1986] 1 Q.B. 669; *Gold* v. *Haringey HA* [1987] 3 W.L.R. 649.

18 See also (at p. 1178) 'abortion and death'. This analysis of abortion is used throughout by Stephenson L.J. There is no explanation of why abortion should be equated with killing, or upon what basis the foetus is accorded personhood.

19 T. Weir, 'Wrongful life – nipped in the bud' *Cambridge Law Journal* [1982], p. 225, at p. 227.

20 ibid., p. 227 – a reference to *Anns* v. *London Borough of Merton* [1978] A.C. 728.

21 *Per* Stephenson L.J. at p. 1181.

22 At p. 1189.

23 At p. 1192.

24 [1979] Q.B. 196 (C.A.); [1980] A.C. 176 (H.L.).

25 [1979] Q.B. 196 at p. 214. 'She was brought back to life. The more's the pity of it! For it was a living death', *per* Lord Denning M.R.: the full quotation may be relevant.

26 [1980] A.C. 176 at p. 182, *per* Lord Scarman.

27 *Per* Griffiths L.J. at p. 1193.

28 *Emeh; Thake*, and see also *Scuriaga*. On this issue generally, see C. R. Symmons, 'Policy factors in actions for wrongful birth', *Modern Law*

*Review*, vol. 50 (1982), p. 269; W. V. Horton Rogers, 'Legal implications of ineffective sterilization', *Legal Studies*, vol. 5 (1985), p. 296.
29 At para. 89.
30 At p. 1184.
31 At p. 1182.
32 See Teff, 'The action for wrongful life' and the American literature cited therein.
33 *Per* Ackner L.J. at p. 1189. The judges in *McKay* equate non-existence with death throughout – a stance which in itself raises interesting philosophical and theological issues.
34 *Per* Stephenson L.J. at p. 1177.
35 See *Cataford* v. *Moreau* (1978) 114 D.L.R. (3d) 585 and G. Robertson, 'Wrongful life', *Modern Law Review*, vol. 45, (1982), pp. 697–701. The case of *Kambouroglou* v. *Crown St. Women's Hospital* 2 Dec. 1980 (NSW Sup. Ct) (unreported, but see P. Hersch, 'Tort liability for "wrongful life" ', *University of New South Wales Law Journal*, vol. 6 (1983), p. 133) would have supported a wrongful life claim on the facts, since having been told of the likely handicap of her child, the plaintiff was mistakenly and negligently told she was not pregnant when she sought an abortion. The child was born handicapped but the plaintiff pursued an action only on her own behalf – i.e. a wrongful birth claim.
36 Allan Hutchinson and Derek Morgan, 'The Canengusian connection: the kaleidoscope of tort theory', *Osgoode Hall Law Journal*, vol. 22 (1984), p. 69, at p. 27.
37 *Per* Stephenson L.J. at p. 1182.
38 (1980) 165 Cal. Rptr 477.
39 At p. 1183. The objections referred to are those in *Gleitman* v. *Cosgrove* (n. 42 below).
40 At p. 1183.
41 *Harbeson* v. *Parke-Davis Inc.* 656 P. (2d) 483 (1983). See also the decision of the Supreme Court of Israel allowing wrongful life, Civil Appeal 518/82, 540/82 noted in *Medicine and Law*, vol. 6 (1987), p. 373.
42 227 A (2d) 689, (1967).
43 410 US 113 (1973).
44 A. M. Capron, 'Tort liability in genetic counselling', *Columbia Law Review*, vol. 79 (1979), p. 618, at p. 635.
45 A. M. Capron, 'Legal rights and moral rights' in J. M. Humber and R. F. Alemeder (eds), *Biomedical Ethics and the Law*, 2nd edn (New York: Plenum Press, 1979), p. 397; Foutz, 'Wrongful life'; Sonnenburg, 'Preference for non-existence', p. 492; Kashi, 'Case of the unwanted blessing'.
46 G. Tedeschi, 'On tort liability for "Wrongful life" ', vol. 1 (1966), p. 529.
47 *Zepeda* v. *Zepeda* 41 Ill. App. (2d) 240, 190 N.E. (2d) 849 (1963) and *Williams* v. *New York* 18 N.Y. (2d) 481, 223 N.E. (2d) 343 (1966).
48 404 A. (2d) 8 (1979). See the judgment of Handler J. in *Procanik* v. *Cillo* 478 A. (2d) 755 at p. 765 (NJ 1984): 'These rulings (in *Berman*) overruled *Gleitman* v. *Cosgrove*.'

49 *Procanik* (n. 48 above). The score now stands at three states in favour of wrongful life and eight against.

50 I am referring here, of course, to the floodgates of the Stockton Waterworks Company – see *Cattle* v. *Stockton Waterworks Co.* (1875) L.R. 10 Q.B. 453 at p. 457 *per* Blackburn J.

51 *Per* Ackner L.J. at p. 1188.

52 At p. 1188; cf. *Young* v. *Rankin* [1934] S.C. 499, 508, *McCallion* v. *Dodd* [1966] NZLR 710.

53 I am referring here, of course, to Burrough J.'s unruly horse; see *Richardson* v. *Mellish* (1824) 2 Bing 229 at p. 252.

54 See n. 10 above.

55 *Scuriaga*, n. 17 above.

56 n. 33 above.

57 n. 17 above.

58 At p. 531.

59 See S. Bloxham, R. Lee, and A. McGee, 'Wrongful birth: the English conception', *Professional Negligence*, vol. 1 (1985), p. 126.

60 n. 17 above.

61 n. 17 above.

62 At p. 668.

63 See *Whitehouse* v. *Jordan* [1980] 1 All E.R. 650 C.A. at p. 658 *per* Denning M.R.: 'We must say, and say firmly, that, in a professional man, an error of judgment is not negligent.'

64 *Royal Commission on Civil Liability and Compensation for Personal Injury,* Cmnd 7054–1 (London: HMSO, 1978), para. 1485.

65 Law Commission, *Injuries to Unborn Children*, para. 89.

66 At p. 1184.

67 At p. 1180.

68 At p. 1188.

69 Teff, 'The action for wrongful life in England and the United States', p. 433; and see Capron, 'Tort liability in genetic counselling', p. 650.

70 *In Re B (A Minor) (Wardship: Medical Treatment)* [1981] 1 W.L.R. 1421.

71 At p. 1422.

72 At p. 1424.

73 *Per* Ackner L.J. at p. 1188.

74 At p. 1188.

75 At p. 1180. This is, of course, a favourite device of courts faced with difficult issues.

76 See *R* v. *Arthur* (1981), *Times*, 6 November 1981, and Chapter 11 in this volume.

77 See Weir, 'Wrongful life – nipped in the bud', p. 227.

78 *Latimer* v. *AEC Ltd* [1953] A.C. 643 in which the appellant was unable to establish that a reasonably careful employer could have guarded against his injury, following a flood at a factory, by closing down the factory for a time.

79 For a similar analysis see Guido Calabresi, 'The gift of the evil deity', in his *Ideals, Beliefs, Attitudes and Law* (New York: Syracuse University Press, 1985).

80 See A. Parkin, 'Public law and the provision of health care', *Urban Law and Policy*, vol. 7 (1985), p. 101.

81 For a clear account of the QUALY, see A. Williams, 'The economic role of "health indicators" ', in G. Teeling-Smith (ed.), *Measuring the Social Benefits of Medicine* (London: OHE, 1983). Readers may care to note that the concept of a QUALY attaches minus scores to certain health states in recognition that there may be fates worse than death; see P. Kind, R. Rosser, and A. Williams, 'Valuation of quality of life: some psychometric evidence', in M. Jones-Lee (ed.), *The Value of Life and Safety* (Amsterdam: North Holland, 1982).

82 A legal fiction is an ancient procedural legal rule which assumes as true without argument something which is in all probability false.

# 11

# 'OTHERWISE KILL ME': MARGINAL CHILDREN AND ETHICS AT THE EDGES OF EXISTENCE

## CELIA WELLS

The appropriate management of handicapped newborn babies presents issues of morality, legality, and economics. It throws into relief judgments made about women and their relationship with childbirth. Whereas infanticide is often represented as an irrational act on the part of a mother disturbed by childbirth, as a rational response to the failure of a baby to fit the appropriate culturally determined criteria it has long historical continuity.[1] Those criteria are now refracted and challenged by developments in western medical technology. Far more low-birthweight babies can be saved than ten or twenty years ago and technological sophistication means that babies with multiple problems can be operated on and live, whereas before they died. Indeed, the survival of many of these babies would have been *unthinkable* a decade ago. Yet, the non-treatment of some physically or mentally handicapped newborn babies is a widespread practice in hospital neonatal units.[2] Is this merely part of our present cultural expression of preference, just as the desire for male progeny is culturally significant in other parts of the world?[3] Or has the introduction of the possibility of life being maintained with only the utmost physical and medical support, introduced questions of a different order? Posed starkly, are some lives destined to be so unthinkably painful, technology-dependent or purposeless that efforts should not be made to save them?

In the United States non-treatment of handicapped newborns has become a matter of Federal intervention.[4] But in the United Kingdom the issue has been largely hidden or ignored. Many people seem unaware of the extent to which non-treatment is, or has until recently, been practised in neonatal intensive care units. The option of sustaining the lives of severely damaged children is one side effect of the significant reduction in infant mortality since the Second World War.[5] Improvements in neonatology techniques have, however, merely exacerbated the problem of 'marginal children' who 'will probably always be a by product of producing more intact children'.[6] Suppose that while before such developments two out of five premature babies might have survived, one intact and one marginal, now five could survive, three intact and two marginal.[7] It would be difficult to argue that this would not represent progress if the production of healthy people is viewed as an inherent good. Yet how do we accommodate the suffering brought to the survivors? And is the sum of extra suffering a net social loss or a gross personal gain, because any sort of life is always worth more than the suffering involved in attaining or sustaining it?

The debate provoked by non-treatment needs to be contextualized. Questions are generated such as whether we subscribe to a belief in the sanctity of life, what that means if we do; what value we place on quality of life; what significance has disability to society, to disabled people and to the people who care for them? Before reviewing the philosophical discussions and considering legal responses, it might then be helpful to map a path between factual medical accounts of decision-making in neonatal intensive care, the stories of some parents of handicapped children and the voices of some adult disabled people; to colour in some contours between the plateaux of medical technology and the foothills of personal experience.

It is only in the last fifteen years that the implications of the increased production of damaged children for practices in neonatal care have begun to be discussed openly, even in medical journals. What has emerged since Duff and Campbell broke 'the public and professional silence on a major social taboo',[8] in 1973 is much less diversity of approach between different hospitals or on international comparisons than might have been expected. There are dissentient voices, of course, both within and between hospitals,[9] but the main impression is that the most forceful opposition to non-treatment comes from those who have the least contact with neonatal units. The core of the dilemma facing paediatricians in neonatal units is twofold: whether to use high-technology life-support machines to prolong the lives of infants with profound neurological or other physical abnormalities, and whether to resuscitate extremely low-birthweight babies. During a four-year period seventy-five infants in the regional neonatal intensive care unit at Hammersmith hospital were assessed as having such poor prognoses that withdrawal of treatment was seriously discussed.[10] The hospital's criterion for non-treatment or withdrawal of treatment has been near-certainty of death or no meaningful life. If all the medical and nursing staff agreed that even with maximum support there was virtual certainty of total incapacity or of a very short survival for only days or weeks, then the parents would be asked whether they agreed to withdrawal of maximum support. In fifty-one of the original seventy-five cases (68 per cent) the medical decision was to cease treatment. The parents agreed in forty-seven (92 per cent) of these and all of the babies died. Of the four for whom the parents wanted treatment to continue, two survived and two died. Of the twenty-four (32 per cent) for whom the medical decision was to continue treatment, seventeen (71 per cent) survived long term, although six had severe disabilities and eight were normal or near normal. And, in an eighteen-month period in their hospital unit in New Haven, Duff and Campbell reported that 14 per cent of deaths were associated with withdrawal of treatment (compared with 66 per cent dying from pathological conditions despite treatment).[11] These acute dilemmas arise in only a tiny proportion of live births; babies born at 27 weeks gestation or earlier represent 0.05 per cent of live births, genetic disorders occur in less than 5 per cent of live births and chromosomal disorders in less than 0.5 per cent.[12] The mortality rate for extremely premature babies of under 25 weeks gestation and weighing less than 1,000 grams can be as high as 90 per cent, with or without intensive care. Babies who manage between 1,000 and 1,500 grams at birth benefit in terms of lower mortality rates from intensive intervention but not in terms of morbidity.[13]

Consistency of neonatal practice in itself may, of course, tell us nothing of moral arguments. The apparent consensus may be attributable to the self-selection of those who are prepared to confront life-and-death issues as part of their working lives in hospitals. But it could be that the general lack of dissent is of significance, that it is part of the context of the debate. Parents of severely defective newborns do not encounter these dilemmas every day, yet the clamour to treat does not usually come from them. They could merely be falling under the spell and informational power of the medical profession, but their responses may tell us something about what people feel about the difficulties facing disabled children, disabled adults, and those who care for them. Especially when those problems are about to invade their own lives.

Neonatal care is 'a social practice that, by its logic, employs both technical and moral languages'.[14] The voice of the parents of one baby maintained through five months of high medical technology speaks eloquently of the suffering that they felt on their own and on their son's behalf. He was born prematurely at 24½ weeks weighing 800 grams (1lb. 12oz.):

> He was 'saved' by the respirator to die 5 long, painful and expensive months later of the respirator's side effects . . . As Andrew's parents, we had a heightened sense of his suffering. Also, we feared the prospect of having to care for the rest of our lives for a pathetically handicapped and retarded child. If this is considered less than noble, what then is the appropriate label for the willingness to apply the latest experimental technology to salvage such a high-risk child and then to hand him over to the life long care of someone else?

> We believe there is a moral and ethical problem of the most fundamental sort involved in a system which allows complicated decisions of this nature to be made unilaterally by people who do not have to live with the consequences of their decisions.[15]

There is certainly support for the conclusion that this is not an isolated viewpoint amongst parents of damaged children, even where those children have survived to become part of a loving family. Parents of Down's syndrome children are more likely to favour abortion (77 per cent of a sample of seventy-eight parents) than euthanasia (48 per cent) of severely handicapped babies, although only 37 per cent thought that an average Down's syndrome child came within the category of severe handicap.[16] A survey of mothers of severely mentally handicapped young adults showed 10 out of 15 wishing in retrospect they could have had an abortion and 12 out of 15 favouring allowing such infants to die in peace rather than have their lives saved by medical treatment.[17] A number of lawsuits challenging the legality of parents' decisions to withhold consent to treatment has led to Federal intervention in the United

States and the promulgation of regulations which more or less require resuscitative efforts to be made with all newborns. In the UK, however, the publicity given to the trial of Leonard Arthur in 1981 for attempted murder after withholding treatment and nutrition from a Down's syndrome baby has not led to similar attempts at control.[18] An opinion poll conducted at the time of the *Arthur* trial revealed that four-fifths of the respondents believed that doctors should not be found guilty of murder in such circumstances.[19] This is despite the fact that few of those who argue that non-treatment can be justified in some circumstances propose criteria which would include the baby in the *Arthur* case. This irony was compounded five years later in the adverse publicity given to the removal for transplant of the heart of an anencephalic baby before it was clinically dead. Such a baby would, on all proponents' criteria, be suitable for non-treatment because its life was not viable.[20]

Is support for non-treatment anything more than a reflection of western society's attitudes to able-bodiedness and able-mindedness? Disability triggers fears in our culture with its obsession with health and well-being. Is institutionalization 'an outgrowth of the assumption that neither the parents nor the community could cope with the child at home: the family, friends and community are never exposed to the child and its actual needs, so dreaded fantasies reinforce stereotypes'?[21] Would the parents in the surveys have different views if women were not oppressed as the under-resourced sole caretakers of children?

Decision-making for women over a broad spectrum of issues connected with reproduction, childbirth and child care is of course mediated by expectations and constructions of their 'true role'. The defective neonate is sometimes the product of the 'technological fix',[22] through which reproduction has become institutionalized as a medical phenomenon,[23] and epitomizes one characteristic of the development of reproductive technologies: that a solution has to be found to every problem. It is not possible, however, simply to solve the dilemma of non-treatment by improving conditions of parenthood nor by restoring power in the reproductive field. High technology brings benefits to viable babies who are going to emerge as healthy, normal children and adults. Where neonatal care is 'successful' (the quotation marks acknowledge the problematic nature of that judgment) it has a higher pay off than any other branch of medicine, ensuring the potential for 60–70 years more life.[24] It is inappropriate, however, to see the issue solely in one set of terms, whether it be medical technology and power or oppressive social structures, which affect women and/or disabled people.

## THE ETHICS

Does non-treatment of a neonate raise the same ethical problems as euthanasia, the idea of which as a relief from chronic pain is widely accepted and has been given some legal endorsement?[25] The question has two dimensions; the first is a general one about whether there is a moral difference between killing and letting die. The second is more particular and relates to whether there are any relevant features distinguishing a newborn baby from other persons, such that action which would be regarded as unacceptable in relation to the latter is not so regarded in relation to the former.

Although *legal* writers often concentrate on the distinction between acts and omissions[26] it is at one and the same time both a non-issue and an extremely powerful cosmetic device. It allows people to condone killing without actually appearing to support it. It has been described as the 'philosophically scandalous but quite proper administrative – ethical distinction'.[27] But such props which facilitate the making of hard choices should be seen for what they are and not as moral determinants in themselves. An additional argument is that the moral response may depend on what is being withheld: is it basic nutrition or an expensive operation?[28] Roman Catholic theology, for instance, recognizes a distinction between ordinary and extraordinary treatment, although this is not necessarily the same as the difference between basic care and more complex forms of treatment. Under this doctrine, efforts to treat a patient can be withheld where the treatment is unlikely significantly to prolong life, is unlikely significantly to correct the patient's condition and is likely to cause more harm than relief. Only where all these criteria are met does the doctrine allow some efforts to preserve life to be abandoned. Of course what is extraordinary treatment is not a fixed variable but depends on the particular context.[29] Although it represents a disciplined attempt to justify non-treatment in *some* cases, the doctrine is difficult to apply in practice.[30] To argue that there can be a moral difference between, on the one hand, withdrawing life-sustaining treatment in the form of surgical operation, ventilation, or antibiotics to combat infection and, on the other, refusing nutrition or actually giving a lethal injection, is not very convincing. The doctrine operates more as a means of authorizing non-treatment in a few hopeless cases than as a useful tool for determining non-treatment in a wider sense. If it involves arguing that there is a difference between sustaining all possible life and withholding antibiotics if an infection should develop, it avoids the central issue. And that is the selectivity by which *some* babies are given the benefit of all the measures available in the intensive care unit while others are not.

Certainly at some point the allocation of resources has to be considered. Assuming limited access to high technology treatment, on what basis should selection be made? This sort of process already occurs in the decision of whether a baby is referred to a regional neonatal unit in the first place. In his extremely sensitive study of one such unit in the United States, Frohock found that admission decisions were based on a principle of triage (that is the selection of those babies who will most benefit, with the best chance for survival), but that once in the nursery treatment decisions were based on need.[31] While resource allocation is a subject which has generated much literature, it does not allow a sufficiently fine focus for the issue of selective non-treatment. It is important to confront this initially outside the constraints of resource allocation in order to discover whether there are any reasons why non-treatment should in itself be a good thing; that is, whether even if resources became plentiful it would be justifiable not to treat some babies. It is because this is the central issue, that distinctions between acts and omissions, between killing and letting die, are irrelevant. Where people are under a duty to care, as are doctors and parents, a decision not to treat is as much a decision to kill as a decision actively to end the baby's life.

The paradox is that hospitals practise *non-treatment* through a mirage of *treatment*. The principles generally applied are that there should be nursing care, feeding on demand (though not by tube) and no antibiotics following infection.[32] There are some disagreements about when to invoke these regimes, or 'bizarre games' as the Stinsons characterize them.[33] In relation to spina bifida many hospitals use the criteria described by Lorber which concentrate on prediction of severe disability and chronic pain.[34] But equally there are doctors who doubt whether accurate prognoses can be made.[35] And prognosis is complicated where the treatment itself becomes a cause of additional damage, as in the development of 'respirator lung syndrome' a condition which was unknown before the use of infant respirators.[36] For the purposes of argument difficulties of prognosis have to be put to one side and the question asked,

## *Are some babies better off dead than alive?*

From this point, then, an attempt has to be made to confront some fundamental notions about the sanctity of life, about personhood and about quality of life. One starting-point would be to assert that all human life is of equal worth. But, as Kuhse and Singer point out, this simple answer does not give an easy solution to hard cases. One such case is that of the anencephalic baby, a condition where most or all of the brain is missing. Such babies would die within days or weeks of birth without life support but they could be kept alive never to become conscious or respond to other human beings. If any and all human life has 'an equal claim to preservation because life is an irreducible value'[37] then anencephalic babies would be entitled to life-sustaining treatment. Yet there would be little point in such an exercise, and this is accepted even by the most ardent opponents of selective non-treatment.[38] The principle of absolute sanctity of life ignores the fact that the concept of life is an historical event, 'an object of economic and political decision making'.[39] So, if all human life is not of equal worth, what criteria can be used to distinguish those lives which are deserving of the protection of life support (in its broadest sense) and those which are not? Clearly in an essay of this length it is not possible to work through all the possible strands of argument. It seems appropriate too in writing on a topic which generates so many intuitive reactions (whether the result of social constructions or not) to state that the conclusion to which I believe I am working is that there *are* circumstances in which *some* babies should not be treated or, once treated, should have that treatment withdrawn.

Simple reliance on arguments based on sentience, or on membership of the human species or on technical differentiation such as viability 'are highly implausible candidates on which to ground the scope of our moral obligations, including our recognition of the right to life'.[40] The issue is more complex. One helpful line of argument distinguishes human beings from persons, whereby certain criteria can be used to separate the species-specific description 'human' from the characteristics on which to base a recognition of a right to life. Foetuses and newborn babies clearly lack certain characteristics and attributes which are commonly associated with human life. To say that they do not have the capacities which might be said to indicate personhood, such as an awareness of self as a present and future being (the precise criteria do not matter for the moment), does not mean that they are entitled to no protection but it allows for the possibility that different moral obligations may be owed to them. It also avoids species-specific distinctions which are unacceptably based on morally irrelevant criteria. Even though foetuses and babies do not have the characteristics of persons, we do not regard their indiscriminate killing as acceptable. We can look for other characteristics to explain their protection, such as sentience or the ability to experience pain (although it can be disputed at what stage foetuses or newborns acquire these).[41] So there may be less compelling reasons for their full protection than there are for protecting fully fledged persons. Certainly, many people regard handicapped newborns, as a group, differently from older children and adults, whether handicapped or not.[42]

For others, however, the recognition that newborns are not persons does not lead to the conclusion that they should be treated any differently. Human life in all forms, whether persons or not, may be viewed as special because of the *potential* to become persons possessed by such life. Although this has an attraction about it, like most initially attractive theories it soon becomes difficult. How far does potentiality go back? From the foetus to the embryo, from the embryo to the zygote, from the zygote to the egg, or to the sperm? Even if one takes a fundamental position in relation to the right to life and opposition to selective non-treatment is accompanied also by opposition to all abortion, these line-drawing difficulties still have to be confronted.

Potentiality should not, however, be dismissed completely. Although it is true that an acorn is not an oak tree,[43] it has more to do with an oak tree than with a privet hedge. So, although a foetus or a newborn baby may not be a person, they belong to a group most of whose members do have the potential to become one, and differ in that respect from, say, a caterpillar.[44] Potentiality can provide both a reason for regarding the killing of a foetus or a newborn as of a different order from killing a fully fledged person, and as a constraint on the circumstances in which that killing is appropriate. In other words, because a potential person is not a person it does not have to be accorded the *same* protection as if it were a person. But the fact that it might become a person means that some conditions should be put on its killing over and above those one might put on the killing of any other life form. For some, the argument will be lost before this point is reached; they do not accept that a potential person should have less protection than a realized person. Others will go as far as accepting that there is a difference between the potential and the actual, but will believe that the only condition under which (a foetus or) a newborn can be killed is when that particular newborn does not *in fact* have the physical attributes to allow it to progress to become a person.[45] Depending on the criteria which are adopted for personhood, this may be the basis on which Dr C. Everett Koop, the US Surgeon General, allows an exception to his 'treat at all costs' philosophy to be made for anencephalic babies.[46]

The next step is more controversial and involves taking the argument beyond justifying the non-treatment of babies who do not have the potentiality for personhood. It involves the assertion that *because* newborn babies are still at the stage of only being potential persons, it can be right in some circumstances to end their lives on the grounds that it is in their best interests not to be allowed to develop into severely damaged persons. Before pursuing that argument I want first to consider what criteria might be used to distinguish persons and non-persons: the personhood argument. Subsequently I will consider the sorts of grounds on which a potential person might be considered to be better served by being killed than by being nurtured to realize that potential: the 'otherwise kill me' argument. Notice that the two arguments developed from the distinction between persons and non-persons can be combined. Non-persons may be entitled to a minimum protectiion from unnecessary pain and suffering but they do not command in addition the full protection of a right to life where reasons suggest otherwise. Deciding when a potential life begins is less problematic where the protection being claimed for the potential person is different from that claimed for the realized person. *Less* is being claimed for the potential *vis-à-vis* the actual, although more is being claimed for the potential *vis-à-vis* other forms of life.

## Personhood

At what stage in development does a baby become a person? Different criteria of course produce different answers. The concept of individualism as it developed in seventeenth-century political thinking is epitomized in Locke's concept of person, which is based on rationality and self-consciousness and the capability to value one's own life. The fine tuning of the concept has led to results which vary from concluding that personhood is reached after twelve weeks of foetal development[47] to a suggestion that it does not occur until a baby is 3 months old.[48] At the one extreme Grobstein has suggested criteria of response to external change, a nervous system and the capacity to be recognized as a self by others. This leads him to conclude that the state of personhood is reached by the end of the first trimester of pregnancy. This is based on a recognition of physiognomy, while Tooley has taken a more physiological approach. For him a concept of person is more akin to the Lockean idea of rationality and self-awareness, rather than Grobstein's concentration on features *recognizable* to others. Harris echoes this by converging what he calls the two strategies to the question of personhood; what is a person and what makes life valuable? He concludes that we do not need to know what it is that makes life valuable for each individual, but rather what persons have in common, which is the capacity to value their own lives and those of others.[49] This requires at least a conception of self-awareness. Tooley suggests that any being which possesses all of the following properties is a person, and that nothing can be a person unless it has at least one of them: a capacity for self-awareness, a capacity to think, a capacity for rational thought, a capacity to arrive at decisions by deliberation, a capacity to envisage a future for oneself, a capacity to remember a past involving oneself, a capacity for being the subject of non-momentary interests and a capacity to use language.[50] This might lead to the conclusion that a baby would have to be considerably older than 3 months, the point at which Tooley suggests it becomes *intrinsically* wrong to kill them.[51] His justification for according babies protection from this stage is that the physiological changes which they have undergone since birth lead at about 10 to 12 weeks to the development of a functioning cortex, and it is the upper layers of the cerebral cortex which are thought to underlie higher mental functions. This coincides with the disappearance of reflexes present at birth such as the Moro and grasping reflex.[52] Although babies are not persons at 3 months, Tooley regards them as quasi-persons and thus worthy of protection on the ground that they have acquired to a degree some qualities of personhood.[53]

A further dimension which can be added to the physiological processes by which newborns acquire the capacity for personhood is the social concept, the point at which a neonate shifts from being of biological to social significance.[54] Engelhardt differs from Tooley in regarding babies as non-persons. Once a foetus becomes viable, although not strictly a biological person, it is seen as a socially significant being entitled to the same rights as a person in the formal sense.[55] It would be possible to adopt a middle ground between these two positions. Tooley, in refusing to acknowledge the social concept of personhood, makes a proposition which is counter-intuitive. Claims that certain ideas are either intuitive or counter-intuitive are always open to attack but, with that reservation in mind, it does not seem too outrageous to suggest that most people *do* have a different kind of respect for viable foetuses and newborn babies than for earlier stages of life. On the other hand, Tooley reminds us that decisions taken about the future of newborn babies relate to a different category of being than those taken in relation to older babies, children, and adults. The interests of a baby which has not yet developed the capacity to have an awareness of self can be considered as less problematic than those of one which has reached the stage at which that capacity begins to develop. The language of rights cannot be asked, as Engelhardt would require of it, to apply both to sentient individuals and to non-autonomous beings.

'A right to life ignores the fact that *health* is the primary goal of medicine, not simply the maintenance of life'.[56] Instead we should be asking how individual interests arise within communities.[57] A harm principle allows this to be done and avoids the right to life which can be transformed into an obligation to live.[58] It could be regarded as a reverse application of the paternalism which prevents euthanasia.

Non-maleficence, the duty to do no harm, is recognized as a crucial principle of medical ethics, but it does not necessarily have priority over doing good.[59] In fact the two will often have to be considered together and harm may be necessary in order to achieve good. But if no good is achieved then the harm of medical inter-vention cannot be justified. However much one talks of harm or good these are concepts which need a context. Generally, a person's assessment of what they find harmful and what they find good is 'intensely personal'.[60] Respect for the patient's autonomy can be invoked in order to justify choice of a treatment with less severe side effects but with less prospect for long-term success. But new-born babies as non-persons do not have autonomy. Their best interests have to be assessed by others. Many of the imperatives to treat which operate in neonatal units

> are drawn from the individualistic languages of recent social theory . . . But patients in neonatal units are not the individuals assumed in recent social thought . . . the staffs are left with a language (of rights, interests, quality) that cannot be used in the way it is typically used – as an instrument to disclose what is of value to autonomous individuals.[61]

This leads to two problems. One, with which I am concerned here, is what criteria can be used to make decisions about someone who is not an autonomous individual. The other is procedural; assuming that some criteria can and have been established, who or what is the appropriate decision-making body to apply those criteria.

### 'Otherwise kill me'

The literature is considerably thinner on the question of *when* the principle of non-treatment should be invoked than on the general issue of whether it can *ever* be justified. Taking a conservative approach, Weir suggests that non-treatment is justified where life can be regarded as an injury rather than a gift because there is no prospect of the baby having a meaningful life.[62] Treatment should be withheld or withdrawn where a baby has an untreatable neuro-logical condition, such as anencephaly, or where the baby has a recessive condition which will develop later, but which involves progressive decline, such as Tay–Sachs disease or Lesch–Nyhan syndrome (the first is a recessive condition the symptoms of which first appear at 6 months and signal inexorable decline of mental and physical ability until death occurs at 3 or 4 years of age; the second is a chromosomal recessive disorder involving physical and mental deterioration from approximately 6 months accompanied by obsessive self-mutilation). The line which divides those for whom Weir regards non-treatment as being in their best interests and those who should be treated is governed by three factors: mental rather than physiological deficits, very short life expectancy and the unavailability of curative or corrective treatments.[63] In other words his concern is with babies who are going to die within a fairly short time anyway (up to about 4 years) and whose lack of prospect of meaningful life is severe at the extreme.

His conclusions offer no solutions to the dilemmas posed by a baby with physical conditions such as spina bifida which can be treated but in their severe forms can, after many painful surgical corrections, lead to a life of immobility and incontinence, sometimes with additional mental impairment. Nor to the question of when to resuscitate a low-birthweight baby. The disagreement amongst pediatricians about the treatment of such babies and children revolves as much (although not totally of course) around difficulties of prognosis as around the question of non-treatment in general. This leads to what might seem alarming variations between rates of treatment of spina bifida infants, from 60–70 per cent non-treatment by John Lorber in Sheffield[64] to 90 per cent treatment by John Freeman in Baltimore.[65] Frohock, who, like Weir, writes as a commentator rather than a participant, takes a broader view of harm and reaches a position closer to that of Lorber. Individuals are not seen as egoistic, their lives primarily benefiting themselves, but as constituent members of a social group, and thus existing as much for the sake of others as for themselves.[66] Reflecting this in his criteria for non-treatment, he suggests that a baby's best interests might combine (a) a cluster of physical condition and prognosis, (b) mental abilities, pain, longevity, mobility, and morphology, (c) the family context and (d) the availability of institutional support.[67] Kuhse and Singer reach a similar position:

> Decisions about severely handicapped infants should not be based on the idea that all life is of equal value, nor on any other version of the principle of the sanctity of human life . . . There is therefore no obligation to do everything possible to keep severely handi-capped infants alive in all possible circumstances. Instead, decisions to keep them alive – or not to do so – should take account of the interests of the infant, the family, the 'next child', and the community as a whole.[68]

By introducing broader criteria, these writers inevitably accept a less clear picture than is drawn by Weir's diagnostic categories or by the amendments to the United States Child Abuse Prevention and Treatment Act which came into force in 1984. Under this, states have been required to develop procedures for responding to reports of cases of 'medically indicated treatment' being withheld. Such treatment is indicated unless the infant is irreversibly coma-tose, or it would merely prolong dying; it would not be effective in correcting all of the infant's life-threatening conditions or it would otherwise be futile in terms of survival. The right-to-life tenor of these rules is breached only by the final provision that treatment is not mandatory where it would be virtually futile in terms of the survival of the infant and the treatment itself under such circum-stances would be inhumane.[69] There are no clear guidelines in the United Kingdom. The British Medical Association's *Handbook of Medical Ethics* devotes less than a page to the subject, stating that a handicapped infant has 'the same rights as a normal infant' and non-medical care necessary for maintenance of life should not be withheld. Where life-saving medical or surgical measures are needed 'every opportunity should be taken for deliberation and discussion'.[70] But little indication is given of the considerations on which the deliberations are to be based:

> The doctor in charge is responsible for the initiation or the with-holding of treatment in the best interests of the infant. He must attend primarily to the needs and rights of the infant, and he must also have concern for the family as a whole.[71]

This lack of clarity reflects a confused legal picture.

## PHILOSOPHICAL INTEGRITY AND LEGAL PRAGMATISM

In so far as the tradition has been for courts in the United Kingdom to allow themselves to be led by the medical profession, it is not necessarily surprising that both appear to pay lip service to the sanctity of life while leaving a vast discretion to the doctor in charge in consultation with the parents. This is unsatisfactory in two respects. It means that some parents who might wish to have treatment withheld for their child are not presented with this option. They are instead subject to the ethical bias of the doctor they encounter and may end up feeling as the Stinsons did, 'Andrew is not our baby any more – he's been taken over by a medical bureaucracy'.[72] More importantly, perhaps, it allows doctors the power to withhold treatment in far less severe cases than any of those discussed above. In *Re B (a minor)*[73] the Court of Appeal decided that a Down's Syndrome baby over whom it was *in loco parentis* should be treated for a life-threatening intestinal blockage because the life of such a child would not be 'demonstrably awful', Lord Justice Templeman recognized that there may be cases 'of severe proved damage where the future is so uncertain that the court may be driven to a different conclusion'.[74] As well as acknowledging that the court might itself contemplate refusal of treatment, the case does not give any further help on the duties of parents or doctors where there is no such intervention.

It is not clear what *legal* consequences can be drawn from the *Arthur* case. The Down's syndrome baby over whose death the prosecution was brought was believed to have no other abnormalities.[75] He was 3 days old when he died, having been prescribed 'nursing care only' and the regular administration of a painkilling drug. Evidence conflicted on whether 'nursing care only' would be interpreted as an instruction not to feed, but in a baby as young as this feeding requirements would be minimal. Breast-fed babies never receive the milk from their mothers until about four days in any case. The painkillers were, however, lethal. The trial judge, Justice Farquarson, distinguished beween murder and the 'setting of conditions' in which death is allowed to occur. The line between murder and the proper practice of medicine appeared to depend on something akin to the distinction between act and omission. The examples which the judge used in the *Arthur* case allowed that neither an omission to treat a Down's syndrome baby with an intestinal obstruction nor the failure to give antibiotics to a handicapped baby with pneumonia would be said by a jury to be murder.[76] But to give painkilling drugs to a baby who was not otherwise going to die might be so regarded. As a moral determinant, however, the act/omission distinction is unsatisfactory. Nor is the raw application of principles of legal causation and mental responsibility much help in making the fine moral distinctions which medical treatment decisions demand. Thus, although legal texts expound the view that *any* acceleration of death is sufficient for causation in homicide, subject to a doctor's freedom to give painkilling drugs where necessary,[77] its application to medical treatment is of singularly little help. It is clear that it is not only medical decisions involving painkillers for the terminally ill which challenge the capacity of the principles of the law of murder to make adequate moral differentiations. If that law does not protect a handicapped baby who 'providentially' develops pneumonia then there is no reason why it should protect that same baby from being actively killed (painlessly). It makes little sense for a less handicapped baby to 'be allowed to die' while enforcing the continued existence of one with severe handicaps who fails to attract the intervention of providence. If the jury in the *Arthur* trial thought painkilling drugs had been given in such amounts intentionally to cause death, then, the judge said, it would be open to them to say it was murder. The moral distinction needs to be based on something less crude. Society needs to face up to 'a central absurdity of modern medicine: the machinery in an intensive care unit is more sophisticated than the codes of law and ethics governing its use'.[78]

It is testimony to the extraordinary power that doctors have over people's moral perceptions that behaviour, which under other circumstances might well have given rise to moral outrage, led to an acquittal. The General Secretary of the British Medical Association thought 'disastrous' the decision of the Director of Public Prosecutions to 'prosecute . . . a consultant paediatrician of Dr Arthur's eminence . . . as a result of medical procedures which to all outward appearances corresponded with accepted medical practice'.[79] The quiet complicity in medical infanticide in the *Arthur* case seems at odds with the agitation caused by the news of the use for transplant of the organs of an anencephalic baby. Obviously *some* people were disturbed by Arthur's treatment regime and that was what led to his prosecution. There are clearly dangers in reading too much into the acquittal, which may have been less a verdict that his action was right and more a reluctance to convict him of attempted murder because of it. On the other hand the case did not lead to the setting up of a Warnock committee or other form of public inquiry, which suggests that the decision was not merely negative in its judgment on him. There are conundrums, however. I do not think that the people who would condone Dr Arthur would necessarily support the anencephalic transplant.[80] As a society we do have deeply conflicting and confused views about the value of babies and children as well as about disability. The rate of death by homicide of children under 12 months is nearly three times that of the population as a whole, while children aged between 5 and 15 years are much less at risk than either those younger or older; the rate for infants is eight times that of the older child.[81] And yet, the prevalent moral climate seems severely condemnatory of those who kill young babies. Perhaps this reflects, at a rough and ready level, a tacit popular acceptance of the sort of argument put forward by Tooley and others and endorsed, in parts, in this essay. The willingness to kill *some* babies for good reason may induce an overreaction to the 'unnecessary' deaths caused 'for no good reason', the baby battering syndrome.

Non-treatment raises many issues which I have not touched on or have dealt with somewhat summarily. I have argued that non-treatment is justified where the continuation of life would not be in the baby's best interests based on a harm principle. I have suggested that there is no moral distinction between letting die and actual killing, which means that implicitly I have argued that there should be nothing to prevent a doctor administering drugs with the purpose of ending the life of a baby who fits the best interests criteria. I have not discussed what the appropriate procedures of decision-making should be, whether the decision is one for the parents and doctors alone, or whether it should be overseen by an ethical committee of the kind employed by many hospitals in the United States. I have not given much attention to arguments about the nature of societal attitudes to disability. This is partly because those who regard non-treatment as resulting from misguided views about the experience of disability are often talking about a much milder degree of handicap than that which would trigger infanticide; and partly because people with disabilities do not talk with one voice. Some say that they wish they had not been treated and maintained to lead a painful life.[82] As much, or possibly even greater, harm is done by preserving an infant in order for it to mature into an unwanted life than by killing a baby which, if left to live, might have been perfectly fulfilled.

## NOTES

My thanks to Keith Smith of Brunel University who made some very useful suggestions on an earlier draft of this chapter.
The title quotation is from Louis MacNeice, 'Prayer Before Birth' (*Selected*

*Poems of Louis MacNeice*, ed. W. H. Auden (London: Faber & Faber, 1964 edn, p. 74).

1 Robert F. Weir, *Selective Non Treatment of Handicapped Newborns*, (London: Oxford University Press, 1984), ch. 1, and Michael Tooley, *Abortion and Infanticide*, (London: Oxford University Press, 1983), p. 315.
2 Weir, *Selective Non Treatment*, ch. 3.
3 Madhu Kishwar, 'The continuing deficit of women in India and the impact of amniocentesis' in G. Corea, R. Duelli Klein, J. Hanmer, H. B. Holmes, B. Hoskins, M. Kishwar, J. Raymond, R. Rowland, and R. Steinbacher, *Man-Made Women: How Reproductive Technologies Affect Women* (London: Hutchinson, 1985), p. 30.
4 Through Amendments to Child Abuse Prevention and Treatment Act, 98 Stat. 1749 (1984) (codified as amended at 42 U.S.C.A. ss. 5101–4, West Supp. 1985).
5 David Armstrong, 'The invention of infant mortality', *Sociology of Health and Illness*, vol. 8 (1968), p. 211.
6 Fred M. Frohock, *Special Care: Medical Decisions at the Beginning of Life* (Chicago: University of Chicago Press, 1986), p. 154.
7 ibid., p. 155.
8 Raymond Duff and A. G. M. Campbell, 'Moral and ethical dilemmas in the special care nursery', *New England Journal of Medicine*, no. 289 (1973), p. 890, extracted in Robert F. Weir (ed.), *Ethical Issues in Death and Dying*, 2nd edn (New York: Columbia University Press, 1986), p. 119; *contra*, see Z. Szawarski and A. Tulczynski, 'Treatment of defective newborns – a survey of paediatricians in Poland', *Journal of Medical Ethics*, vol. 14 (1988), p. 11.
9 For an account of some of the differences see Weir, *Selective Non Treatment*, ch. 3, and Joseph E. Magnet and Eike-Henner W. Kluge, *Withholding Treatment from Defective Newborn Children* (Cowansville Quebec: Brown Legal Publications, 1985), Nancy K. Rhoden, 'Treating Baby Doe: the ethics of uncertainty', *Hastings Center Report*, vol. 16, (1986), p. 34, and Robert and Peggy Stinson, *The Long Dying of Baby Andrew* (Boston: Little, Brown, 1983 edn), pp. 146, 326.
10 Andrew Whitelaw, 'Death as an option in neonatal intensive care', *Lancet*, 9 August 1986, p. 328.
11 Duff and Campbell, 'Moral and ethical dilemmas in the special care nursery'. Rhoden, 'Treating Baby Doe', describes practices in the United States, the United Kingdom, and Sweden, p. 37.
12 Frohock, *Special Care*, p. vii.
13 Alistair G. S. Philip, George A. Little, Denise R. Polivy, and Jerald F. Lucey, 'Neonatal risk for the eighties: the importance of birthweight/gestational age groups', *Pediatrics*, vol. 68 (1981), p. 124, and Sargant P. Horwood, Michael H. Boyle, George W. Torrance, and John C. Sinclair, 'Mortality and morbidity of 500–1499 gram birth weight infants live born to residents of a defined geographic region before and after neonatal intensive care', *Pediatrics*, vol. 69 (1982),

p. 613. The latter reported major damage in about 12 per cent of the survivors.

14 Frohock, *Special Care*, p. ix.

15 Robert and Peggy Stinson, 'On the death of a baby', *Journal of Medical Ethics*, vol. 7 (1981), p. 18, and see the same authors' *The Long Dying of Baby Andrew*.

16 B. Sheppardson, 'Abortion and euthanasia of Down's syndrome children – the parents' view', *Journal of Medical Ethics*, vol. 9 (1983), p. 152.

17 Madeleine Sims, 'Informed dissent: the views of some mothers of severely mentally handicapped young adults', *Journal of Medical Ethics*, vol. 12 (1986), pp. 72–4.

18 Discussed in Helen Beynon, 'Doctors as murderers', *Criminal Law Review* (1982), p. 17; M. J. Gunn and J. C. Smith, 'Arthur's case and the rights to life of a Down's syndrome child', *Criminal Law Review* (1985), p. 706; and Helga Kuhse and Peter Singer, *Should the Baby Live?* (London: Oxford University Press, 1985), pp. 1–11.

19 MORI poll, *Times*, 10 November 1981.

20 *Guardian*, 15 December 1986.

21 Marsha Saxton, 'Born and unborn: the implications of reproductive technologies for people with disabilities', in R. Arditti, R. Duelli Klein, and S. Minden (eds), *Test-Tube Women*, (London: Pandora Press, 1984), p. 306.

22 Renate Duelli Klein, 'What's new about the "new" reproductive technologies?', in Corea *et al.* (eds), *Man-Made Women*, pp. 64, 66.

23 ibid., p.67.

24 Frohock, *Special Care*, p. viii.

25 Eighty-five per cent of those surveyed favoured voluntary euthanasia for a person with a painful incurable disease, but 85 per cent opposed it where a person is merely 'tired of living'. Roger Jowell, Sharon Witherspoon, and Lindsay Brook (eds), *British Social Attitudes: The 1986 Report* (Aldershot: Gower, 1986), p. 15. A New York court has refused to order the force-feeding of a competent 85-year-old stroke victim; Frohock, *Special Care*, p. 76. The trial of Dr Bodkin Adams in England in 1957 is widely cited as endorsing the practice of shortening of life in order to alleviate pain: see Patrick Devlin, *Easing the Passing* (London: Bodley Head, 1985).

26 Beynon, 'Doctors as murderers', pp. 19ff; Gunn and Smith, 'Arthur's case', pp. 707ff.

27 Jeffrey Minson, *Genealogies of Morals* (Basingstoke: Macmillan, 1985), p. 172.

28 Smith and Gunn, 'Arthur's case'.

29 Raanan Gillon, 'Ordinary and extraordinary means', *British Medical Journal*, vol. 292, (25 January 1986), p. 259.

30 Kuhse and Singer, *Should the Baby Live?* p. 36. See Z. Szawarski and A. Tulczynski, 'Treatment of defective newborns', pp. 13–14, for very different interpretations between Australian and Polish paediatricians.

31 Frohock, *Special Care*, p. 10.

32 J. K. Mason and D. W. Meyers, 'Parental choice and selective non-

treatment of deformed newborns: a view from mid-atlantic', *Journal of Medical Ethics*, vol. 12 (1986), p. 67.

33 *The Long Dying*, p. 288.

34 'Selective treatment of myelomeningocele: to treat or not to treat?', *Pediatrics*, vol. 53 (1974), p. 307. See also J. Lorber and S. Salfield, 'Result of selective treatment of spina bifida cystica', *Archives of Diseases of Childhood*, vol. 56 (1981), pp. 822, 830.

35 Weir, *Selective Non Treatment*, p. 231. Prognosis is particularly difficult in very low birthweight babies; Rhoden, 'Treating Baby Doe', p. 34.

36 Bronchopulmonary dysplasia, damage to lung tissue caused by the use of positive pressure respirators and oxygen on immature infants. Stinson and Stinson, *The Long Dying*, p. 372.

37 Sanford H. Kadish, 'Respect for life and regard for rights in the criminal law', in S. F. Barker (ed.), *Respect for Life in Medicine, Philosophy and the Law* (Baltimore: Johns Hopkins University Press, 1977), p. 72.

38 C. Everett Koop, cited in Kuhse and Singer, *Should the Baby Live?*, p. 25.

39 Minson, *Genealogies*, p. 172.

40 Raanan Gillon, 'To what do we have moral obligations and why? II', *British Medical Journal*, vol. 290 (8 June 1985), p. 1735, reprinted in his *Philosophical Medical Ethics* (Chichester: John Wiley, 1986), ch. 8.

41 Magnet and Kluge report that painkillers are not used in most Canadian neonatal units, *Withholding Treatment*, p. 34.

42 MORI poll referred to above. A Gallup poll conducted in Australia in 1978 found that 55 per cent of those interviewed thought that the law should allow life to be terminated painlessly in the case of babies who are 'mentally abnormal' or 'physically seriously deformed'; quoted in Tooley, *Abortion and Infanticide*, p. 311.

43 Judith Jarvis Thomson, 'A defense of abortion', in Joel Feinberg (ed.), *The Problem of Abortion* (Belmont, Calif.: Wadsworth Publishing, 1973), p. 121.

44 John Harris, *The Value of Life* (London: Routledge & Kegan Paul, 1985), p. 11.

45 In the case of a foetus, because by definition it is still maintained in another's body, the limitations on its being killed may themselves be countered by arguments about the mother's right to determine what happens in her own body; see Jarvis Thomson, 'A defense of abortion', p. 137.

46 C. Everett Koop, quoted in Kuhse and Singer, *Should the Baby Live?*, p. 25.

47 Clifford Grobstein, *From Chance to Purpose* (Reading, Mass.: Addison-Wesley, 1981), p. 353.

48 Tooley, *Abortion and Infanticide*, p. 408.

49 Harris, *The Value of Life*, p. 16.

50 Tooley, p. 349.

51 ibid., p. 408.

52 ibid., p. 397.

53 The inner world of some brain-damaged people is revealingly explored

in Oliver Sacks, *The Man Who Mistook His Wife for a Hat* (London: Picador, 1986).

54 H. Tristram Engelhardt, 'Medicine and the concept of the person', in Tom Beauchamp and Seymour Perlin (eds), *Ethical Issues in Death and Dying* (Hemel Hempstead: Prentice-Hall, 1978), p. 278.

55 Engelhardt, 'Medicine and the concept of the person', p. 267.

56 Frohock, *Special Care*, p. 214, and Minson, *Genealogies*.

57 Frohock p. 214.

58 ibid., p. 204.

59 Raanan Gillon, ' "Primum non nocere" and the principle of non maleficence', *British Medical Journal*, vol. 291 (13 July 1985), *Philosophical Medical Ethics*, ch. 13.

60 Raanan Gillon, 'Beneficence: doing good for others', *British Medical Journal*, vol. 291 (16 July 1985); *Philosophical Medical Ethics*, ch. 12, p. 45.

61 Frohock, pp. 200–1.

62 Weir, *Selective Non Treatment*, p, 183.

63 ibid., pp. 238–9.

64 Lorber and Salfield, 'Result of selective treatment', p. 830.

65 'Ethics and the decision making process for defective children', in David Roy (ed.), *Medical Wisdom and Ethics in the Treatment of Severely Defective Newborn and Young Children* (Montreal: Eden Press, 1978), pp. 27–8.

66 Frohock, p. 119. As in Japan where the Confucian philosophical tradition emphasizes group harmony at the expense of individualism; Rihito Kimura, 'In Japan, parents participate but doctors decide', *Hastings Center Report*, vol. 16 (1986), p. 22.

67 Frohock, p. 118. Doubt has been expressed at the suggestion that death could be in a person's interest, but 'You can certainly say that in some circumstances the misery of human life can be judged to outweigh its happiness, actual or potential', D. D. Raphael, 'Handicapped infants: medical ethics and the law', *Journal of Medical Ethics*, vol. 14 (1988), p. 7.

68 *Should the Baby Live?*, p. 172.

69 Amendments to Child Abuse Prevention and Treatment Act, 98 Stat. 1749 (1984). The original Baby Doe regulations which were even stricter were finally struck down by the Supreme Court, *Bowen* v. *American Hospital Association* 106 S. Ct. 2101 (1986), affirming *American Hospital Association* v. *Heckler*, 585 F. Supp. 541 (S.D.N.Y.).

70 British Medical Association, *Handbook of Medical Ethics* (London: British Medical Association, 1984), p. 63.

71 ibid.

72 *The Long Dying*, p. 115.

73 [1981] 1 W.L.R. 1421.

74 *Re B*, p. 1424.

75 It emerged in the forensic evidence at the trial that there were other life-threatening abnormalities. It was for this reason that the charge of attempted murder was substituted. See Diana Brahams and Michael Brahams, 'The Arthur case – a proposal for legislation', *Journal of Medical Ethics*, vol. 9 (1983), p. 12.

76 Kuhse and Singer, *Should the Baby Live?*, p. 7.
77 For example, Glanville Williams, *Textbook of Criminal Law*, 2nd edn (London: Stevens, 1983) p. 385.
78 Stinson and Stinson, *The Long Dying*, p. 288.
79 J. Havard, *Journal of Medical Ethics*, vol. 9 (1983), p. 18.
80 The reason an anencephalic baby is not brain dead is that the criteria rely on a 'whole brain' definition developed to protect comatose patients who might recover brain function. The anencephalic may have some brain stem but has no brain to be activated or reactivated. See Michael R. Harrison, 'The anencephalic newborn as organ donor', *Hastings Center Report*, vol. 16 (1986), p. 21.
81 R. Walmsley, *Personal Violence* (London: HMSO, 1986). The average in 1984 was 11 per million; for those under 12 months it was 32 per million, and for those aged 5–15, 4 per million.
82 See Kuhse and Singer, *Should the Baby Live?*, p. 145.

# INDEX

abnormality 40, 44; congenital 40; foetal 44

abortion 4, 6, 7, 10, 24, 44, 45, 58, 74, 86, 88ff., 106, 136, 155ff., 163, 173–5, 180; amniocentesis and 86; competing rights and 10, 168; mental handicap and 136; private clinics in 106; selective feticide and 44, 45

Abortion Law Reform Association (ALRA) 156

adoption 48, 73, 74, 75, 76, 96, 97ff., 157; British agencies for 74; children by donation 96; decline in 73, 76, 157; Scotland in 99; secrecy and 97ff.

adult training centres 141, 145

adultery (AID and) 117, 121

agnosia, visual 5

AID *see* artificial insemination by donor

AIDS 142

Alton, David 167

amniocentesis 86, 172

anencephaly 7, 202

Angell, R. R. 40

antibiotics 201

Archbishop of Canterbury's Commission on Artificial Human Insemination 120, 123

Aristotle 91

Arthur, Leonard 199, 210–11

artificial insemination by donor (AID) 1, 7, 30, 61, 75, 96, 105, 110; in France 110; self-insemination 111, 115ff., 116, 119; social workers advice on 107

artificial insemination by husband (AIH) 118

Atkins, Susan 23

*Babies for Burning* 156

Baby M 32

Barrett, Michelle 124

Bayh, Senator 26

Bell, Carrie 135

Benyon, W. 156

*Bible*, surrogacy and the 63

Biggers, J. D. 40, 42

Bill of Rights 18

birth: certificates, access to 97, 100, 104; choices regarding 189; marked 'by donation' 109; multiple order 3, 40, 42, 48; premature 40, 42, 196; registration, AID and 120, 126

Bok, Sissela 99

bonding, maternal 59

Bowlby, John 105

Brahams, D. 45

British Medical Association (BMA) 66, 122; AID and 118; Arthur trial and 211; *Handbook of Medical Ethics* 209

British Pregnancy Advisory Service (BPAS) 119, 120

Brophy, J. 24

Brown, Louise 39

Caesarian section 29, 143

Campbell, A. G. M. 196–7

Campbell, Tom 9

Capron, Alexander 180

care order 159

Chernobyl 87

Childlessness Overcome Through Surrogacy (COTS) 70

chromosomes, aberrations in 40; imbalance in 40